UNTOLD COMIC TALES FROM THE HIT TV SERIES ON THE CW

RIVERDALE®

ALL-NEW STORIES

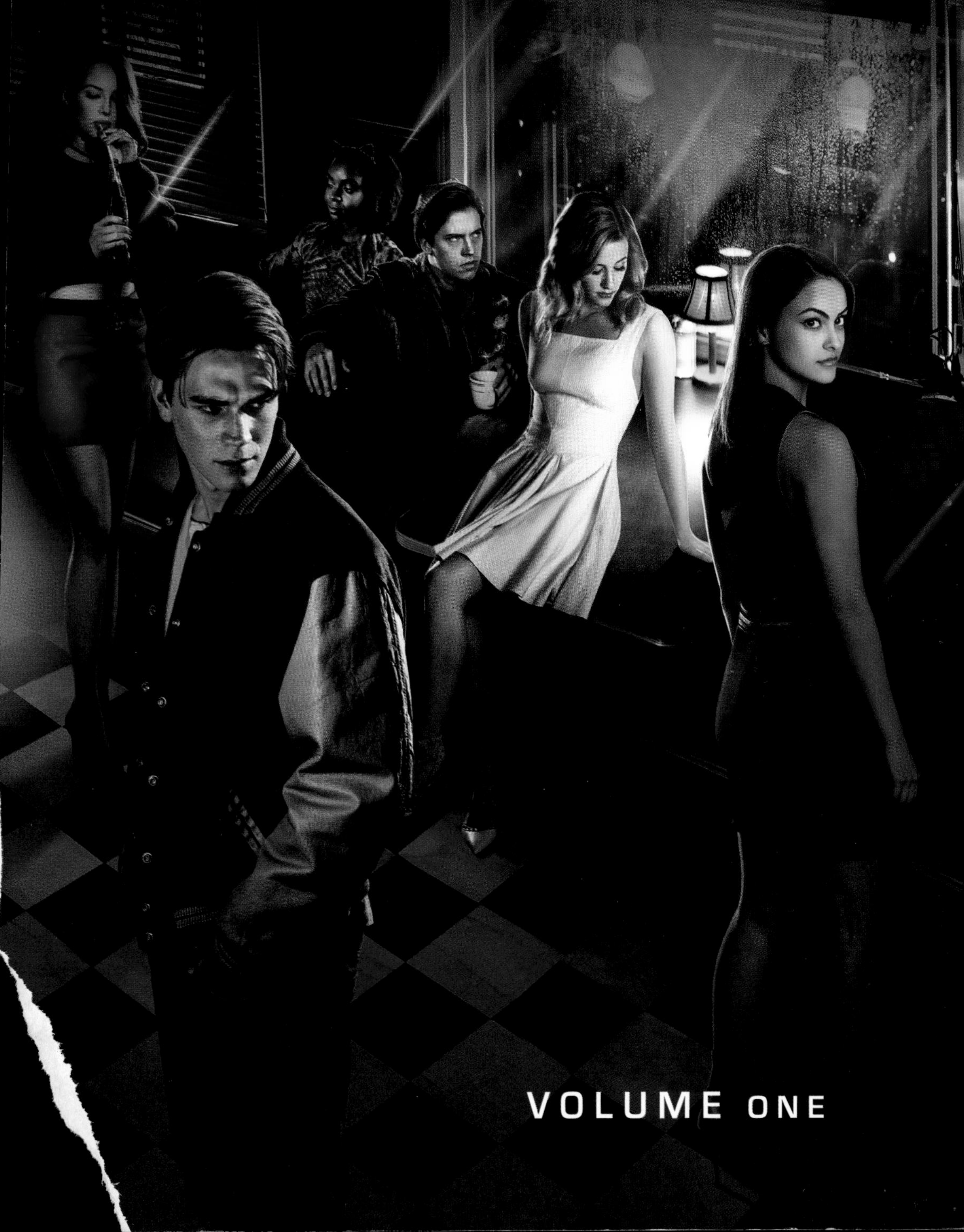

VOLUME ONE

RIVERDALE®

STORIES BY:
ROBERTO AGUIRRE-SACASA

WRITTEN BY:
JAMES DEWILLE, WILL EWING, MICHAEL GRASSI, DANIEL KING, BRITTA LUNDIN, GREG MURRAY & BRIAN E. PATERSON.

WITH ART BY:
JOE EISMA, ELLIOT FERNANDEZ, ALITHA MARTINEZ, THOMAS PITILLI, JIM TOWE, JANICE CHIANG, THOMAS CHU, BOB SMITH, ANDRE SZYMANOWICZ, GLENN WHITMORE & JOHN WORKMAN.

CHIEF EXECUTIVE OFFICER/PUBLISHER:
JON GOLDWATER

CHIEF CREATIVE OFFICER:
ROBERTO AGUIRRE-SACASA

EDITOR-IN-CHIEF:
VICTOR GORELICK

EDITOR:
MIKE PELLERITO

ASSOCIATE EDITOR:
STEPHEN OSWALD

ASSISTANT EDITOR:
JAMIE LEE ROTANTE

LEAD DESIGNER:
KARI MCLACHLAN

All photos courtesy of The CW/Warner Bros.

Welcome, Readers, to a comic book based on a TV show based on a comic book.

The show is the CW's *Riverdale*, a darker take on Archie, Betty, Veronica, and the rest of the gang. This book contains stories set in the *Riverdale* "universe." So you may notice that things are a bit more macabre, a bit sexier, and a bit more...*off*. Like a strawberry milkshake that's on the verge of curdling.

Riverdale, the television series, almost died on the vine numerous times. Every step of the way felt like a brush with death; we'd clear one hurdle—barely—and ten more would materialize before us. The biggest one came early, when an executive told me that whatever show I had in mind, it would need some kind of high-concept hook or genre element. Because it couldn't *just* be a coming-of-age show, as I'd imagined it. *Riverdale* needed something...*extra*.

I went back to the drawing board, and—after flailing around for a while (portals! time-travel!)—I remembered something the uber-producer Greg Berlanti had mentioned to me a couple of months earlier: *What if there's a dead body in the town of Riverdale?* I began to think about movies like *Stand By Me, Donnie Darko,* and *River's Edge*. They were coming-of-age movies set in high schools, for sure, but they also all had...at least one dead body.

And then there's *Twin Peaks*. The holiest of holies. The show that changed television and inspired countless imitators. When I talked to people about *Riverdale* and the show it was becoming

they often said to me. "Oh, it's Archie meets *Twin Peaks*." As elevator pitches go, it was a good one. Its central mystery, after all, hinged on the murder of a high school student: Homecoming Queen Laura Palmer. Well, if it was good enough for David Lynch, it would be good enough for me, but *maybe* instead of Queen Bee Cheryl Blossom dying, it's her twin brother Jason, and *maybe* that's just the tip of a hamburger-shaped iceberg...

Somewhat paradoxically, Jason's death breathed life into *Riverdale*. His murder gave us "permission" to tell the stories in these pages. They're tales that exist "in between"—in between the Archie comic books of yore and the CW's *Riverdale* of today. They were written like episodes of a television show. One writer pitched an idea, other writers helped him or her flesh it out. Then they were drawn and inked and colored and lettered and published and, ultimately, collected. Like the DVD box set of a beloved TV series.

A lot of people worked hard to make *Riverdale* the show—and now, *Riverdale* the comic book series—happen. My deepest thanks to all of them, especially those writers toiling with me, day in and day out, in the sweltering shadow of the Warner Brothers water tower. And an extra special thanks to...Jason Blossom. Who gave so much to make this whole thing possible...and who still haunts our dreams.

From the depths
of the Burbank Studios,

—Roberto Aguirre-Sacasa

CHAPTER ONE

ARCHIE IN SWEETWATER

WRITER:
BRIAN E. PATERSON

ART:
ELLIOT FERNANDEZ

COLORS:
THOMAS CHU

LETTERS:
JOHN WORKMAN

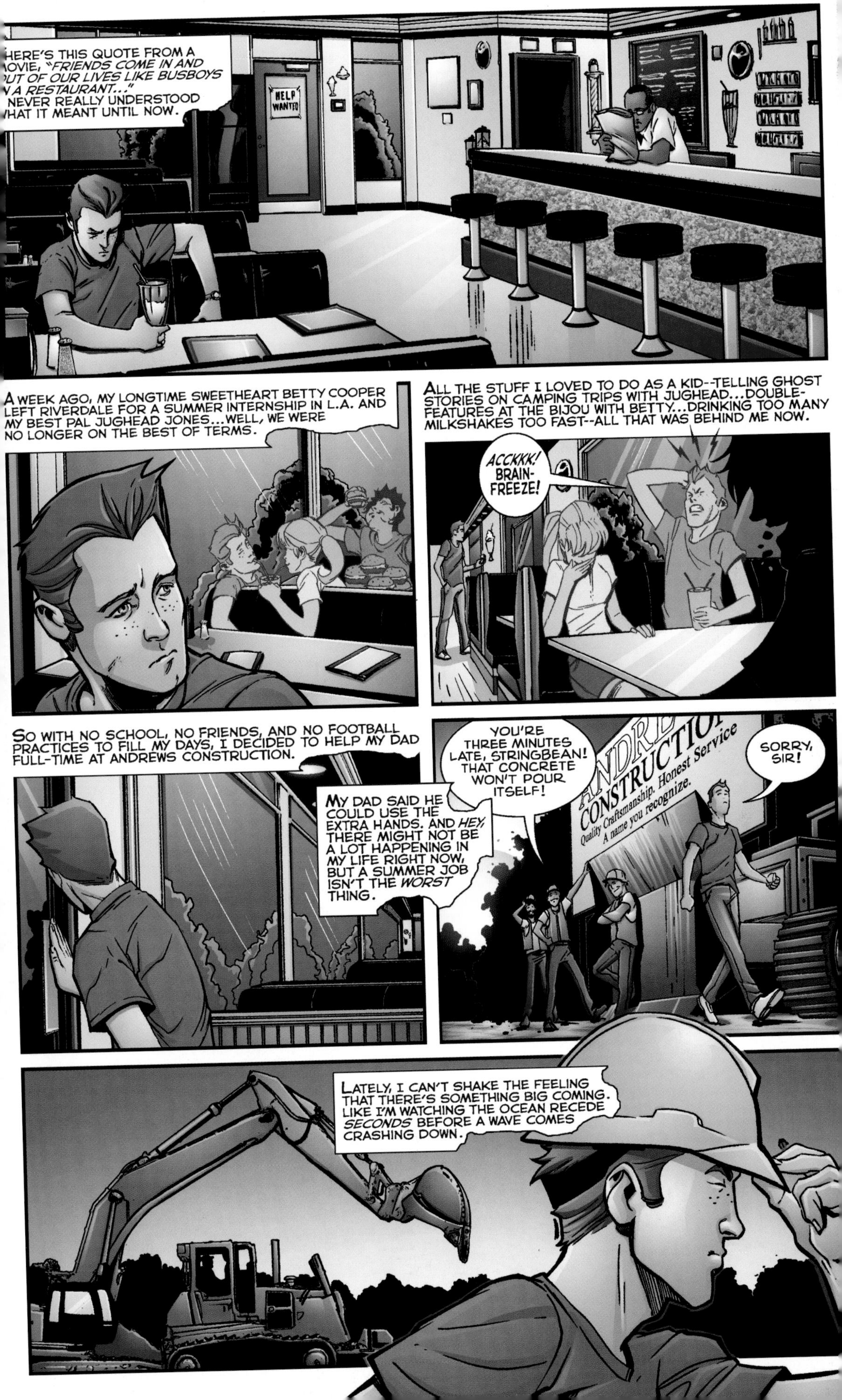

HERE'S THIS QUOTE FROM A MOVIE, "FRIENDS COME IN AND OUT OF OUR LIVES LIKE BUSBOYS IN A RESTAURANT..." I NEVER REALLY UNDERSTOOD WHAT IT MEANT UNTIL NOW.
HELP WANTED
A WEEK AGO, MY LONGTIME SWEETHEART BETTY COOPER LEFT RIVERDALE FOR A SUMMER INTERNSHIP IN L.A. AND MY BEST PAL JUGHEAD JONES...WELL, WE WERE NO LONGER ON THE BEST OF TERMS.
ALL THE STUFF I LOVED TO DO AS A KID--TELLING GHOST STORIES ON CAMPING TRIPS WITH JUGHEAD...DOUBLE-FEATURES AT THE BIJOU WITH BETTY...DRINKING TOO MANY MILKSHAKES TOO FAST--ALL THAT WAS BEHIND ME NOW.
ACCKKK! BRAIN-FREEZE!
SO WITH NO SCHOOL, NO FRIENDS, AND NO FOOTBALL PRACTICES TO FILL MY DAYS, I DECIDED TO HELP MY DAD FULL-TIME AT ANDREWS CONSTRUCTION.
MY DAD SAID HE COULD USE THE EXTRA HANDS. AND HEY, THERE MIGHT NOT BE A LOT HAPPENING IN MY LIFE RIGHT NOW, BUT A SUMMER JOB ISN'T THE WORST THING.
YOU'RE THREE MINUTES LATE, STRINGBEAN! THAT CONCRETE WON'T POUR ITSELF!
CONSTRUCTION
Quality Craftsmanship. Honest Service
A name you recognize.
SORRY, SIR!
LATELY, I CAN'T SHAKE THE FEELING THAT THERE'S SOMETHING BIG COMING. LIKE I'M WATCHING THE OCEAN RECEDE SECONDS BEFORE A WAVE COMES CRASHING DOWN.

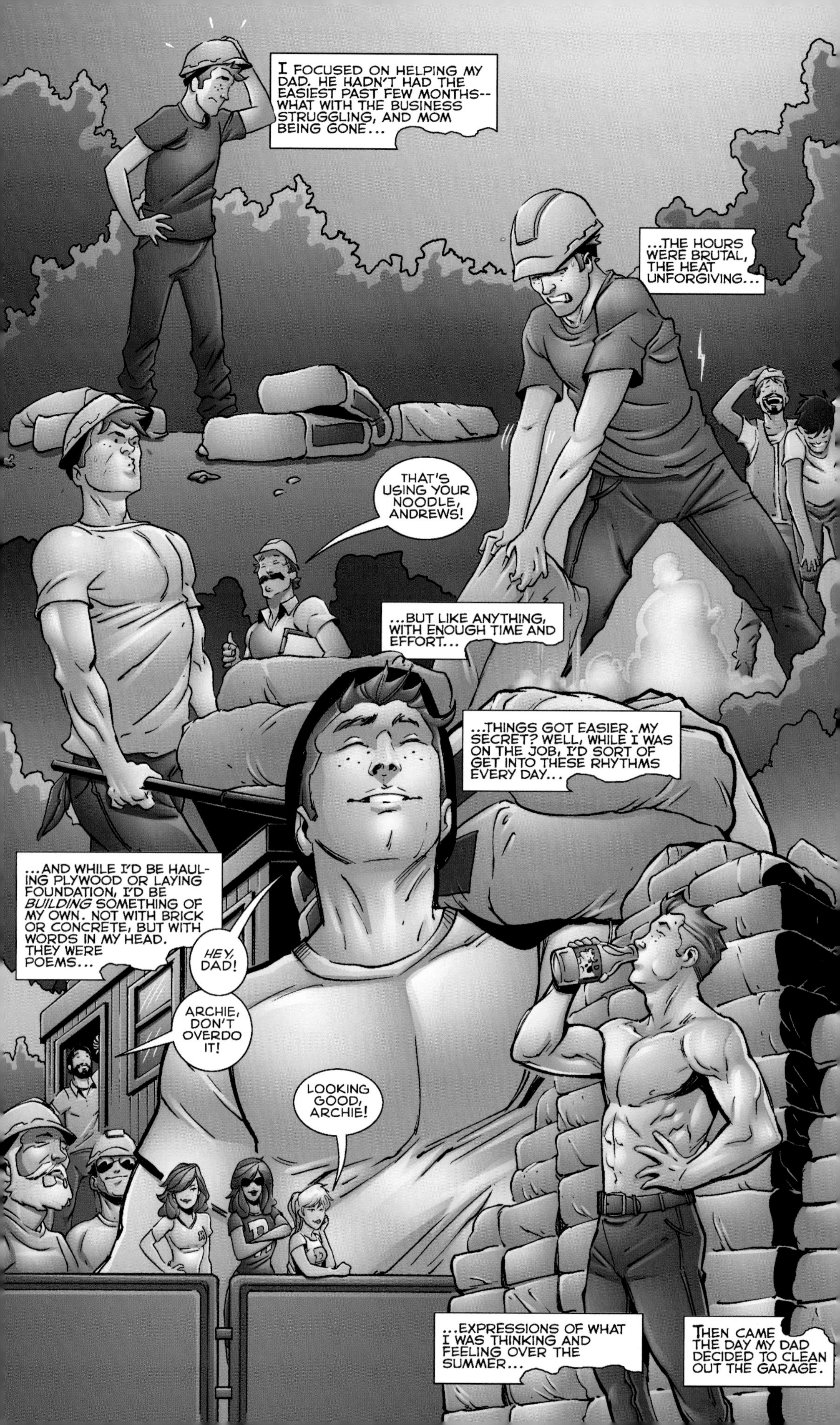
I FOCUSED ON HELPING MY DAD. HE HADN'T HAD THE EASIEST PAST FEW MONTHS-- WHAT WITH THE BUSINESS STRUGGLING, AND MOM BEING GONE...
...THE HOURS WERE BRUTAL, THE HEAT UNFORGIVING...
THAT'S USING YOUR NOODLE, ANDREWS!
...BUT LIKE ANYTHING, WITH ENOUGH TIME AND EFFORT...
...THINGS GOT EASIER. MY SECRET? WELL, WHILE I WAS ON THE JOB, I'D SORT OF GET INTO THESE RHYTHMS EVERY DAY...
...AND WHILE I'D BE HAULING PLYWOOD OR LAYING FOUNDATION, I'D BE *BUILDING* SOMETHING OF MY OWN. NOT WITH BRICK OR CONCRETE, BUT WITH WORDS IN MY HEAD. THEY WERE POEMS...
HEY, DAD!
ARCHIE, DON'T OVERDO IT!
LOOKING GOOD, ARCHIE!
...EXPRESSIONS OF WHAT I WAS THINKING AND FEELING OVER THE SUMMER...
THEN CAME THE DAY MY DAD DECIDED TO CLEAN OUT THE GARAGE.

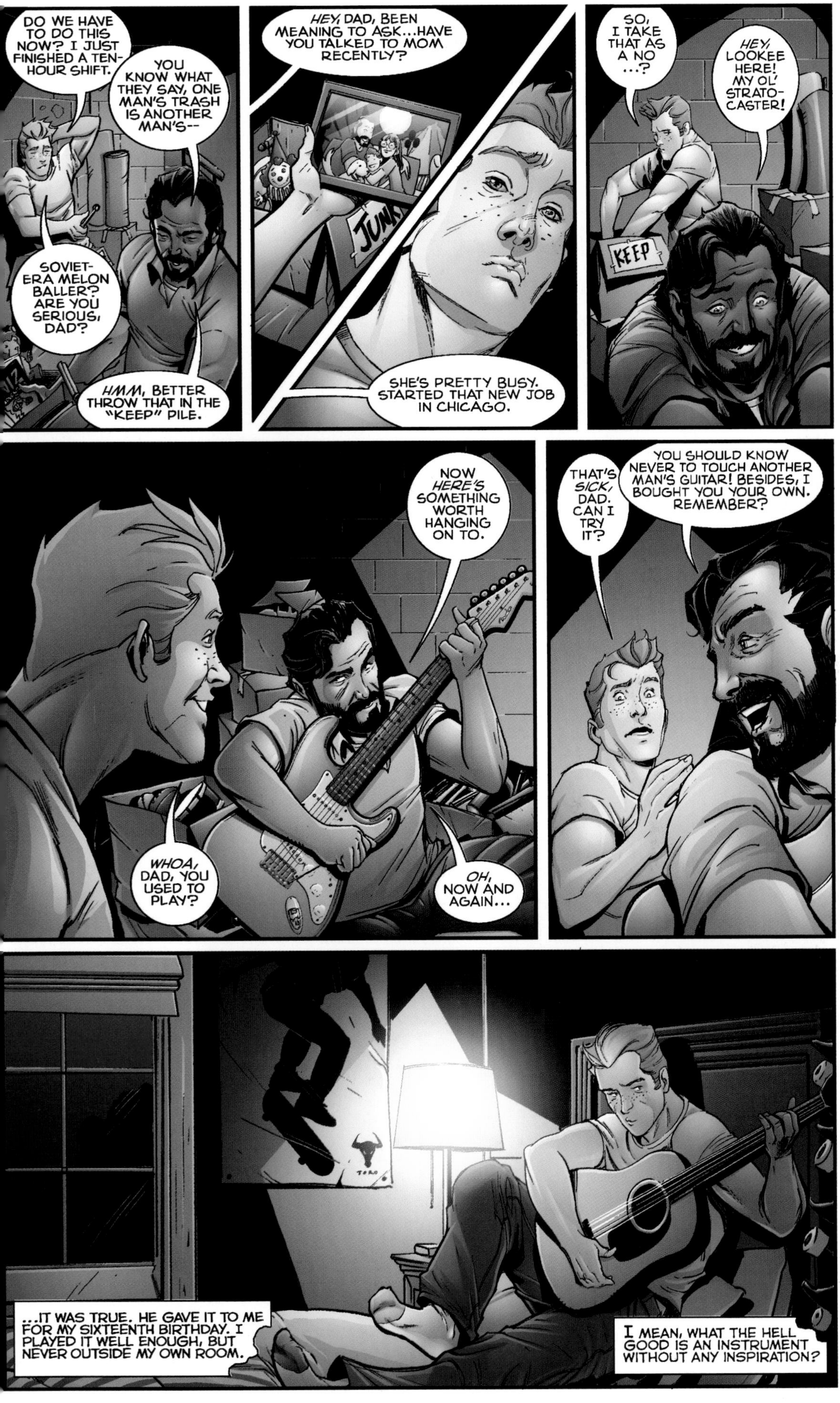
DO WE HAVE TO DO THIS NOW? I JUST FINISHED A TEN-HOUR SHIFT.
YOU KNOW WHAT THEY SAY, ONE MAN'S TRASH IS ANOTHER MAN'S--
SOVIET-ERA MELON BALLER? ARE YOU SERIOUS, DAD?
HMM, BETTER THROW THAT IN THE "KEEP" PILE.
HEY, DAD, BEEN MEANING TO ASK...HAVE YOU TALKED TO MOM RECENTLY?
JUNK
SHE'S PRETTY BUSY. STARTED THAT NEW JOB IN CHICAGO.
SO, I TAKE THAT AS A NO ...?
HEY, LOOKEE HERE! MY OL' STRATO-CASTER!
KEEP
NOW HERE'S SOMETHING WORTH HANGING ON TO.
WHOA, DAD, YOU USED TO PLAY?
OH, NOW AND AGAIN...
THAT'S SICK, DAD. CAN I TRY IT?
YOU SHOULD KNOW NEVER TO TOUCH ANOTHER MAN'S GUITAR! BESIDES, I BOUGHT YOU YOUR OWN. REMEMBER?
TORO
...IT WAS TRUE. HE GAVE IT TO ME FOR MY SIXTEENTH BIRTHDAY. I PLAYED IT WELL ENOUGH, BUT NEVER OUTSIDE MY OWN ROOM.
I MEAN, WHAT THE HELL GOOD IS AN INSTRUMENT WITHOUT ANY INSPIRATION?

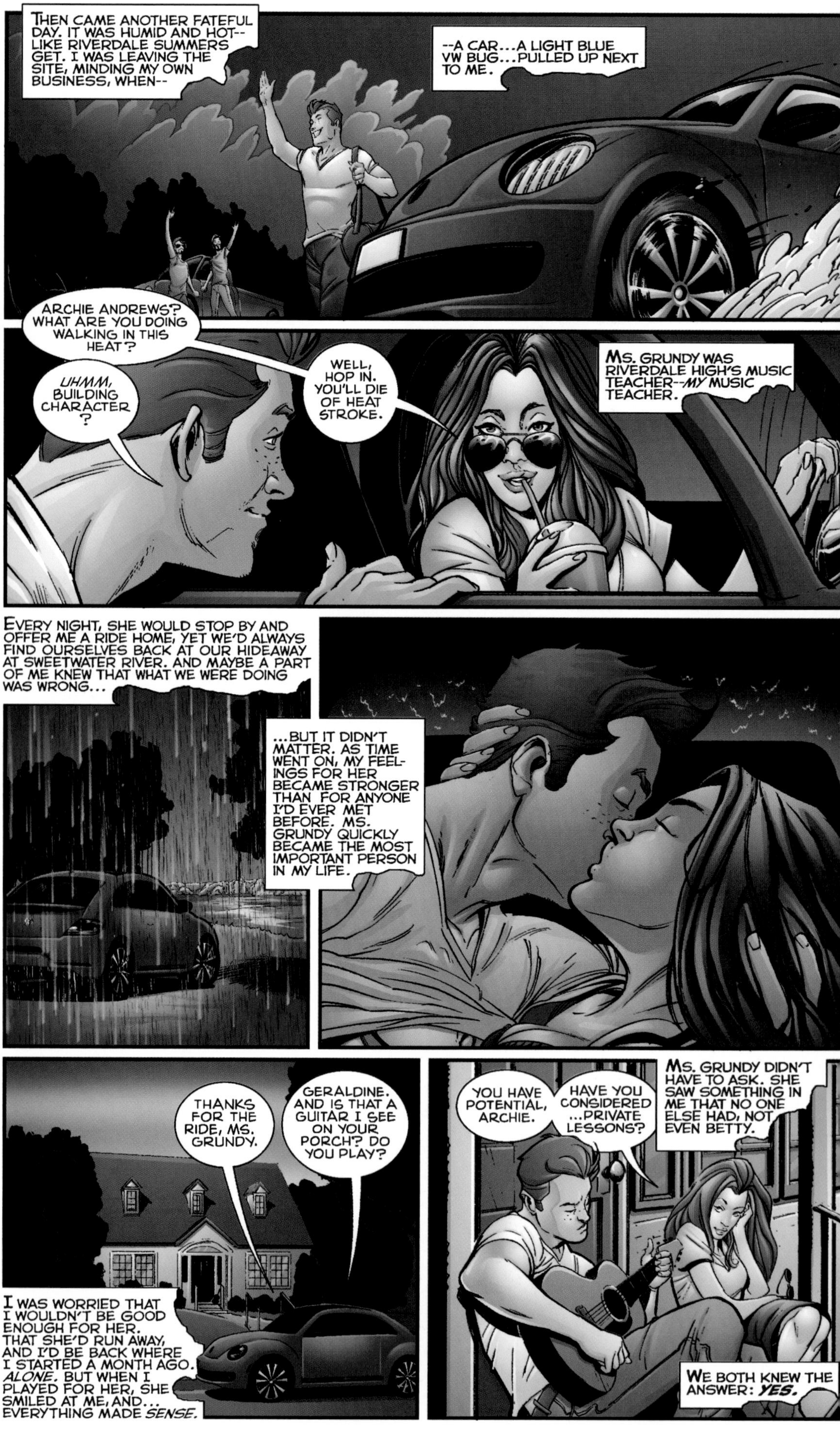
THEN CAME ANOTHER FATEFUL DAY. IT WAS HUMID AND HOT--LIKE RIVERDALE SUMMERS GET. I WAS LEAVING THE SITE, MINDING MY OWN BUSINESS, WHEN--
--A CAR...A LIGHT BLUE VW BUG...PULLED UP NEXT TO ME.
ARCHIE ANDREWS? WHAT ARE YOU DOING WALKING IN THIS HEAT?
UHMM, BUILDING CHARACTER?
WELL, HOP IN. YOU'LL DIE OF HEAT STROKE.
MS. GRUNDY WAS RIVERDALE HIGH'S MUSIC TEACHER--MY MUSIC TEACHER.
EVERY NIGHT, SHE WOULD STOP BY AND OFFER ME A RIDE HOME, YET WE'D ALWAYS FIND OURSELVES BACK AT OUR HIDEAWAY AT SWEETWATER RIVER. AND MAYBE A PART OF ME KNEW THAT WHAT WE WERE DOING WAS WRONG...
...BUT IT DIDN'T MATTER. AS TIME WENT ON, MY FEELINGS FOR HER BECAME STRONGER THAN FOR ANYONE I'D EVER MET BEFORE. MS. GRUNDY QUICKLY BECAME THE MOST IMPORTANT PERSON IN MY LIFE.
THANKS FOR THE RIDE, MS. GRUNDY.
GERALDINE. AND IS THAT A GUITAR I SEE ON YOUR PORCH? DO YOU PLAY?
I WAS WORRIED THAT I WOULDN'T BE GOOD ENOUGH FOR HER. THAT SHE'D RUN AWAY, AND I'D BE BACK WHERE I STARTED A MONTH AGO. ALONE. BUT WHEN I PLAYED FOR HER, SHE SMILED AT ME, AND... EVERYTHING MADE SENSE.
YOU HAVE POTENTIAL, ARCHIE.
HAVE YOU CONSIDERED ...PRIVATE LESSONS?
MS. GRUNDY DIDN'T HAVE TO ASK. SHE SAW SOMETHING IN ME THAT NO ONE ELSE HAD, NOT EVEN BETTY.
WE BOTH KNEW THE ANSWER: YES.

ONE DAY, TOWARDS THE END OF JUNE, I STOPPED BY POP'S AFTER WORK 'CAUSE I WANTED TO SURPRISE MS. GRUNDY WITH DINNER. THAT'S WHEN I SAW JUGHEAD FOR THE FIRST TIME ALL SUMMER. HE LOOKED...TIRED.

HELP WANTED

WELL, WELL, LOOK WHO'S BEEN HITTING THE GYM. SPARE A FEW MINUTES FOR YOUR OLD PAL?

I WAS SORT OF IN A RUSH, AND WASN'T PARTICU-LARLY IN THE MOOD TO REMINISCE, BUT A PART OF ME REALLY MISSED HIM.

SO I SAT.

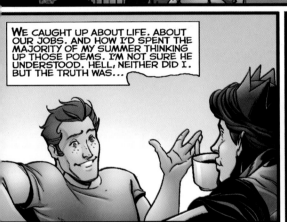

WE CAUGHT UP ABOUT LIFE. ABOUT OUR JOBS. AND HOW I'D SPENT THE MAJORITY OF MY SUMMER THINKING UP THOSE POEMS. I'M NOT SURE HE UNDERSTOOD. HELL, NEITHER DID I. BUT THE TRUTH WAS...

...MY MIND WAS ELSEWHERE. IT WAS WITH MS. GRUNDY. IN THAT VOLKS-WAGEN BUG NEAR SWEETWATER. THAT'S WHEN HE ASKED ME...

HEY!

REMEMBER WHEN WE WERE KIDS, HOW WE USED TO ROAD TRIP DOWN TO CENTERVILLE EVERY FOURTH OF JULY TO SEE THE FIREWORKS? WHY DON'T WE GO AGAIN THIS YEAR--YOU KNOW, LIKE OLD TIMES?

SOUNDS GREAT, JUG.

I HAVE NO IDEA WHY I SAID THOSE WORDS-- MAYBE BECAUSE I WAS THINKING OF THAT MOVIE QUOTE...

SO I'LL SEE YOU ON THE FOURTH.

SEE YA, PAL.

OUR NEXT MEET-ING WOULDN'T BE NEARLY AS FRIENDLY.

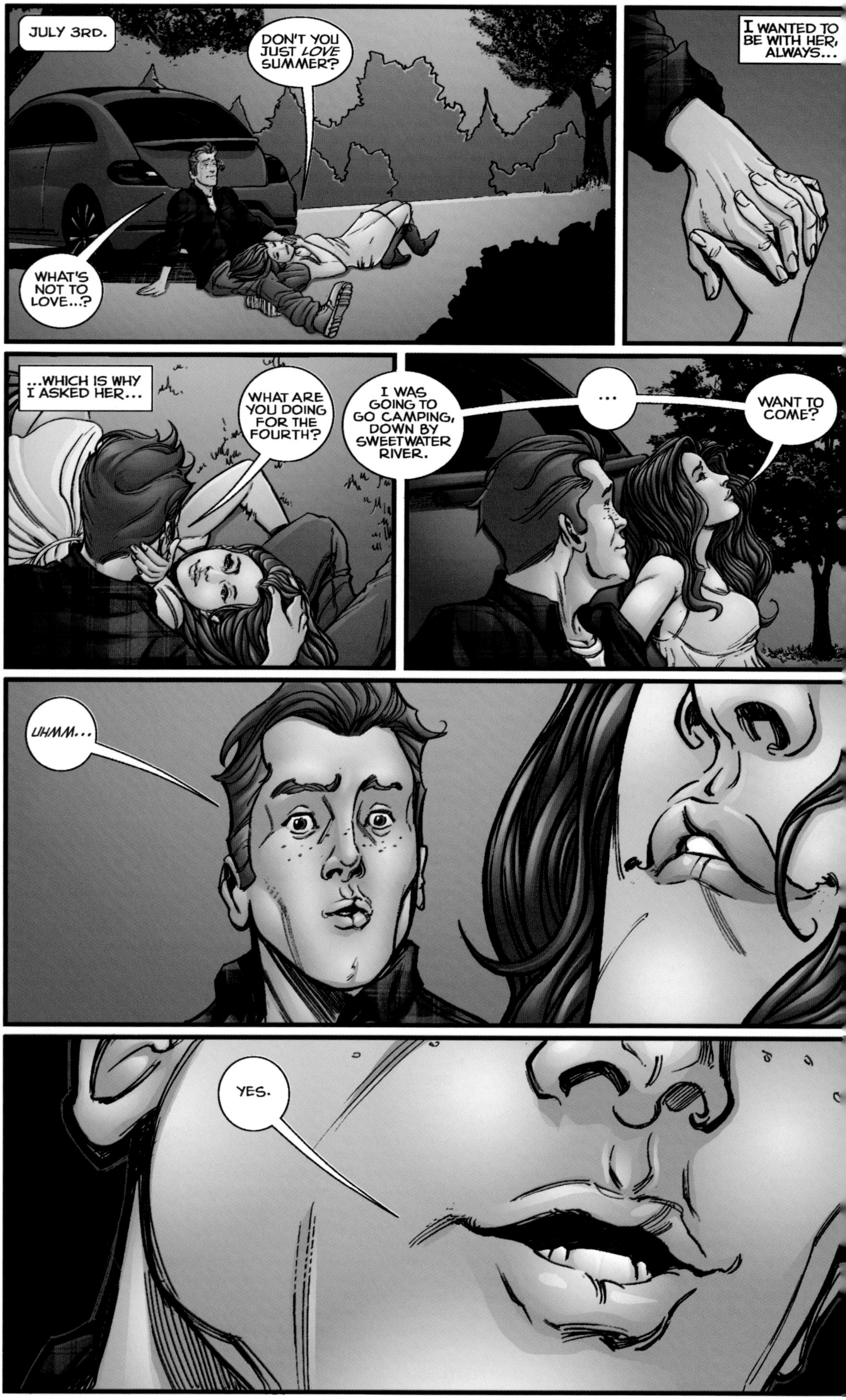
JULY 3RD.
DON'T YOU JUST *LOVE* SUMMER?
WHAT'S NOT TO LOVE...?
I WANTED TO BE WITH HER, ALWAYS...
...WHICH IS WHY I ASKED HER...
WHAT ARE YOU DOING FOR THE FOURTH?
I WAS GOING TO GO CAMPING, DOWN BY SWEETWATER RIVER.
...
WANT TO COME?
UHMM...
YES.

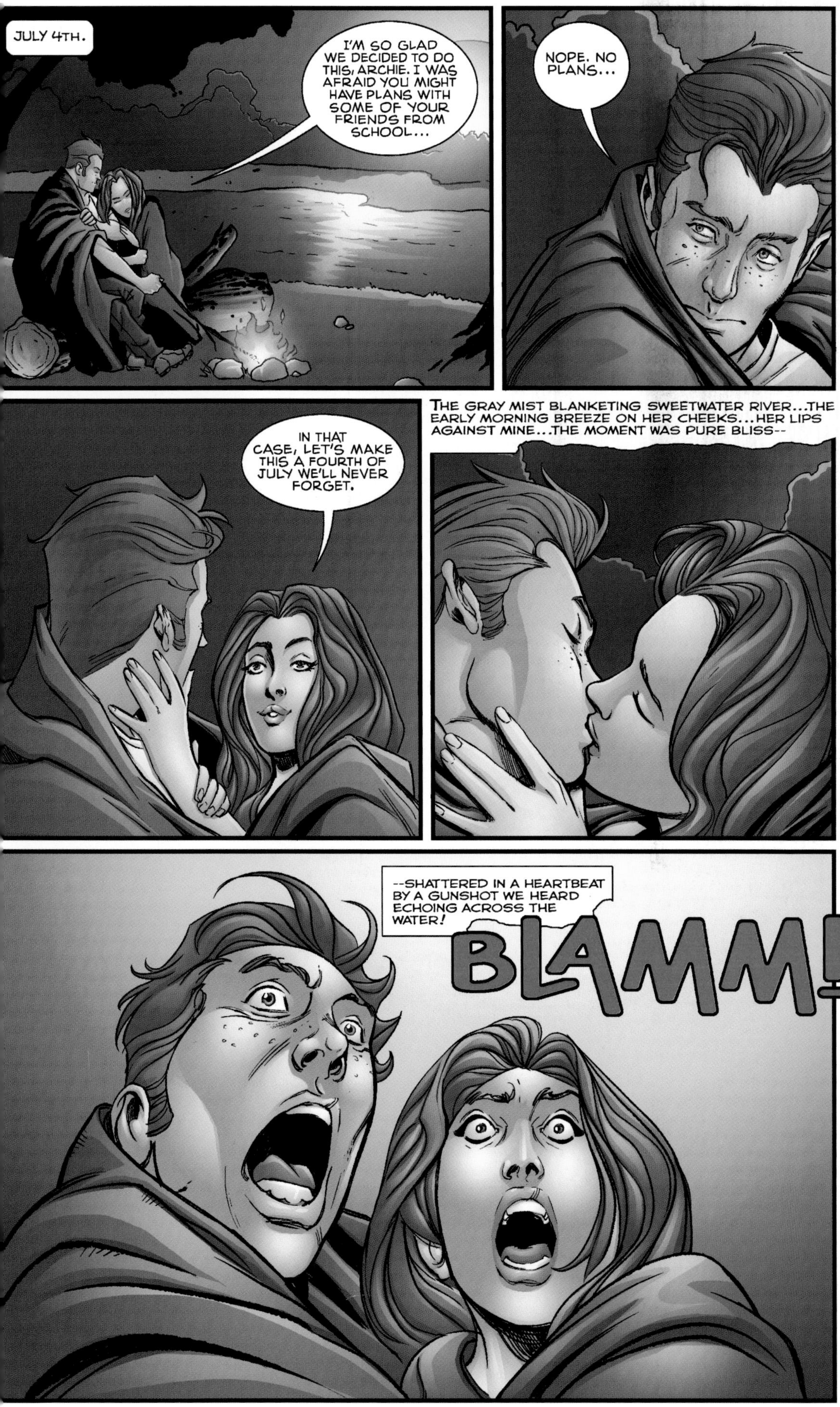
JULY 4TH.
I'M SO GLAD WE DECIDED TO DO THIS, ARCHIE. I WAS AFRAID YOU MIGHT HAVE PLANS WITH SOME OF YOUR FRIENDS FROM SCHOOL...
NOPE. NO PLANS...
IN THAT CASE, LET'S MAKE THIS A FOURTH OF JULY WE'LL NEVER FORGET.
THE GRAY MIST BLANKETING SWEETWATER RIVER...THE EARLY MORNING BREEZE ON HER CHEEKS...HER LIPS AGAINST MINE...THE MOMENT WAS PURE BLISS--
--SHATTERED IN A HEARTBEAT BY A GUNSHOT WE HEARD ECHOING ACROSS THE WATER!
BLAMM!

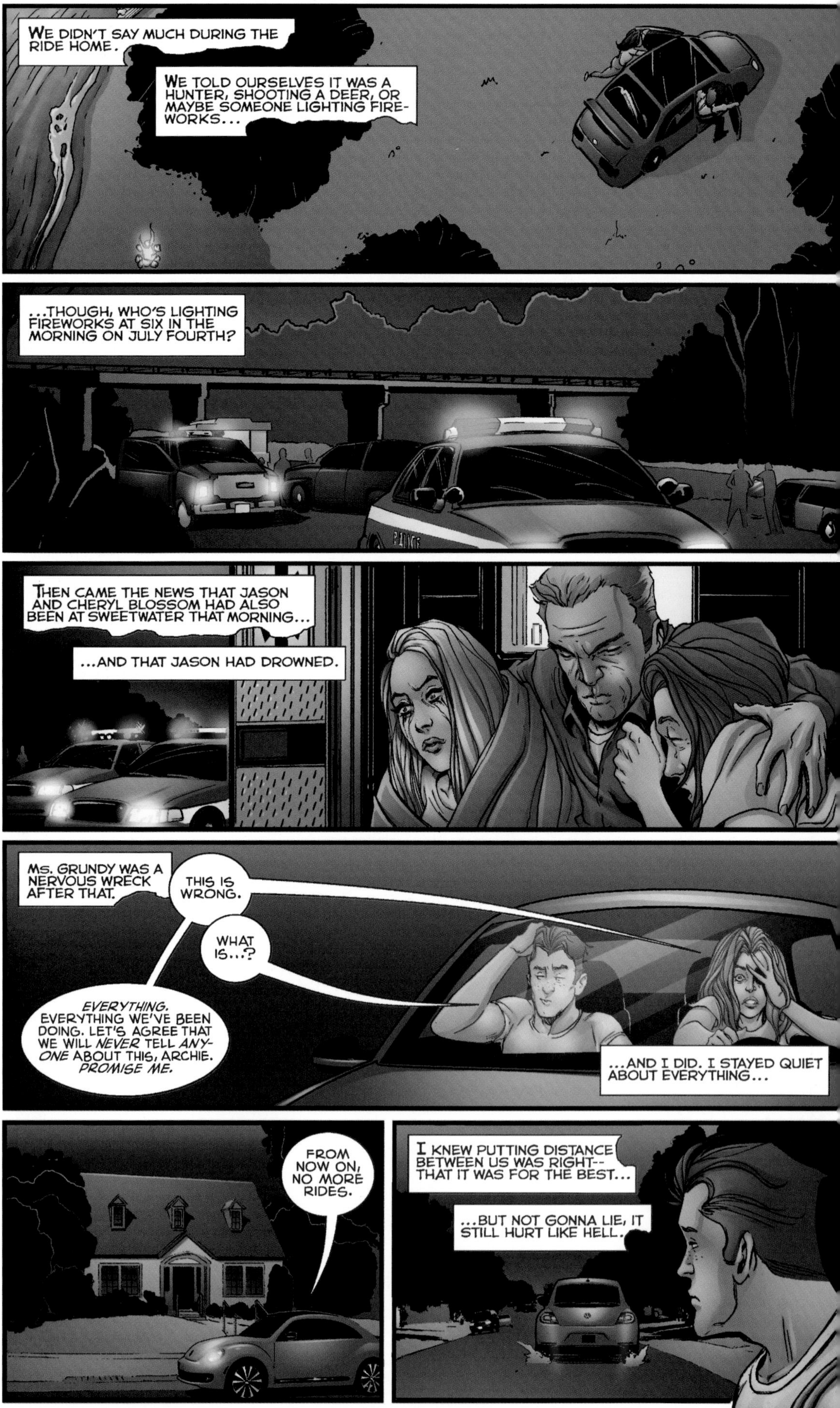
WE DIDN'T SAY MUCH DURING THE RIDE HOME.
WE TOLD OURSELVES IT WAS A HUNTER, SHOOTING A DEER, OR MAYBE SOMEONE LIGHTING FIRE-WORKS...
...THOUGH, WHO'S LIGHTING FIREWORKS AT SIX IN THE MORNING ON JULY FOURTH?
THEN CAME THE NEWS THAT JASON AND CHERYL BLOSSOM HAD ALSO BEEN AT SWEETWATER THAT MORNING...
...AND THAT JASON HAD DROWNED.
MS. GRUNDY WAS A NERVOUS WRECK AFTER THAT.
THIS IS WRONG.
WHAT IS...?
EVERYTHING. EVERYTHING WE'VE BEEN DOING. LET'S AGREE THAT WE WILL NEVER TELL ANY-ONE ABOUT THIS, ARCHIE. PROMISE ME.
...AND I DID. I STAYED QUIET ABOUT EVERYTHING...
FROM NOW ON, NO MORE RIDES.
I KNEW PUTTING DISTANCE BETWEEN US WAS RIGHT--THAT IT WAS FOR THE BEST...
...BUT NOT GONNA LIE, IT STILL HURT LIKE HELL.

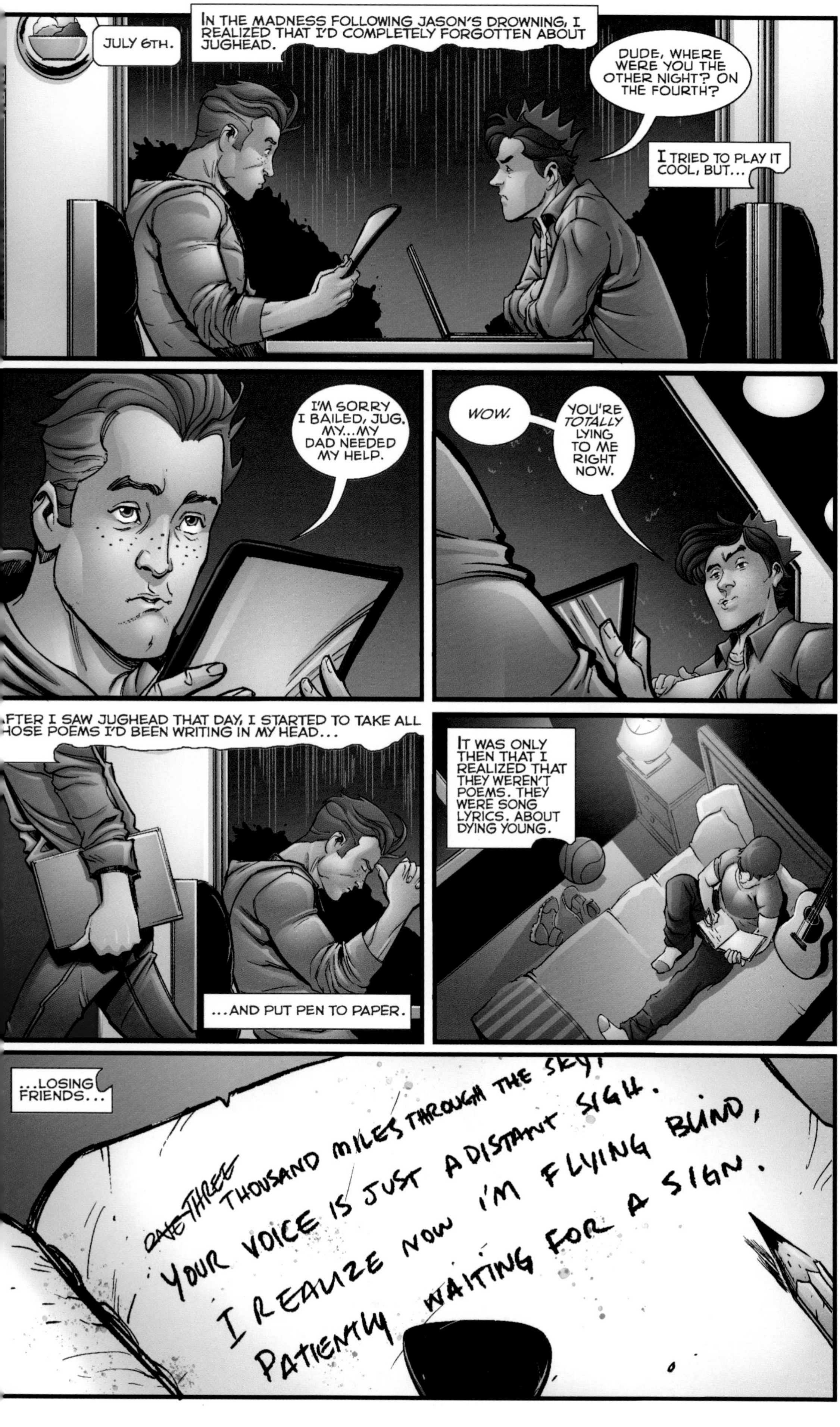
JULY 6TH.
IN THE MADNESS FOLLOWING JASON'S DROWNING, I REALIZED THAT I'D COMPLETELY FORGOTTEN ABOUT JUGHEAD.
DUDE, WHERE WERE YOU THE OTHER NIGHT? ON THE FOURTH?
I TRIED TO PLAY IT COOL, BUT...
I'M SORRY I BAILED, JUG. MY...MY DAD NEEDED MY HELP.
WOW.
YOU'RE TOTALLY LYING TO ME RIGHT NOW.
FTER I SAW JUGHEAD THAT DAY, I STARTED TO TAKE ALL HOSE POEMS I'D BEEN WRITING IN MY HEAD...
...AND PUT PEN TO PAPER.
IT WAS ONLY THEN THAT I REALIZED THAT THEY WEREN'T POEMS. THEY WERE SONG LYRICS. ABOUT DYING YOUNG.
...LOSING FRIENDS...
~~ONE~~ THREE THOUSAND MILES THROUGH THE SKY,
YOUR VOICE IS JUST A DISTANT SIGH.
I REALIZE NOW I'M FLYING BLIND,
PATIENTLY WAITING FOR A SIGN.

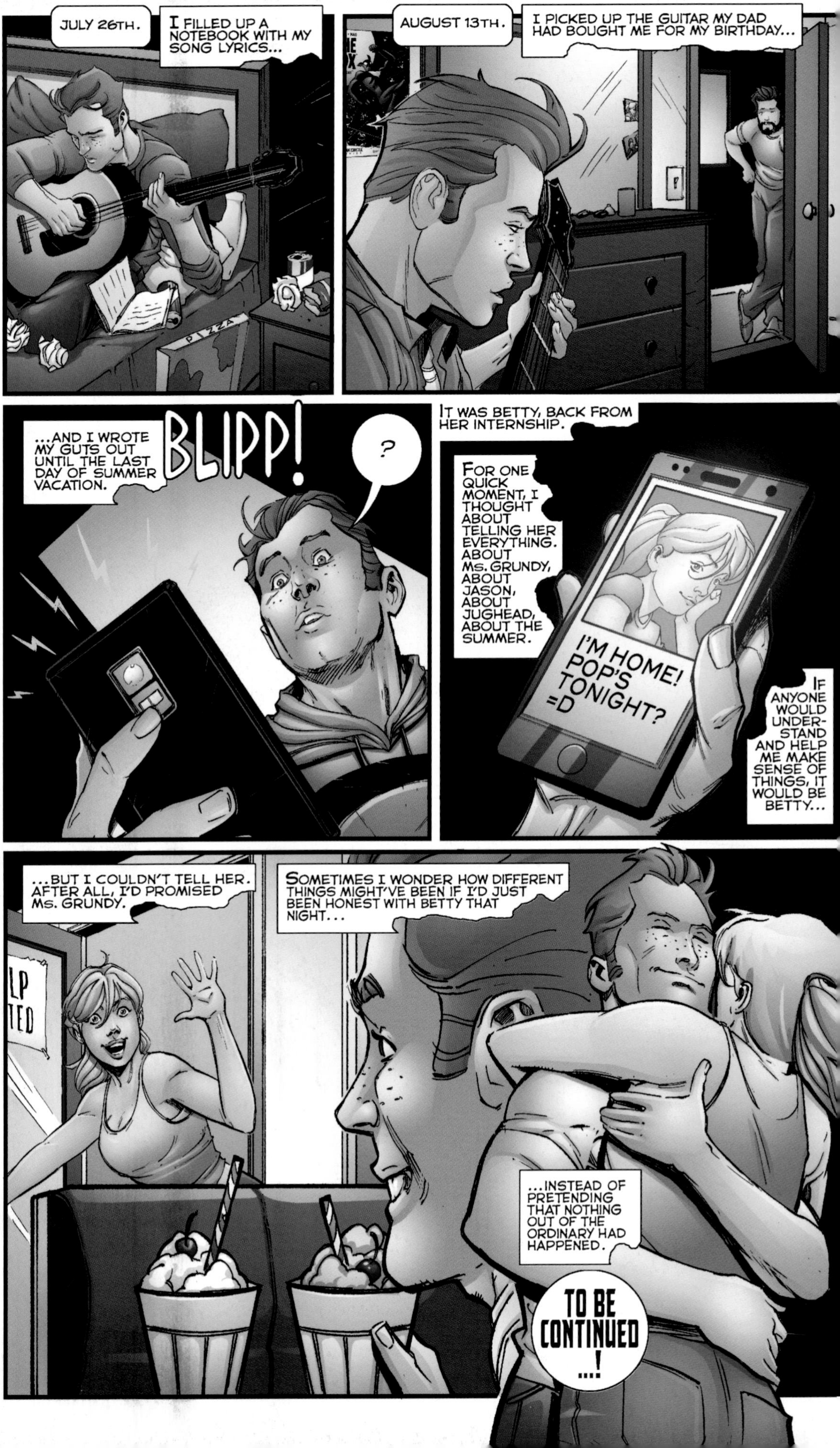

JULY 26TH.
I FILLED UP A NOTEBOOK WITH MY SONG LYRICS...
AUGUST 13TH.
I PICKED UP THE GUITAR MY DAD HAD BOUGHT ME FOR MY BIRTHDAY...
...AND I WROTE MY GUTS OUT UNTIL THE LAST DAY OF SUMMER VACATION.
BLIPP!
?
IT WAS BETTY, BACK FROM HER INTERNSHIP.
FOR ONE QUICK MOMENT, I THOUGHT ABOUT TELLING HER EVERYTHING. ABOUT MS. GRUNDY, ABOUT JASON, ABOUT JUGHEAD, ABOUT THE SUMMER.
I'M HOME! POP'S TONIGHT? =D
IF ANYONE WOULD UNDER-STAND AND HELP ME MAKE SENSE OF THINGS, IT WOULD BE BETTY...
...BUT I COULDN'T TELL HER. AFTER ALL, I'D PROMISED MS. GRUNDY.
SOMETIMES I WONDER HOW DIFFERENT THINGS MIGHT'VE BEEN IF I'D JUST BEEN HONEST WITH BETTY THAT NIGHT...
...INSTEAD OF PRETENDING THAT NOTHING OUT OF THE ORDINARY HAD HAPPENED.
TO BE CONTINUED ...!

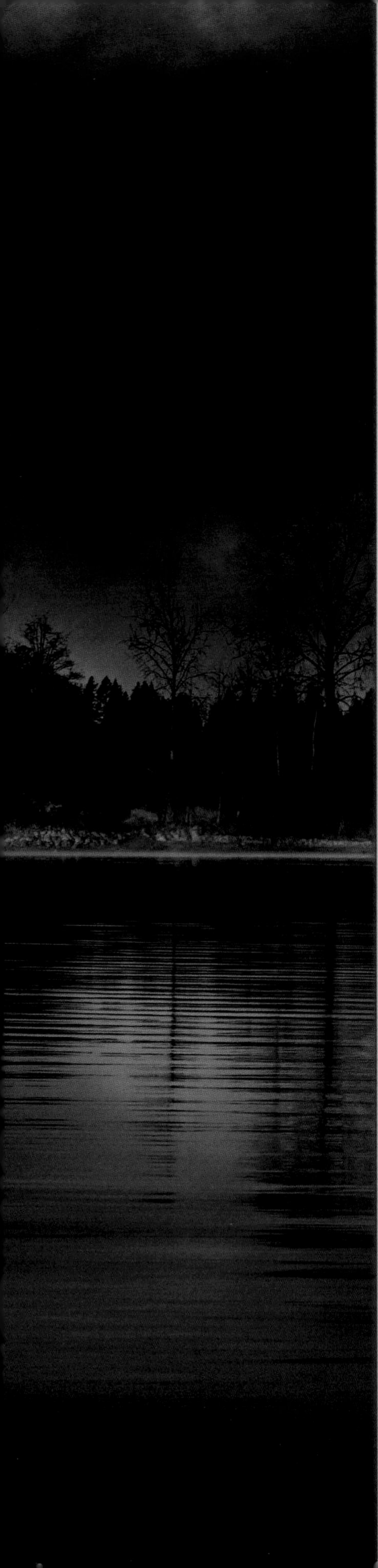

CHAPTER TWO

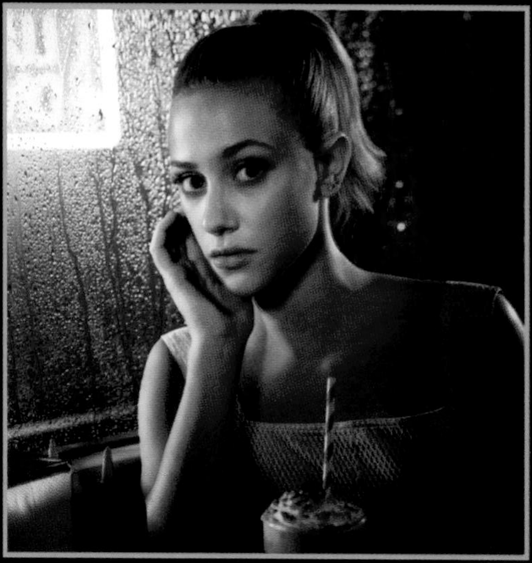

BETTY IN SUMMER NIGHTS

WRITER:
BRITTA LUNDIN

ART:
JIM TOWE

COLORS:
GLENN WHITMORE

LETTERS:
JANICE CHIANG

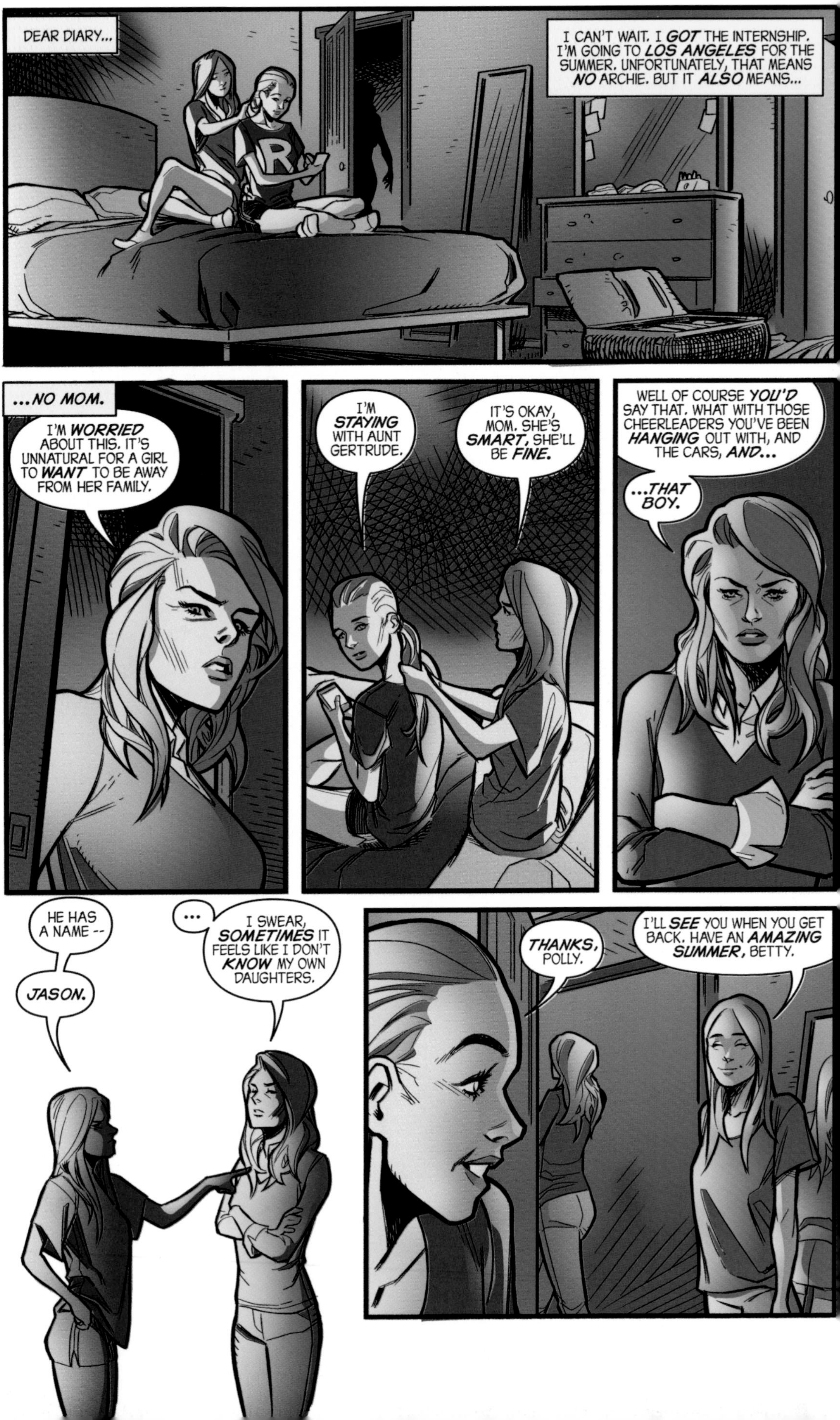
DEAR DIARY...
I CAN'T WAIT. I GOT THE INTERNSHIP. I'M GOING TO LOS ANGELES FOR THE SUMMER. UNFORTUNATELY, THAT MEANS NO ARCHIE. BUT IT ALSO MEANS...
...NO MOM.
I'M WORRIED ABOUT THIS. IT'S UNNATURAL FOR A GIRL TO WANT TO BE AWAY FROM HER FAMILY.
I'M STAYING WITH AUNT GERTRUDE.
IT'S OKAY, MOM. SHE'S SMART, SHE'LL BE FINE.
WELL OF COURSE YOU'D SAY THAT. WHAT WITH THOSE CHEERLEADERS YOU'VE BEEN HANGING OUT WITH, AND THE CARS, AND...
...THAT BOY.
HE HAS A NAME --
JASON.
...
I SWEAR, SOMETIMES IT FEELS LIKE I DON'T KNOW MY OWN DAUGHTERS.
THANKS, POLLY.
I'LL SEE YOU WHEN YOU GET BACK. HAVE AN AMAZING SUMMER, BETTY.

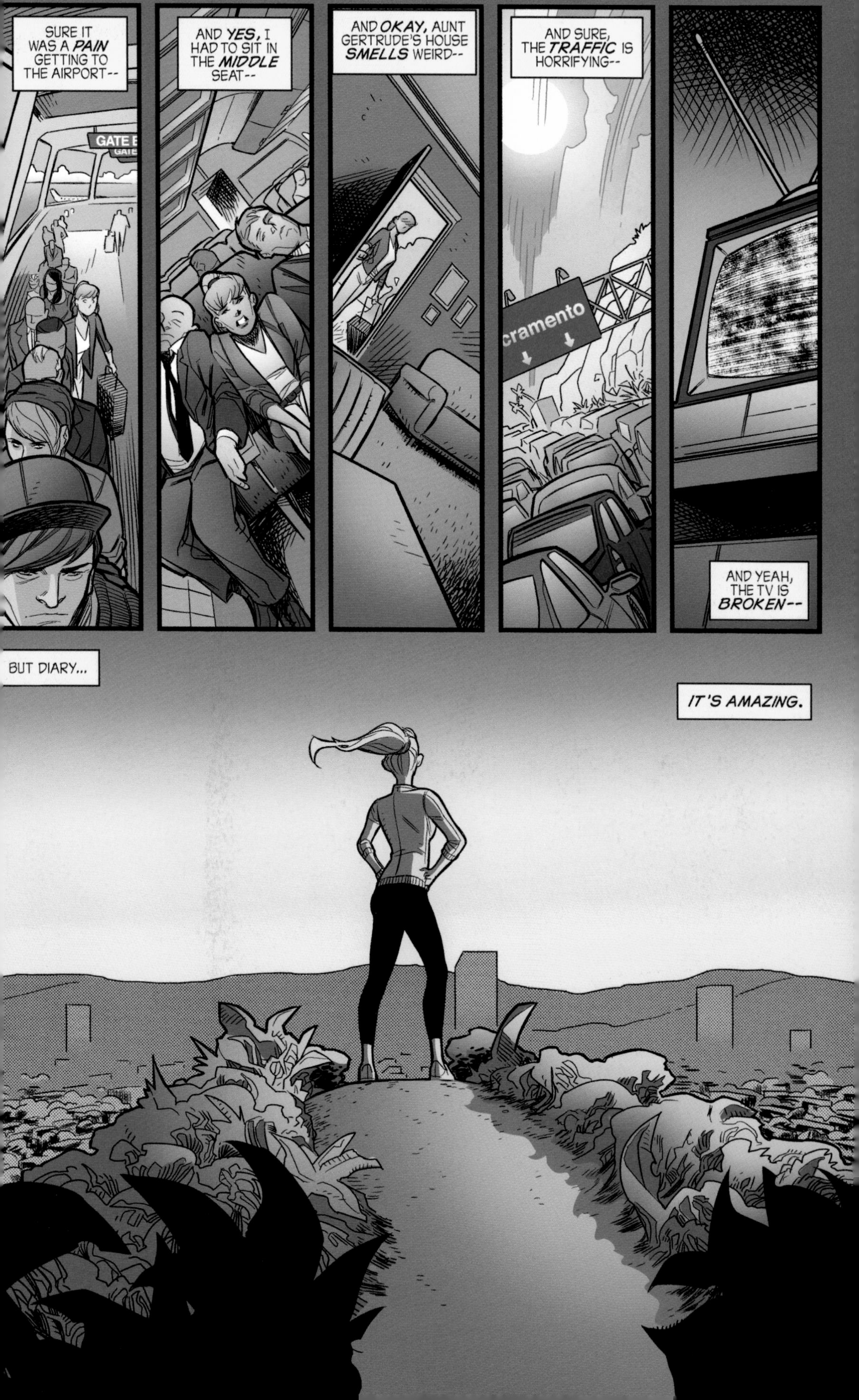

SURE IT WAS A PAIN GETTING TO THE AIRPORT--
GATE B
AND YES, I HAD TO SIT IN THE MIDDLE SEAT--
AND OKAY, AUNT GERTRUDE'S HOUSE SMELLS WEIRD--
AND SURE, THE TRAFFIC IS HORRIFYING--
cramento
AND YEAH, THE TV IS BROKEN--
BUT DIARY...
IT'S AMAZING.

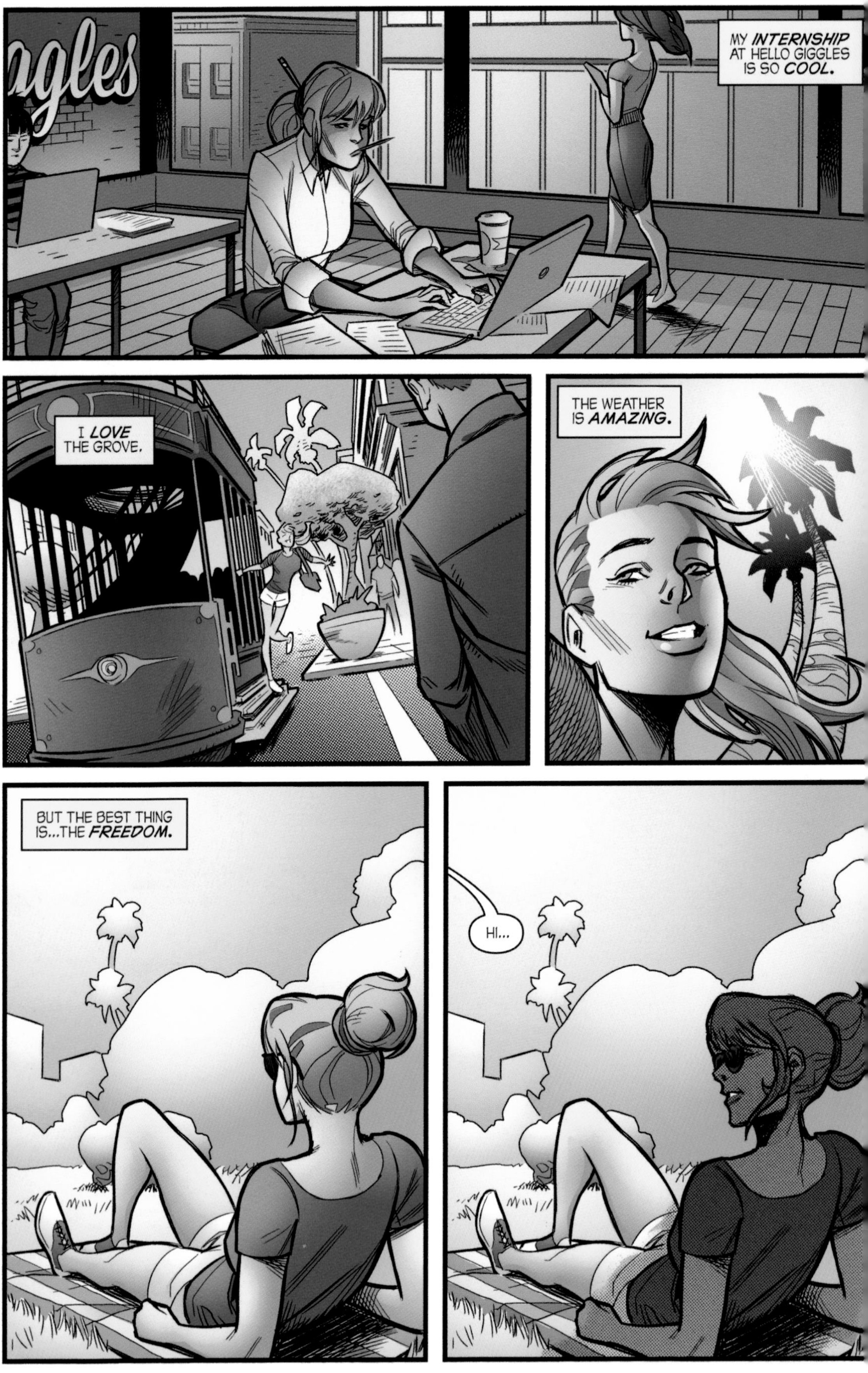

MY INTERNSHIP AT HELLO GIGGLES IS SO COOL.
I LOVE THE GROVE.
THE WEATHER IS AMAZING.
BUT THE BEST THING IS...THE FREEDOM.
HI...

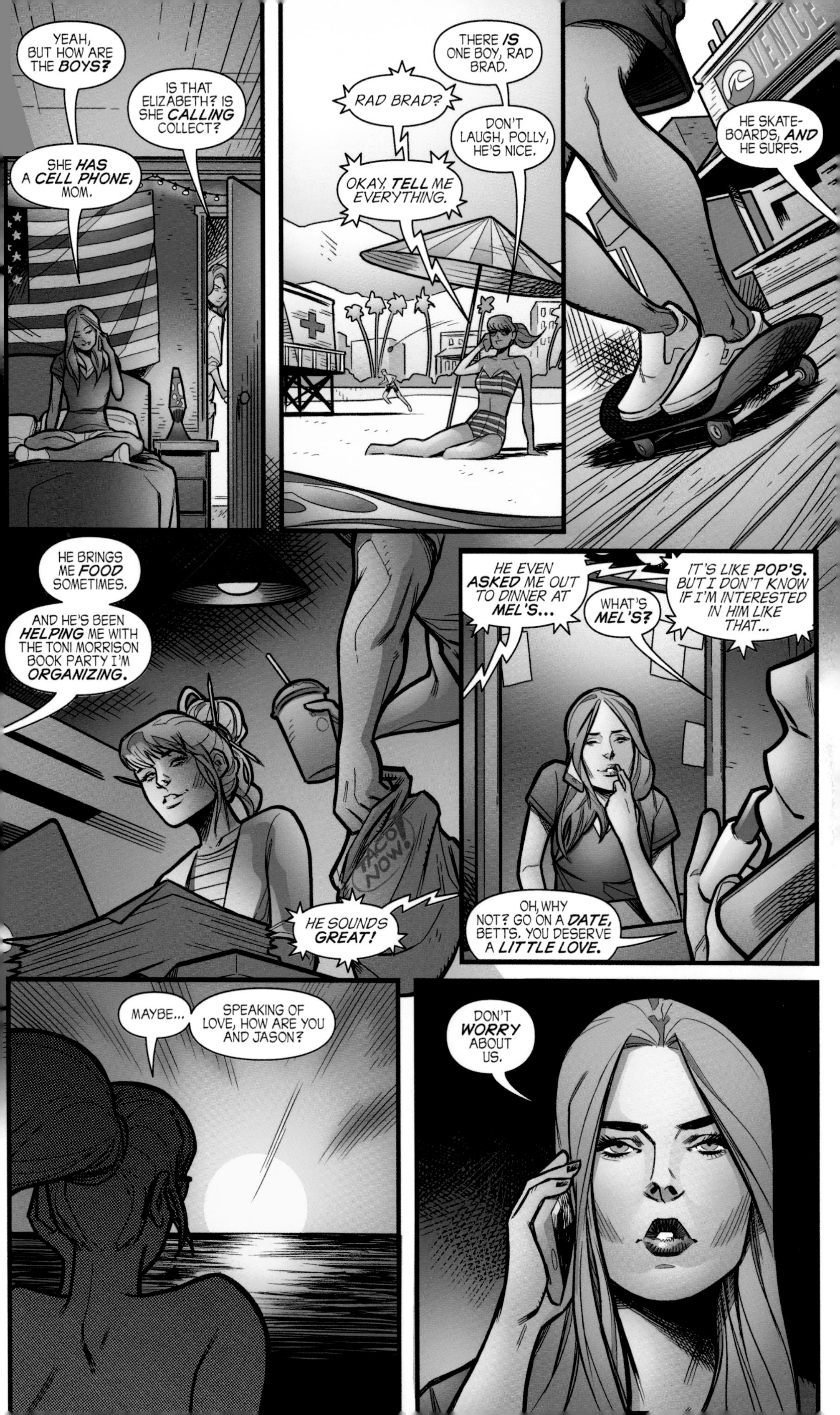
YEAH, BUT HOW ARE THE BOYS?
IS THAT ELIZABETH? IS SHE CALLING COLLECT?
SHE HAS A CELL PHONE, MOM.
THERE IS ONE BOY, RAD BRAD.
RAD BRAD?
DON'T LAUGH, POLLY, HE'S NICE.
OKAY, TELL ME EVERYTHING.
VENICE
HE SKATE-BOARDS, AND HE SURFS.
HE BRINGS ME FOOD SOMETIMES.
AND HE'S BEEN HELPING ME WITH THE TONI MORRISON BOOK PARTY I'M ORGANIZING.
TACO NOW!
HE SOUNDS GREAT!
HE EVEN ASKED ME OUT TO DINNER AT MEL'S...
WHAT'S MEL'S?
IT'S LIKE POP'S. BUT I DON'T KNOW IF I'M INTERESTED IN HIM LIKE THAT...
OH, WHY NOT? GO ON A DATE, BETTS. YOU DESERVE A LITTLE LOVE.
MAYBE...
SPEAKING OF LOVE, HOW ARE YOU AND JASON?
DON'T WORRY ABOUT US.

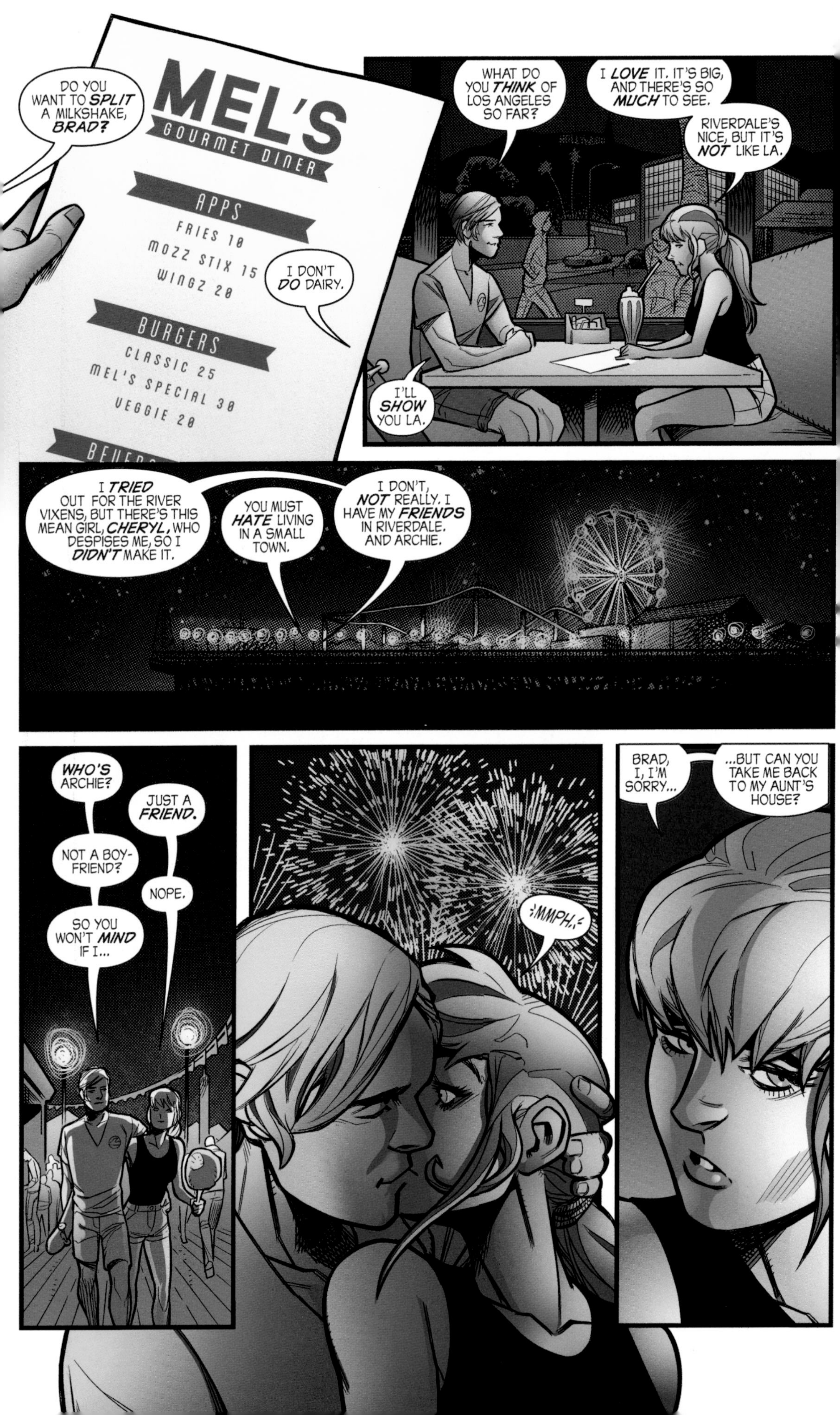
MEL'S
GOURMET DINER
APPS
FRIES 10
MOZZ STIX 15
WINGZ 20
BURGERS
CLASSIC 25
MEL'S SPECIAL 30
VEGGIE 20
DO YOU WANT TO SPLIT A MILKSHAKE, BRAD?
I DON'T DO DAIRY.
WHAT DO YOU THINK OF LOS ANGELES SO FAR?
I LOVE IT. IT'S BIG, AND THERE'S SO MUCH TO SEE.
RIVERDALE'S NICE, BUT IT'S NOT LIKE LA.
I'LL SHOW YOU LA.
I TRIED OUT FOR THE RIVER VIXENS, BUT THERE'S THIS MEAN GIRL, CHERYL, WHO DESPISES ME, SO I DIDN'T MAKE IT.
YOU MUST HATE LIVING IN A SMALL TOWN.
I DON'T, NOT REALLY. I HAVE MY FRIENDS IN RIVERDALE. AND ARCHIE.
WHO'S ARCHIE?
JUST A FRIEND.
NOT A BOY-FRIEND?
NOPE.
SO YOU WON'T MIND IF I...
MMPH!
BRAD, I, I'M SORRY...
...BUT CAN YOU TAKE ME BACK TO MY AUNT'S HOUSE?

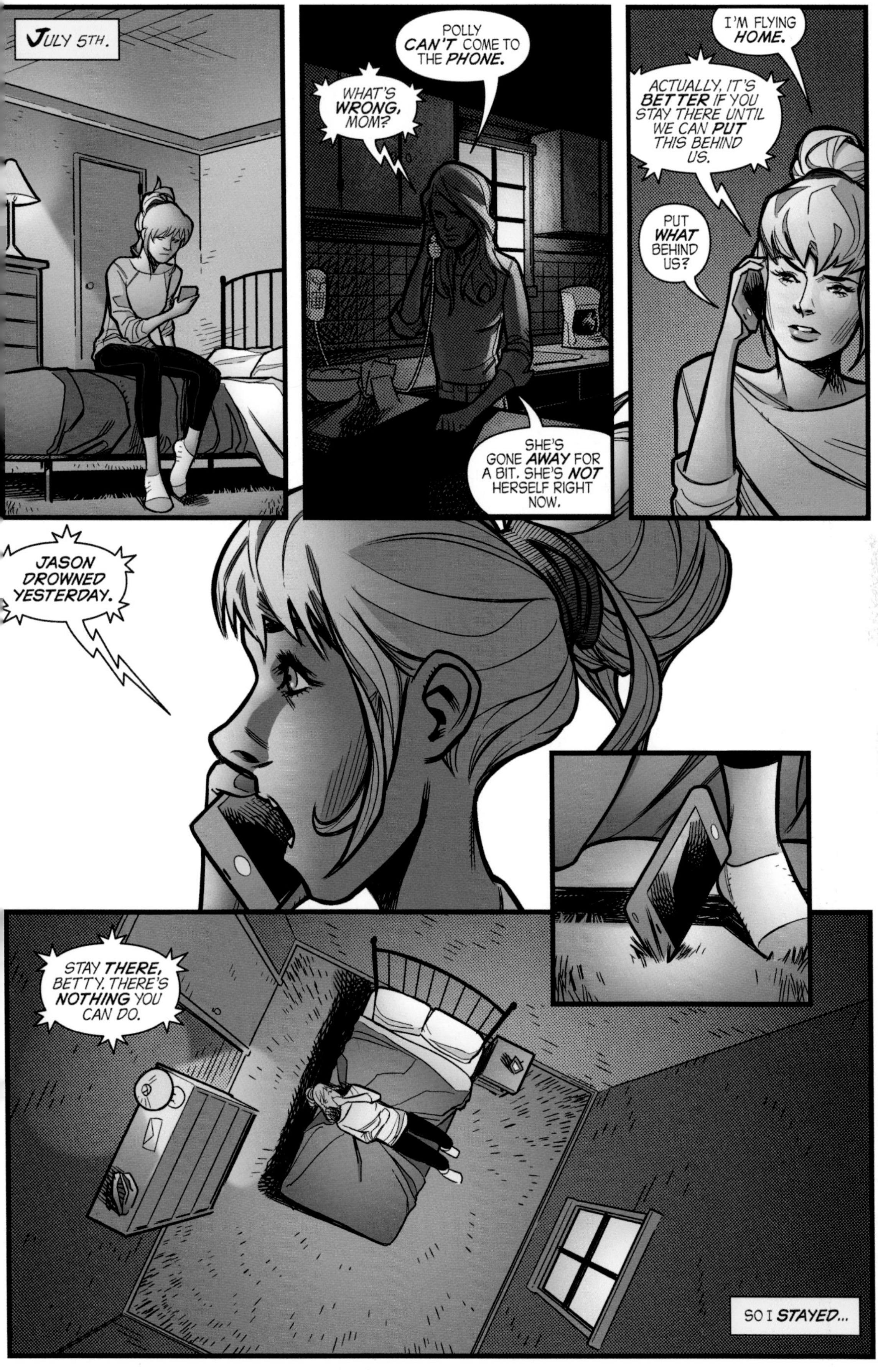
JULY 5TH.
WHAT'S WRONG, MOM?
POLLY CAN'T COME TO THE PHONE.
SHE'S GONE AWAY FOR A BIT. SHE'S NOT HERSELF RIGHT NOW.
I'M FLYING HOME.
ACTUALLY, IT'S BETTER IF YOU STAY THERE UNTIL WE CAN PUT THIS BEHIND US.
PUT WHAT BEHIND US?
JASON DROWNED YESTERDAY.
STAY THERE, BETTY. THERE'S NOTHING YOU CAN DO.
SO I STAYED...

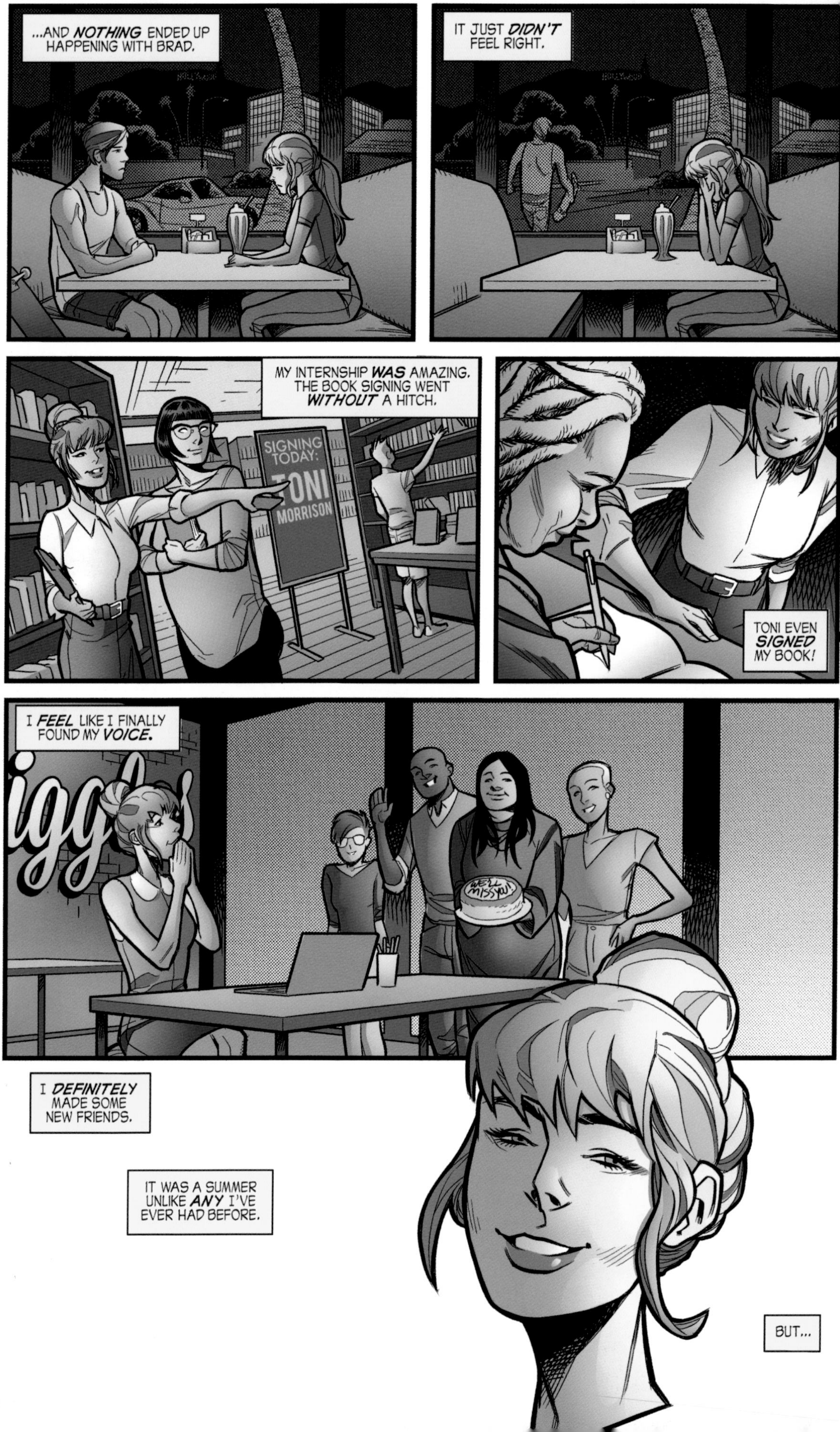
...AND NOTHING ENDED UP HAPPENING WITH BRAD.
IT JUST DIDN'T FEEL RIGHT.
MY INTERNSHIP WAS AMAZING. THE BOOK SIGNING WENT WITHOUT A HITCH.
SIGNING TODAY: TONI MORRISON
TONI EVEN SIGNED MY BOOK!
I FEEL LIKE I FINALLY FOUND MY VOICE.
WE'LL MISS YOU!
I DEFINITELY MADE SOME NEW FRIENDS.
IT WAS A SUMMER UNLIKE ANY I'VE EVER HAD BEFORE.
BUT...

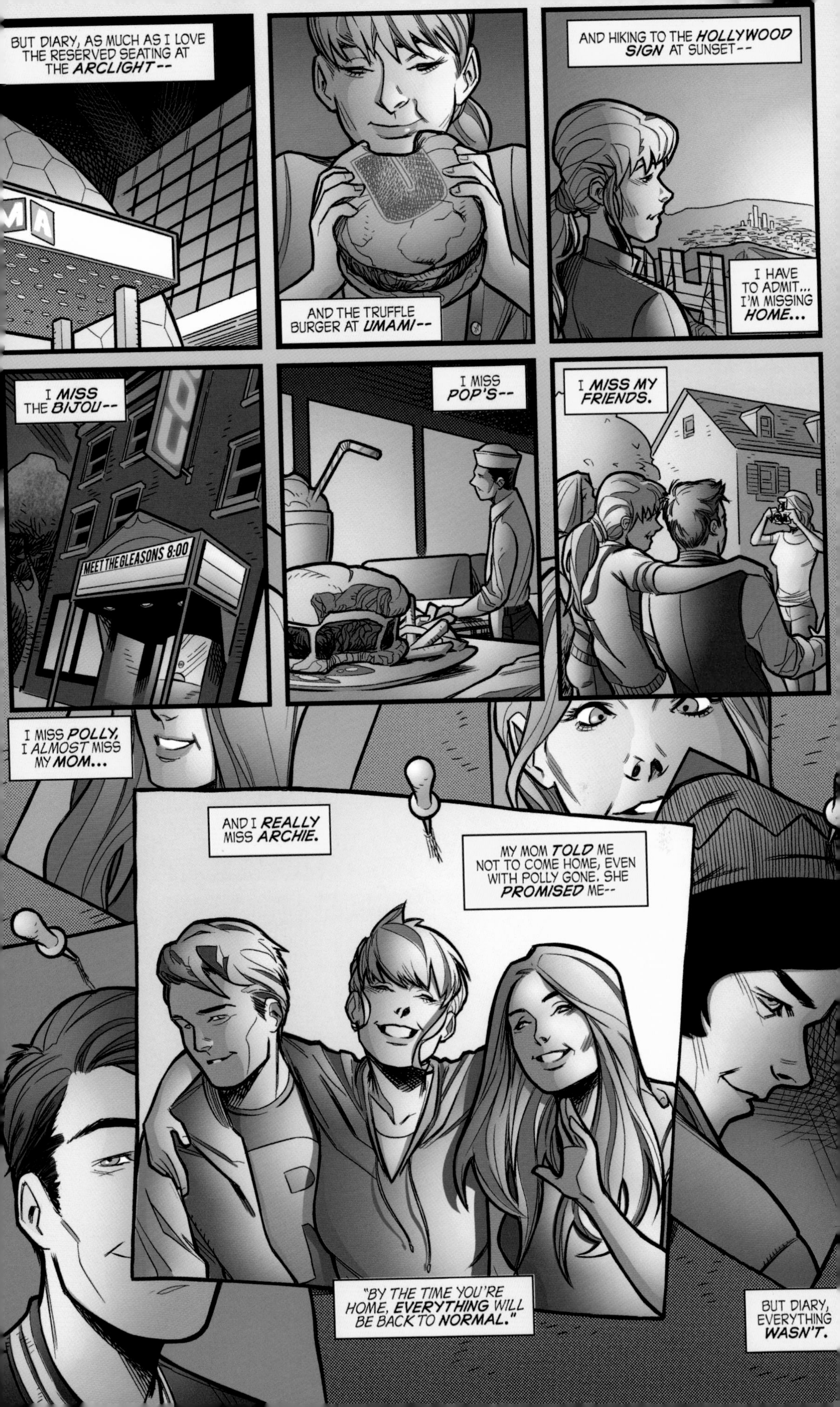
BUT DIARY, AS MUCH AS I LOVE THE RESERVED SEATING AT THE ARCLIGHT--
AND THE TRUFFLE BURGER AT UMAMI--
AND HIKING TO THE HOLLYWOOD SIGN AT SUNSET--
I HAVE TO ADMIT... I'M MISSING HOME...
I MISS THE BIJOU--
MEET THE GLEASONS 8:00
I MISS POP'S--
I MISS MY FRIENDS.
I MISS POLLY. I ALMOST MISS MY MOM...
AND I REALLY MISS ARCHIE.
MY MOM TOLD ME NOT TO COME HOME, EVEN WITH POLLY GONE. SHE PROMISED ME--
"BY THE TIME YOU'RE HOME, EVERYTHING WILL BE BACK TO NORMAL."
BUT DIARY, EVERYTHING WASN'T.

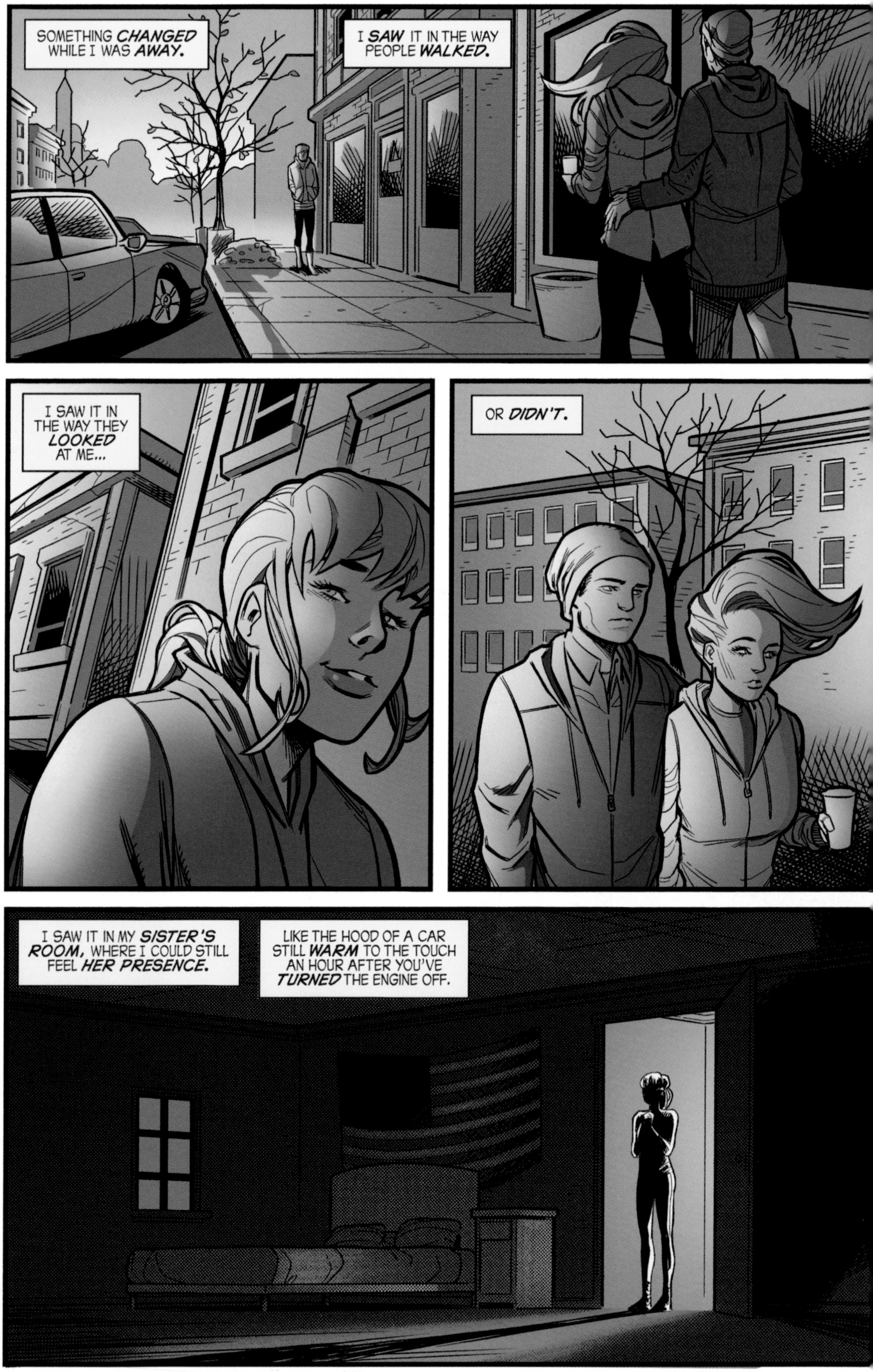
SOMETHING CHANGED WHILE I WAS AWAY.
I SAW IT IN THE WAY PEOPLE WALKED.
I SAW IT IN THE WAY THEY LOOKED AT ME...
OR DIDN'T.
I SAW IT IN MY SISTER'S ROOM, WHERE I COULD STILL FEEL HER PRESENCE.
LIKE THE HOOD OF A CAR STILL WARM TO THE TOUCH AN HOUR AFTER YOU'VE TURNED THE ENGINE OFF.

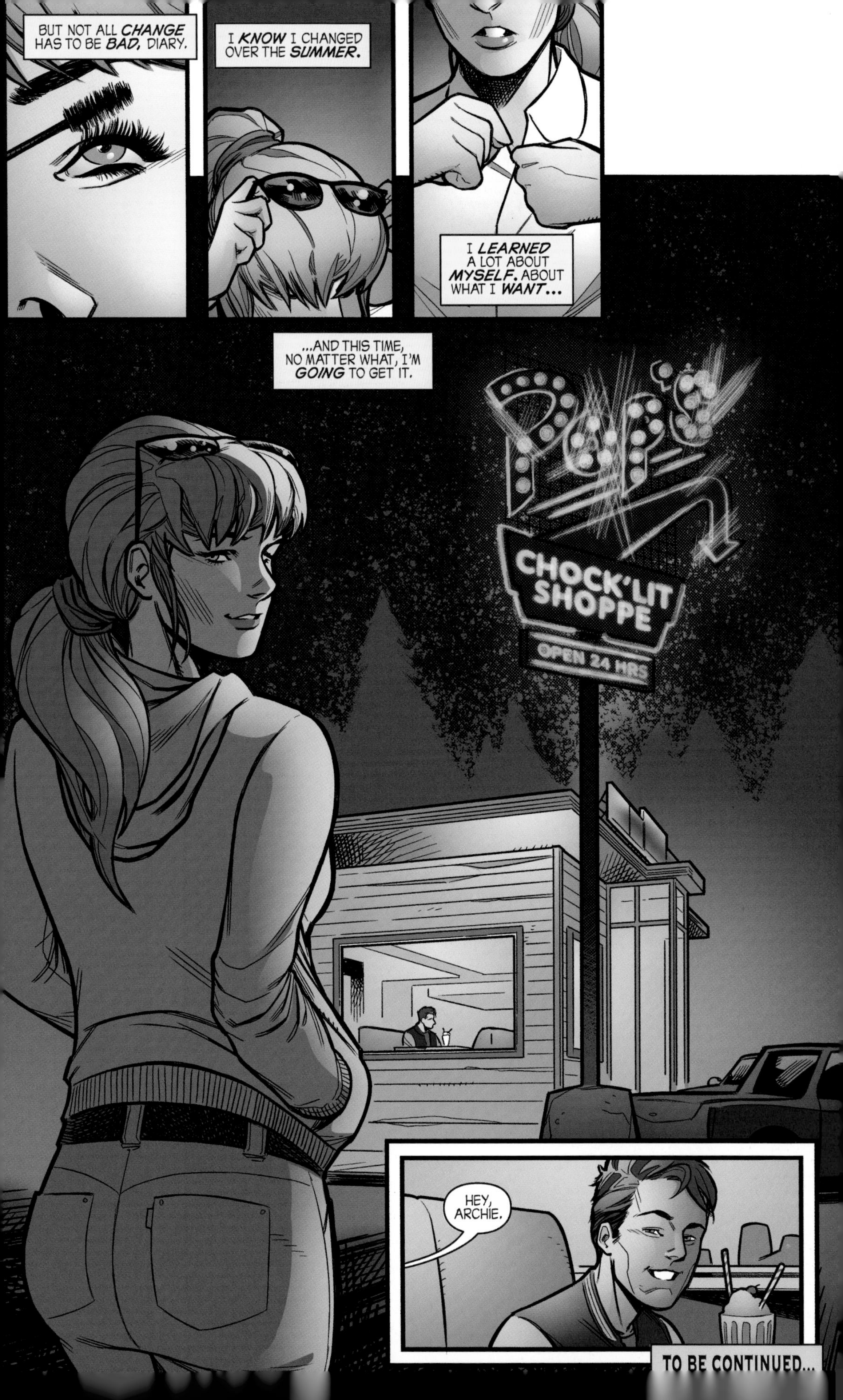
BUT NOT ALL CHANGE HAS TO BE BAD, DIARY.
I KNOW I CHANGED OVER THE SUMMER.
I LEARNED A LOT ABOUT MYSELF. ABOUT WHAT I WANT...
...AND THIS TIME, NO MATTER WHAT, I'M GOING TO GET IT.
CHOCK'LIT SHOPPE
OPEN 24 HRS
HEY, ARCHIE.
TO BE CONTINUED...

CHAPTER THREE

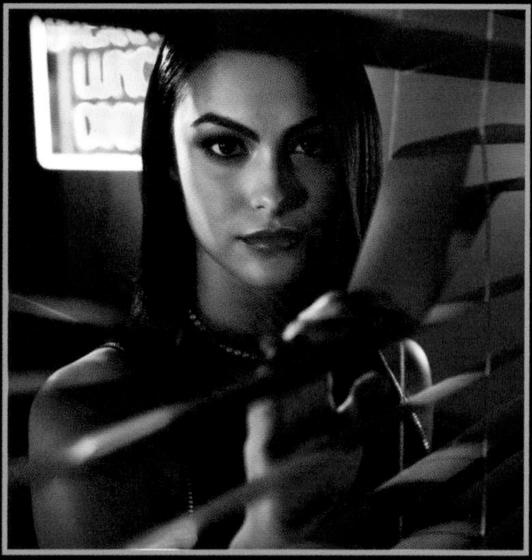

VERONICA IN FALL FROM GRACE

WRITER:
JAMES DEWILLE

ART:
THOMAS PITILLI

COLORS:
ANDRE SZYMANOWICZ

LETTERS:
JOHN WORKMAN

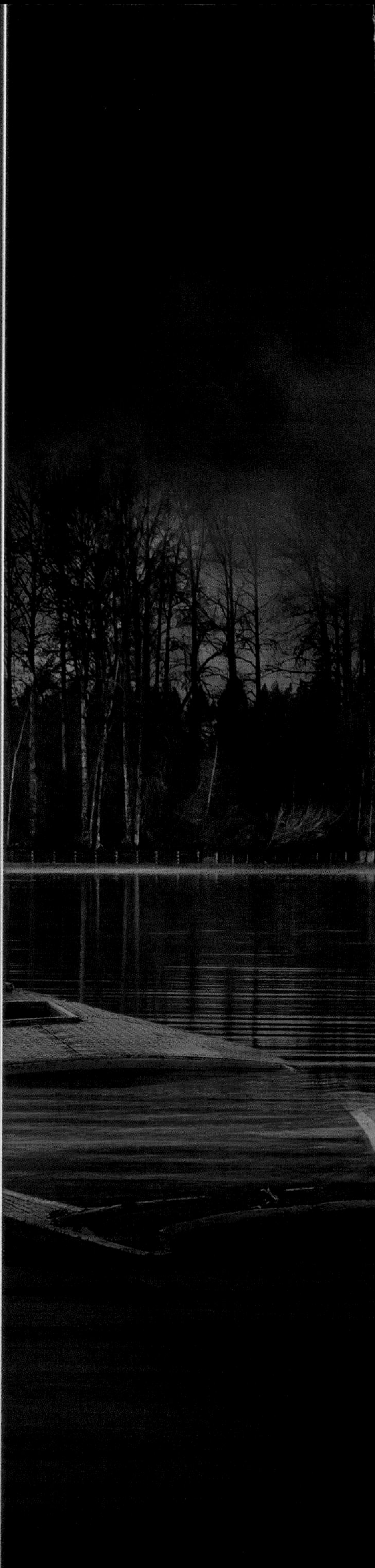

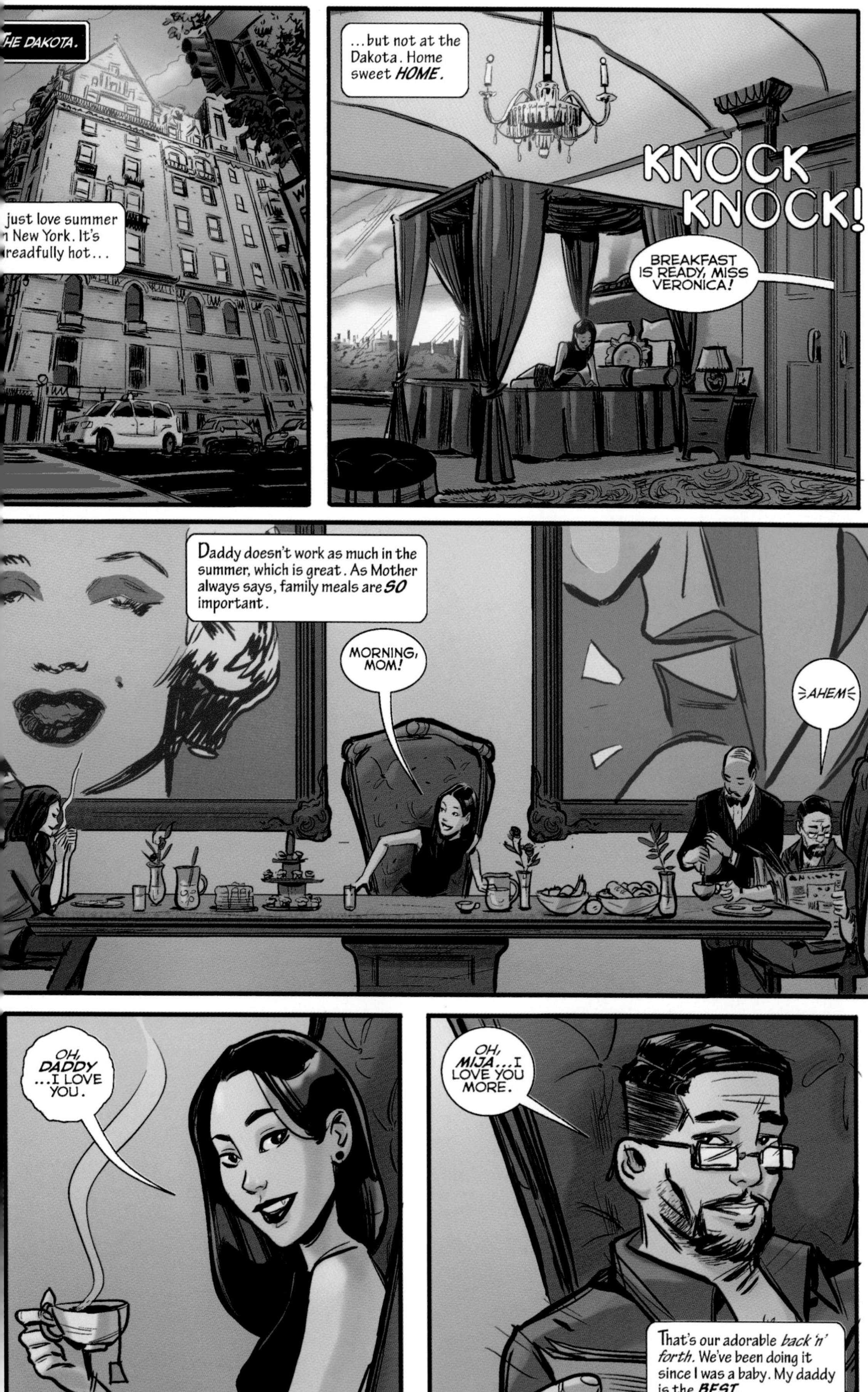
HE DAKOTA.
just love summer
n New York. It's
readfully hot...
...but not at the Dakota. Home sweet HOME.
KNOCK KNOCK!
BREAKFAST IS READY, MISS VERONICA!
Daddy doesn't work as much in the summer, which is great. As Mother always says, family meals are SO important.
MORNING, MOM!
AHEM
OH, DADDY ...I LOVE YOU.
OH, MIJA...I LOVE YOU MORE.
That's our adorable back 'n' forth. We've been doing it since I was a baby. My daddy is the BEST.

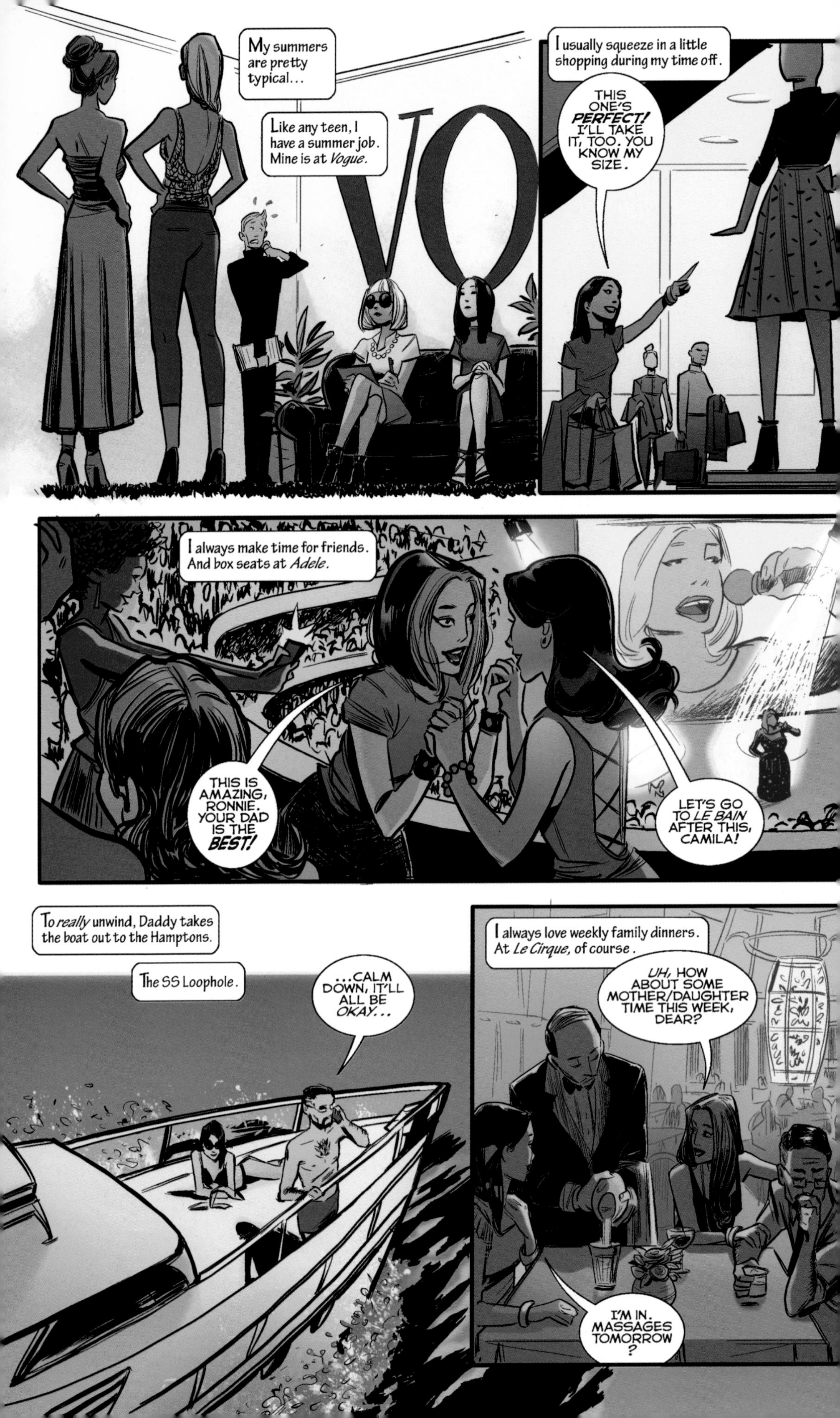

My summers are pretty typical...
Like any teen, I have a summer job. Mine is at *Vogue.*
I usually squeeze in a little shopping during my time off.
THIS ONE'S ***PERFECT!*** I'LL TAKE IT, TOO. YOU KNOW MY SIZE.
I always make time for friends. And box seats at *Adele.*
THIS IS AMAZING, RONNIE. YOUR DAD IS THE ***BEST!***
LET'S GO TO *LE BAIN* AFTER THIS, CAMILA!
To *really* unwind, Daddy takes the boat out to the Hamptons.
The SS Loophole.
...CALM DOWN, IT'LL ALL BE *OKAY...*
I always love weekly family dinners. At *Le Cirque,* of course.
UH, HOW ABOUT SOME MOTHER/DAUGHTER TIME THIS WEEK, DEAR?
I'M IN. MASSAGES TOMORROW?

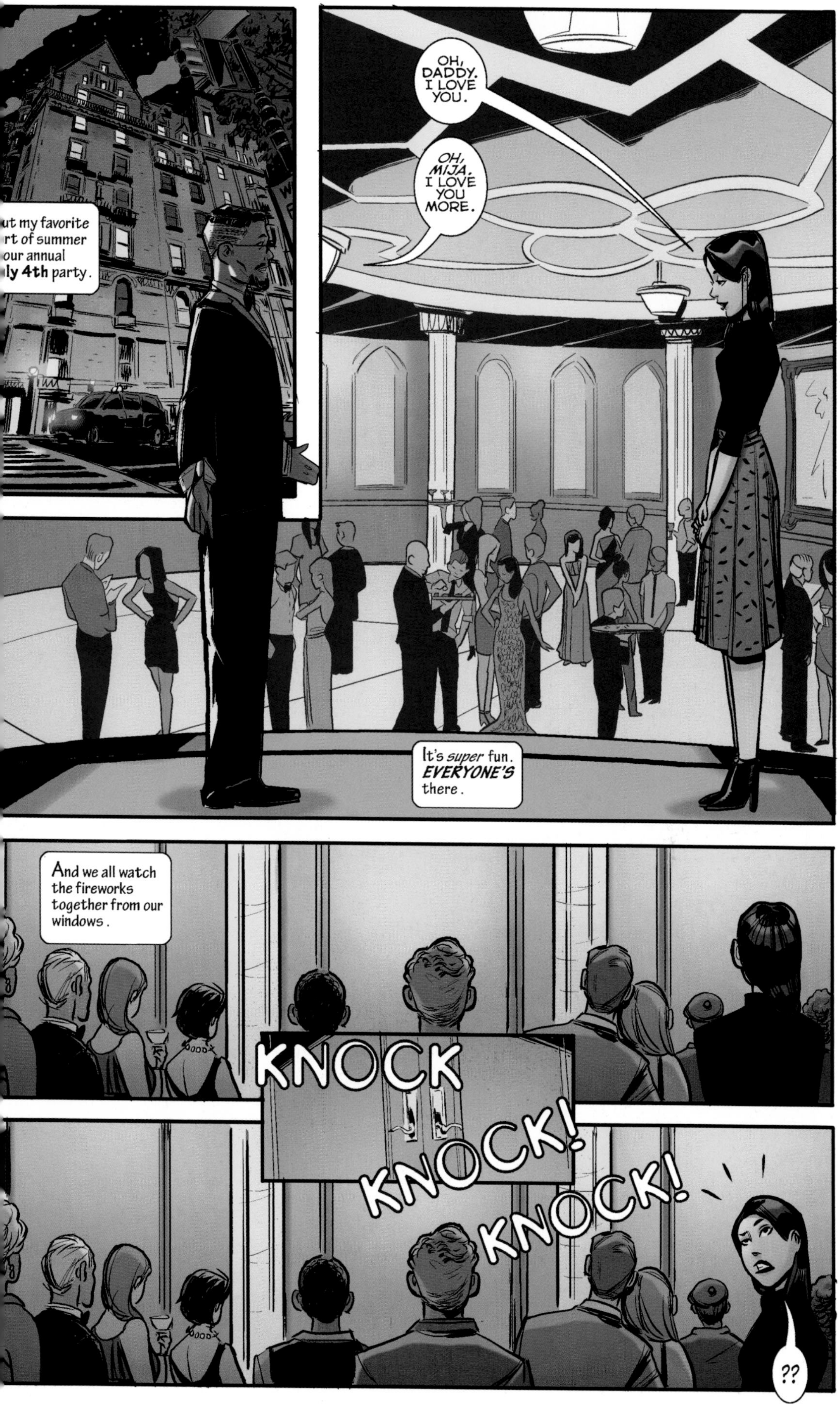
ut my favorite
rt of summer
our annual
ly **4th** party.
OH, DADDY. I LOVE YOU.
OH, MIJA. I LOVE YOU MORE.
It's *super* fun. ***EVERYONE'S*** there.
And we all watch the fireworks together from our windows.
KNOCK
KNOCK!
KNOCK!
??

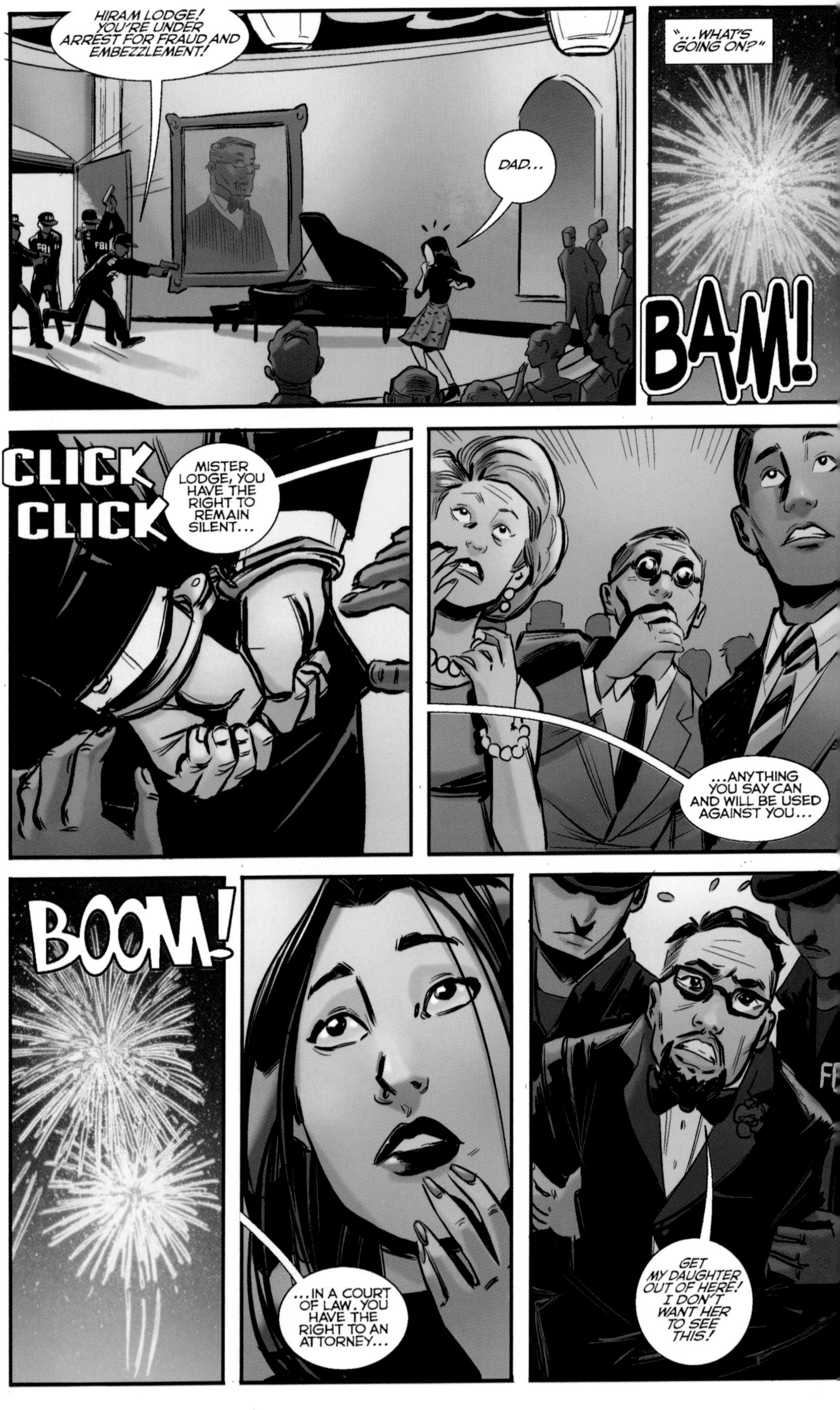
HIRAM LODGE! YOU'RE UNDER ARREST FOR FRAUD AND EMBEZZLEMENT!
DAD...
"...WHAT'S GOING ON?"
BAM!
CLICK CLICK
MISTER LODGE, YOU HAVE THE RIGHT TO REMAIN SILENT...
...ANYTHING YOU SAY CAN AND WILL BE USED AGAINST YOU...
BOOM!
...IN A COURT OF LAW. YOU HAVE THE RIGHT TO AN ATTORNEY...
GET MY DAUGHTER OUT OF HERE! I DON'T WANT HER TO SEE THIS!

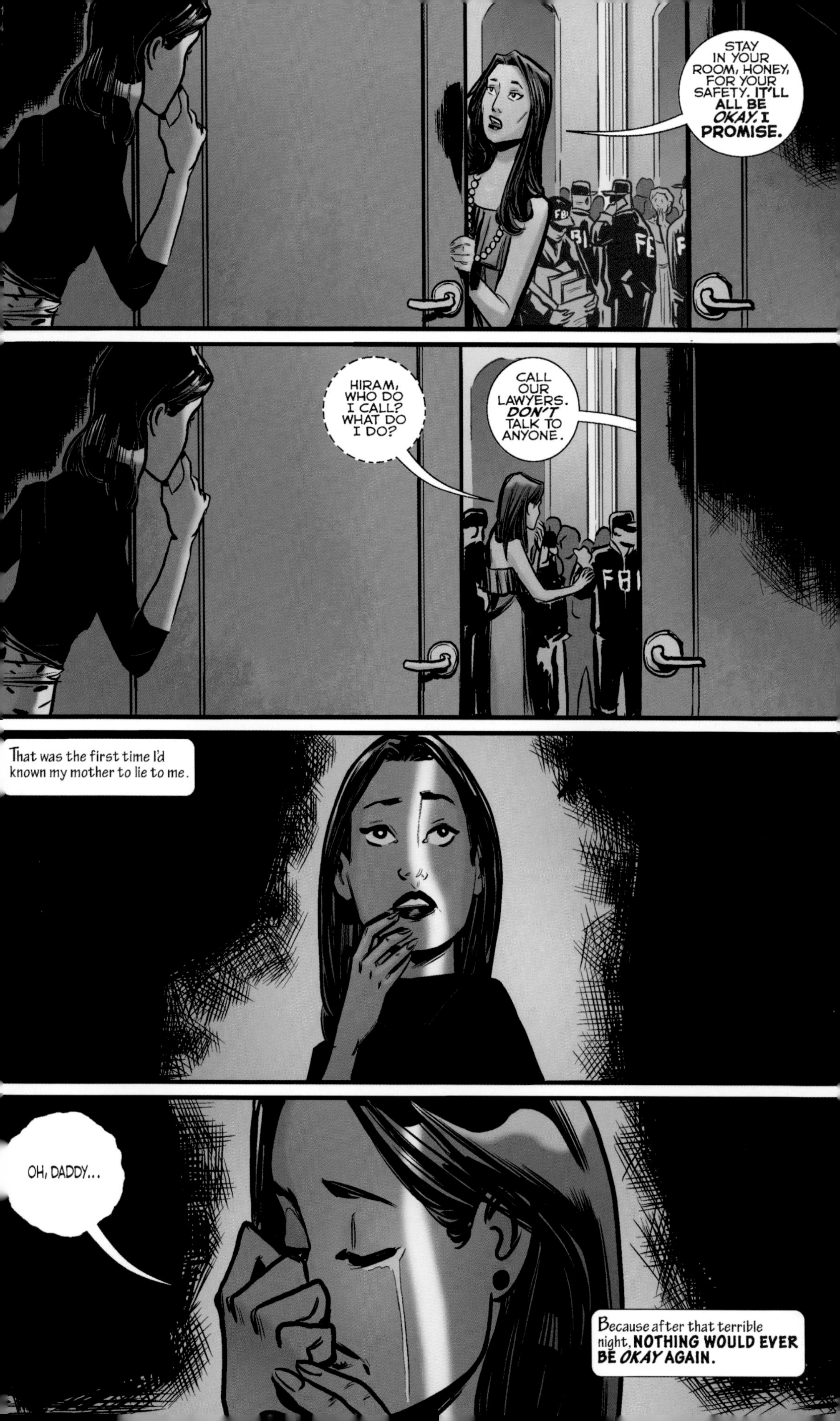
STAY IN YOUR ROOM, HONEY, FOR YOUR SAFETY. IT'LL ALL BE OKAY. I PROMISE.
HIRAM, WHO DO I CALL? WHAT DO I DO?
CALL OUR LAWYERS. DON'T TALK TO ANYONE.
That was the first time I'd known my mother to lie to me.
OH, DADDY...
Because after that terrible night, NOTHING WOULD EVER BE OKAY AGAIN.

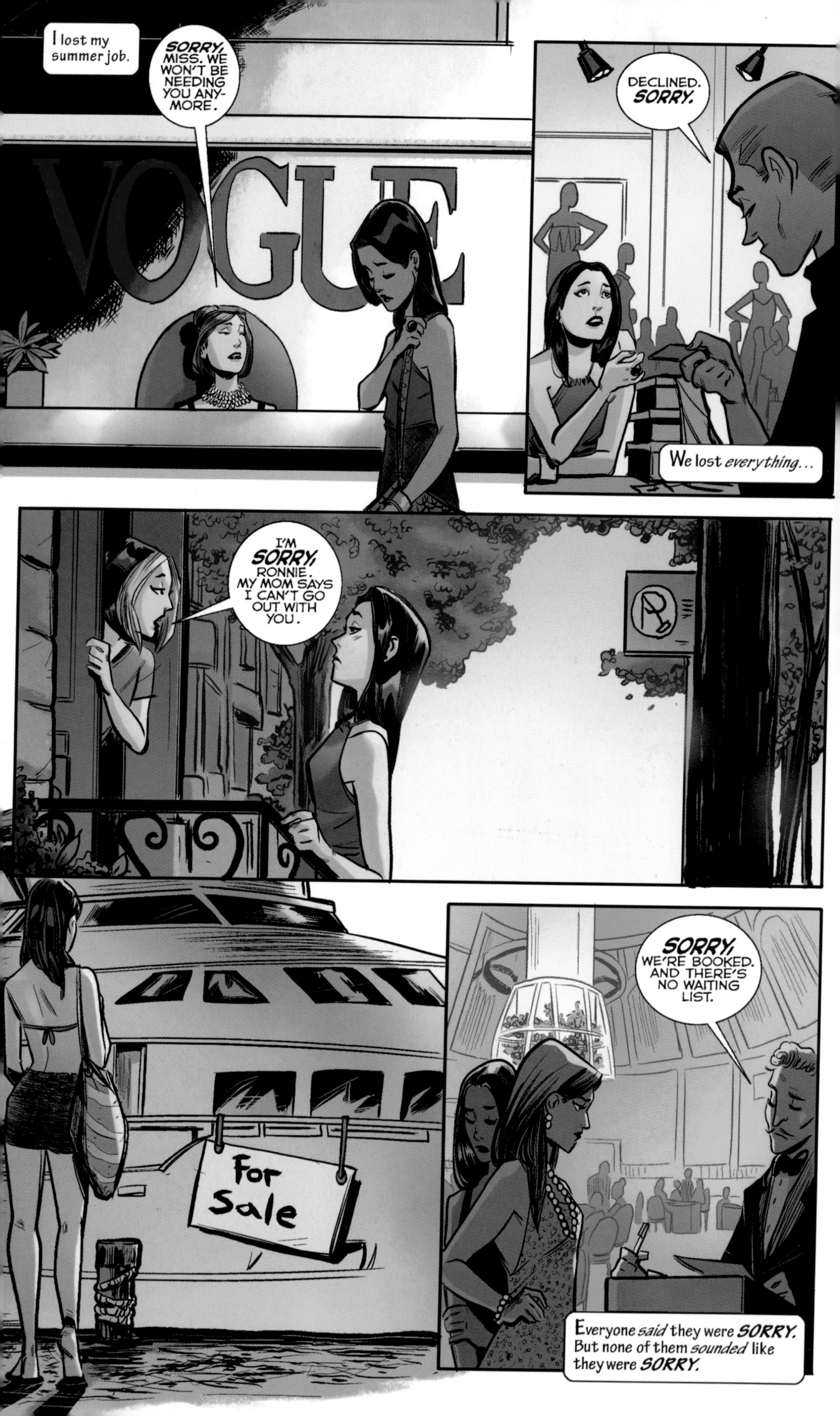

I lost my summer job.
SORRY, MISS. WE WON'T BE NEEDING YOU ANY-MORE.
DECLINED. SORRY.
We lost *everything*...
I'M SORRY, RONNIE. MY MOM SAYS I CAN'T GO OUT WITH YOU.
VOGUE
For Sale
SORRY, WE'RE BOOKED. AND THERE'S NO WAITING LIST.
Everyone *said* they were **SORRY**. But none of them *sounded* like they were **SORRY**.

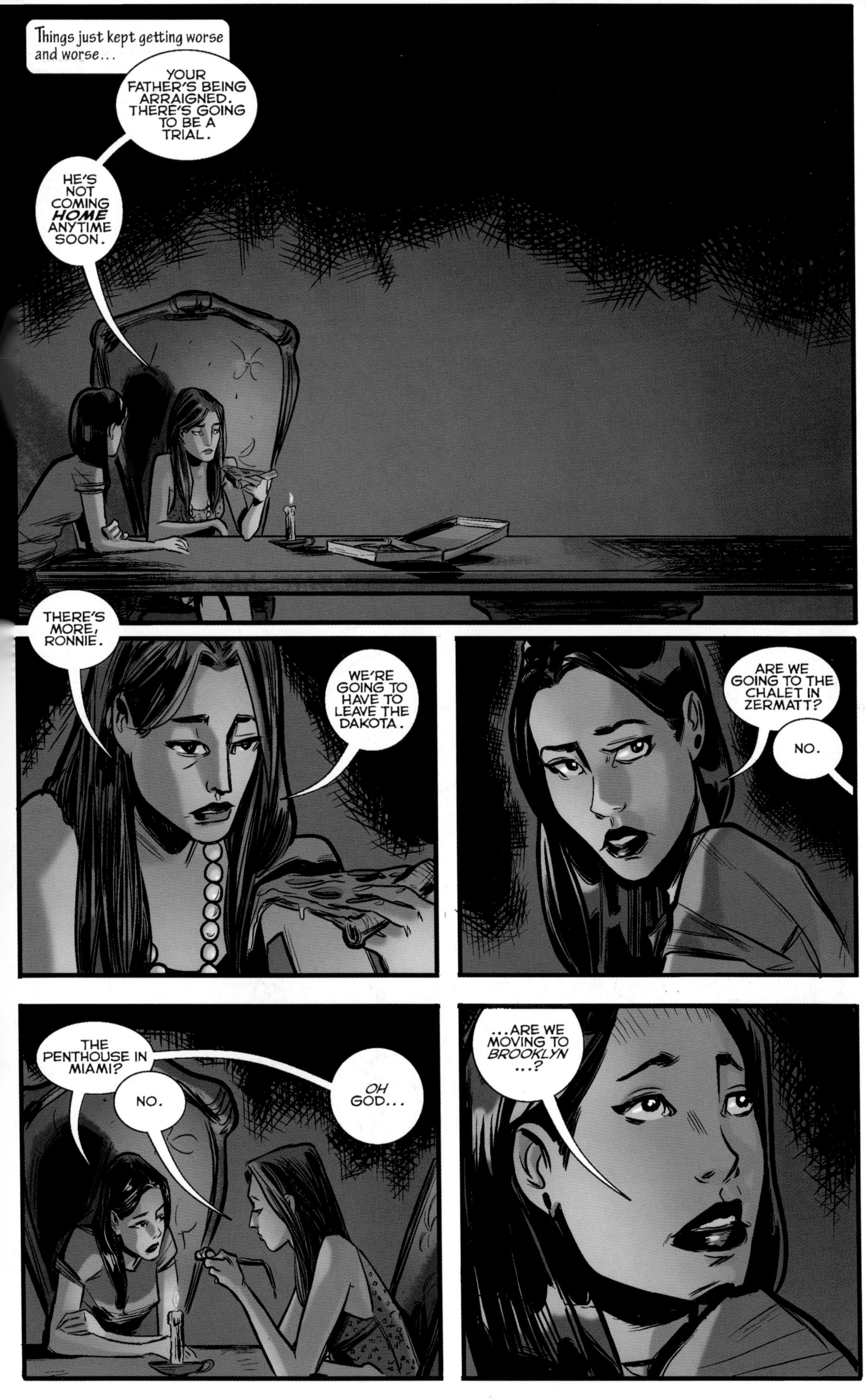
Things just kept getting worse and worse...
YOUR FATHER'S BEING ARRAIGNED. THERE'S GOING TO BE A TRIAL.
HE'S NOT COMING HOME ANYTIME SOON.
THERE'S MORE, RONNIE.
WE'RE GOING TO HAVE TO LEAVE THE DAKOTA.
ARE WE GOING TO THE CHALET IN ZERMATT?
NO.
THE PENTHOUSE IN MIAMI?
NO.
OH GOD...
...ARE WE MOVING TO BROOKLYN ...?

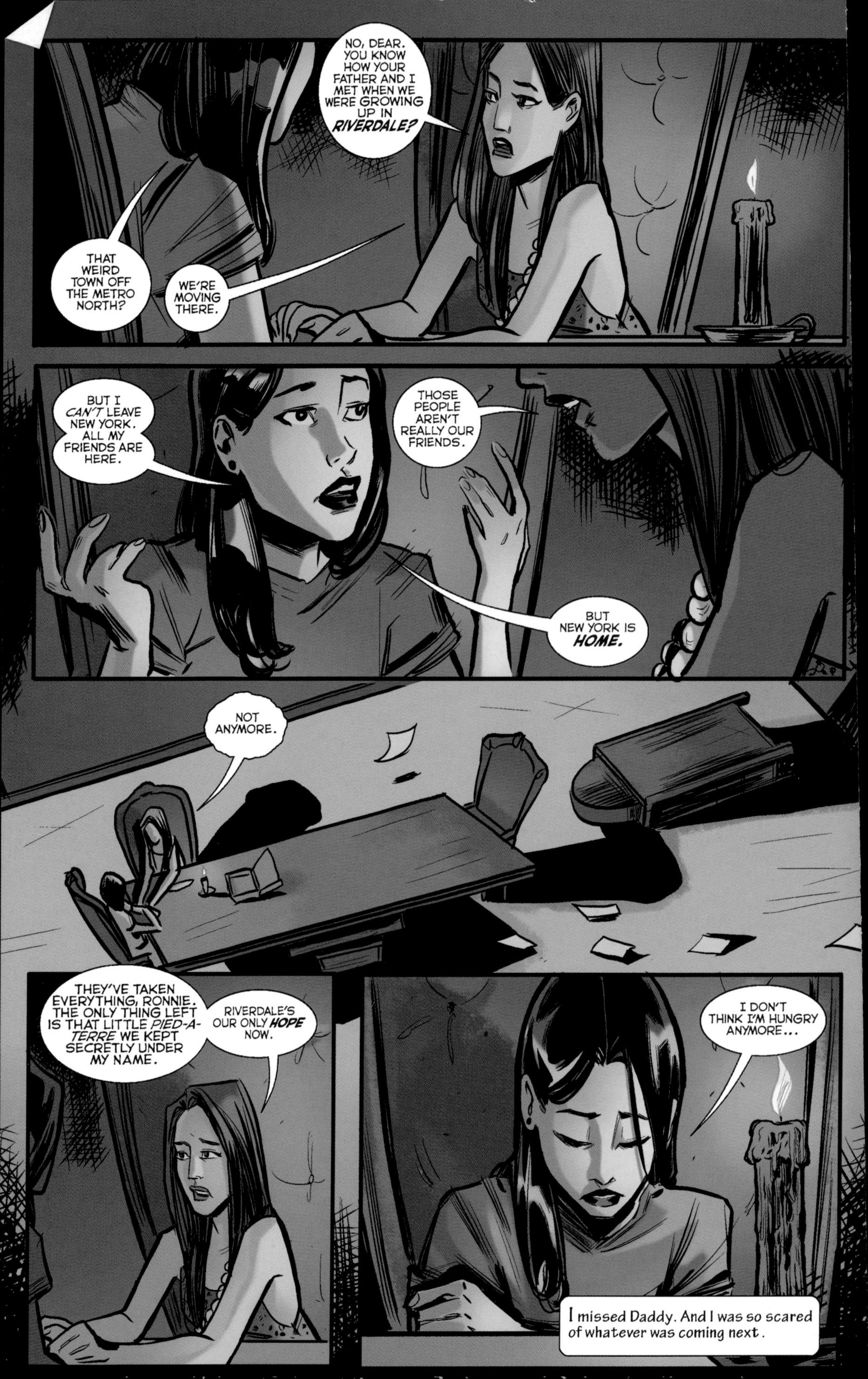
NO, DEAR. YOU KNOW HOW YOUR FATHER AND I MET WHEN WE WERE GROWING UP IN RIVERDALE?
THAT WEIRD TOWN OFF THE METRO NORTH?
WE'RE MOVING THERE.
BUT I CAN'T LEAVE NEW YORK. ALL MY FRIENDS ARE HERE.
THOSE PEOPLE AREN'T REALLY OUR FRIENDS.
BUT NEW YORK IS HOME.
NOT ANYMORE.
THEY'VE TAKEN EVERYTHING, RONNIE. THE ONLY THING LEFT IS THAT LITTLE PIED-A-TERRE WE KEPT SECRETLY UNDER MY NAME.
RIVERDALE'S OUR ONLY HOPE NOW.
I DON'T THINK I'M HUNGRY ANYMORE...
I missed Daddy. And I was so scared of whatever was coming next.

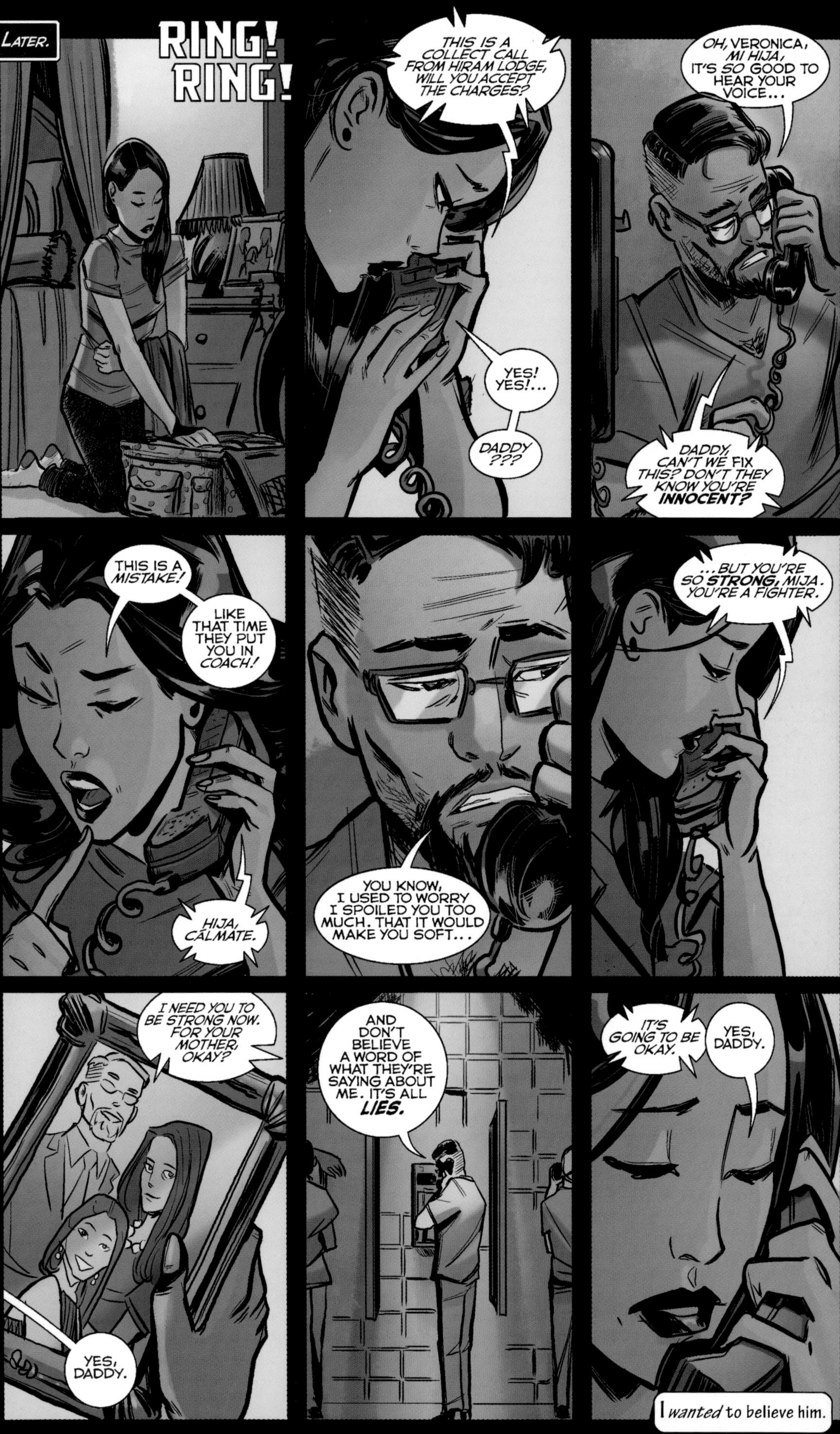

LATER.
RING! RING!
THIS IS A COLLECT CALL FROM HIRAM LODGE, WILL YOU ACCEPT THE CHARGES?
YES! YES!...
DADDY???
OH, VERONICA, MI HIJA, IT'S SO GOOD TO HEAR YOUR VOICE...
DADDY, CAN'T WE FIX THIS? DON'T THEY KNOW YOU'RE INNOCENT?
THIS IS A MISTAKE!
LIKE THAT TIME THEY PUT YOU IN COACH!
HIJA, CÁLMATE.
YOU KNOW, I USED TO WORRY I SPOILED YOU TOO MUCH. THAT IT WOULD MAKE YOU SOFT...
...BUT YOU'RE SO STRONG, MIJA. YOU'RE A FIGHTER.
I NEED YOU TO BE STRONG NOW. FOR YOUR MOTHER, OKAY?
YES, DADDY.
AND DON'T BELIEVE A WORD OF WHAT THEY'RE SAYING ABOUT ME. IT'S ALL LIES.
IT'S GOING TO BE OKAY.
YES, DADDY.
I wanted to believe him.

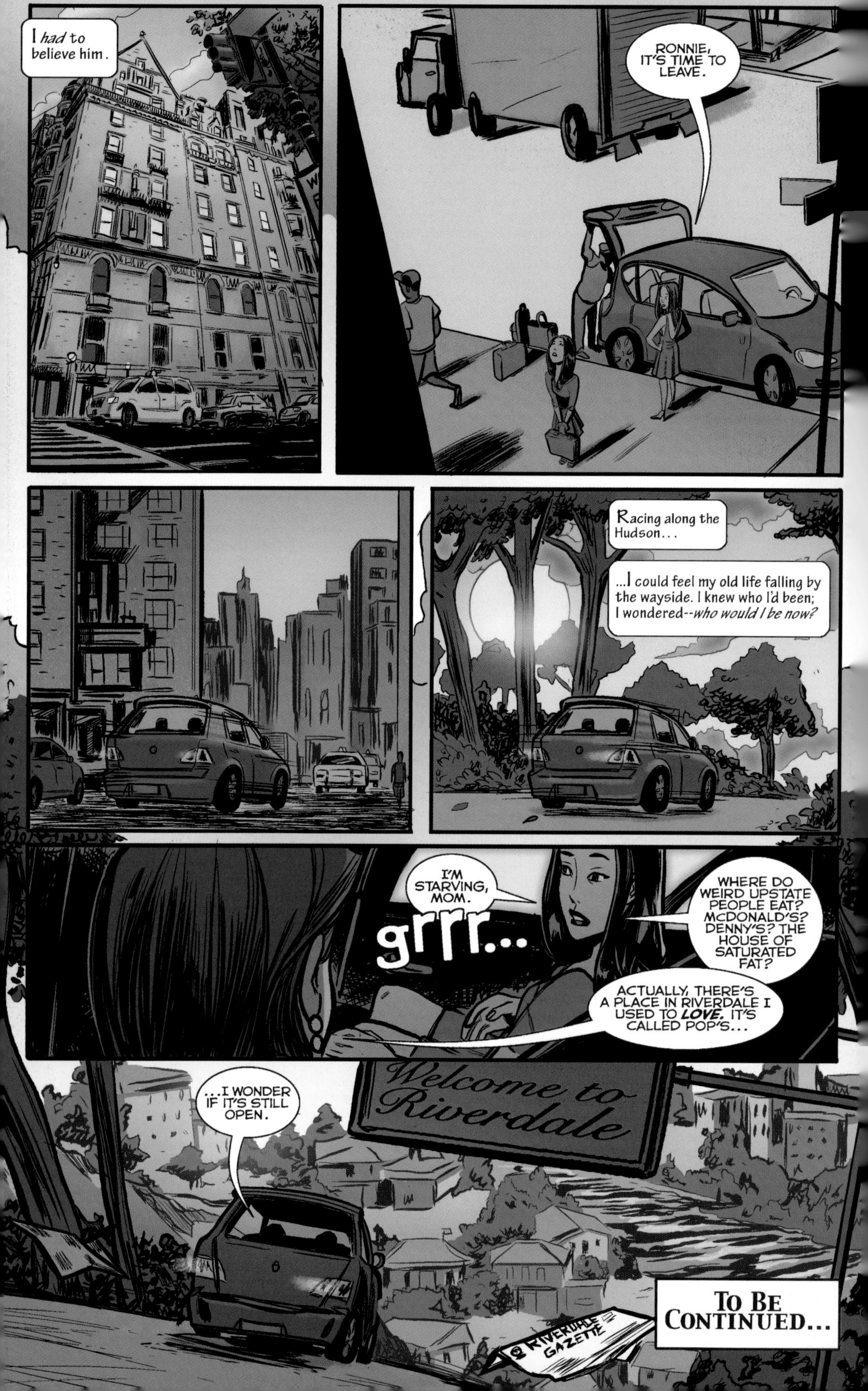
I *had* to believe him.
RONNIE, IT'S TIME TO LEAVE.
Racing along the Hudson...
...I could feel my old life falling by the wayside. I knew who I'd been; I wondered--*who would I be now?*
I'M STARVING, MOM.
grrr...
WHERE DO WEIRD UPSTATE PEOPLE EAT? McDONALD'S? DENNY'S? THE HOUSE OF SATURATED FAT?
ACTUALLY, THERE'S A PLACE IN RIVERDALE I USED TO ***LOVE.*** IT'S CALLED POP'S...
Welcome to Riverdale
...I WONDER IF IT'S STILL OPEN.
RIVERDALE GAZETTE
TO BE CONTINUED...

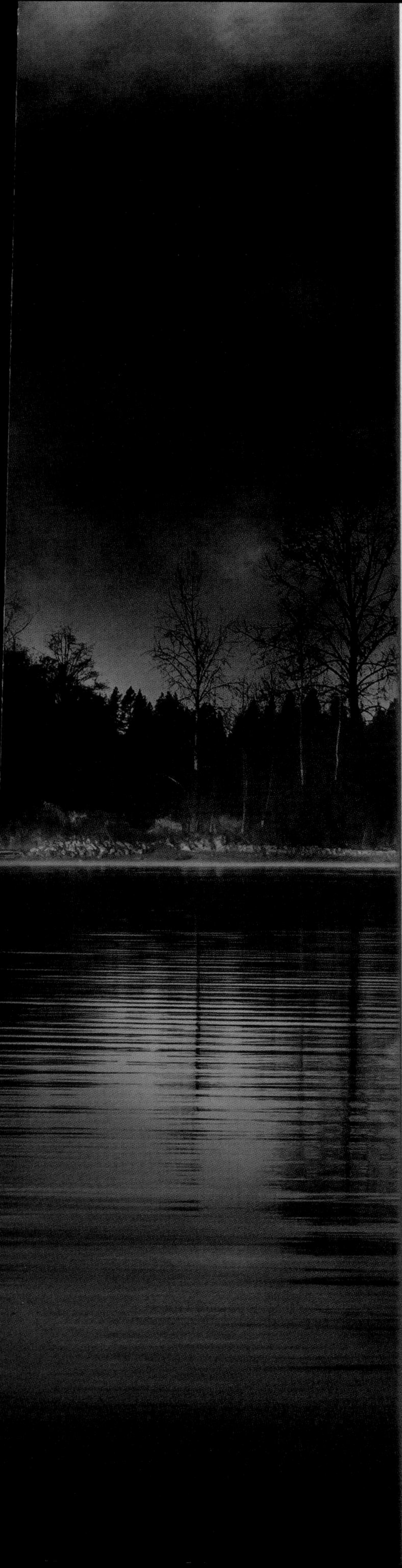

CHAPTER FOUR

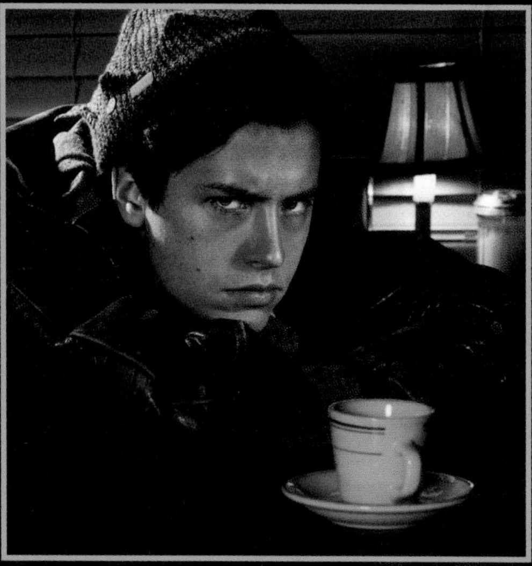

JUGHEAD IN IT WAS A DARK AND STORMY NIGHT

WRITER:
WILL EWING

ART:
ALITHA MARTINEZ

INKS:
BOB SMITH

COLORS:
ANDRE SZYMANOWICZ
WITH **THOMAS CHU**

LETTERS:
JANICE CHIANG

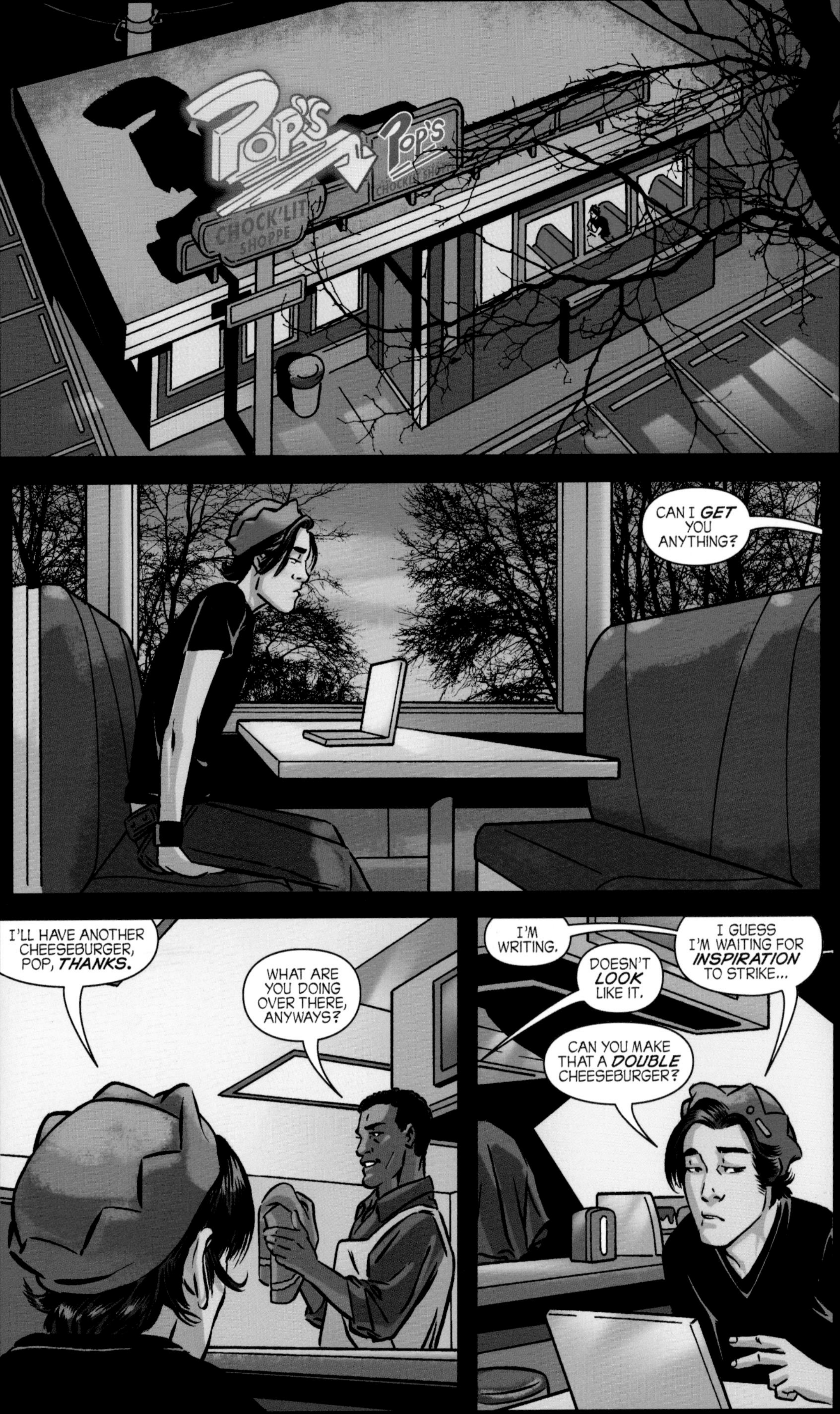
POP'S
CHOCK'LIT SHOPPE
CAN I *GET* YOU ANYTHING?
I'LL HAVE ANOTHER CHEESEBURGER, POP, ***THANKS.***
WHAT ARE YOU DOING OVER THERE, ANYWAYS?
I'M WRITING.
DOESN'T *LOOK* LIKE IT.
I GUESS I'M WAITING FOR *INSPIRATION* TO STRIKE...
CAN YOU MAKE THAT A *DOUBLE* CHEESEBURGER?

≥sigh≤

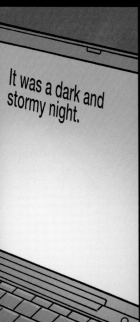

It was a dark and stormy night.

It was a dark and stormy night.

Clack clack clack

HEEEEERE'S...

ALL WORK AND NO PLAY
ALL WORK AND NO PLAY
ALL WORK AND NO PLAY
ALL WORK AND NO PLAY

...POPPY!

≥Hehehehe!≤

DROLL, POP. *VERY* DROLL.

YOU REALLY DO *LOVE* YOUR BURGERS, HUH, JUGHEAD?

EATING THEM, *YEAH.* SERVING THEM, *NOT* SO MUCH.

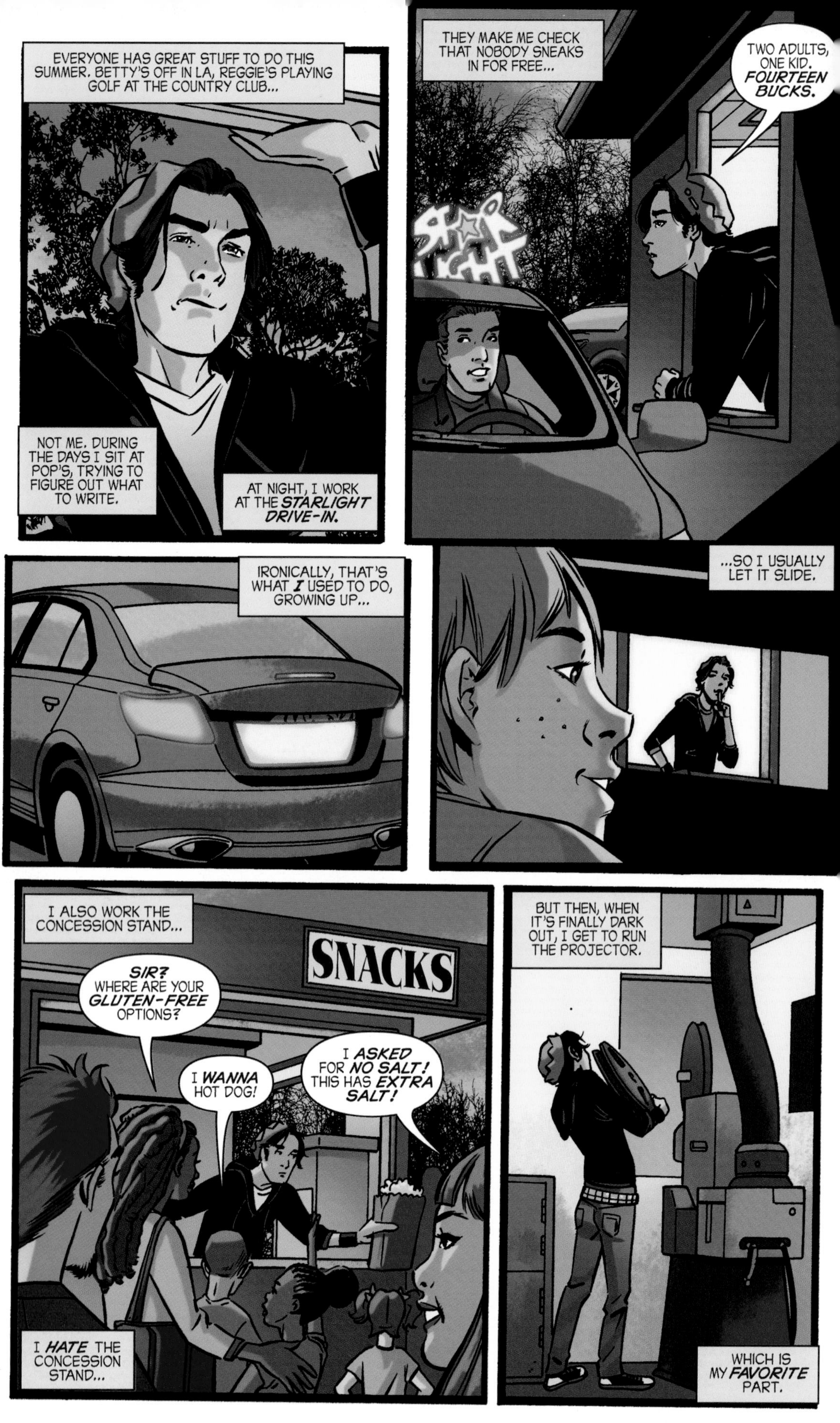
EVERYONE HAS GREAT STUFF TO DO THIS SUMMER. BETTY'S OFF IN LA, REGGIE'S PLAYING GOLF AT THE COUNTRY CLUB...
NOT ME. DURING THE DAYS I SIT AT POP'S, TRYING TO FIGURE OUT WHAT TO WRITE.
AT NIGHT, I WORK AT THE STARLIGHT DRIVE-IN.
THEY MAKE ME CHECK THAT NOBODY SNEAKS IN FOR FREE...
TWO ADULTS, ONE KID. FOURTEEN BUCKS.
IRONICALLY, THAT'S WHAT I USED TO DO, GROWING UP...
...SO I USUALLY LET IT SLIDE.
I ALSO WORK THE CONCESSION STAND...
SNACKS
SIR? WHERE ARE YOUR GLUTEN-FREE OPTIONS?
I WANNA HOT DOG!
I ASKED FOR NO SALT! THIS HAS EXTRA SALT!
I HATE THE CONCESSION STAND...
BUT THEN, WHEN IT'S FINALLY DARK OUT, I GET TO RUN THE PROJECTOR.
WHICH IS MY FAVORITE PART.

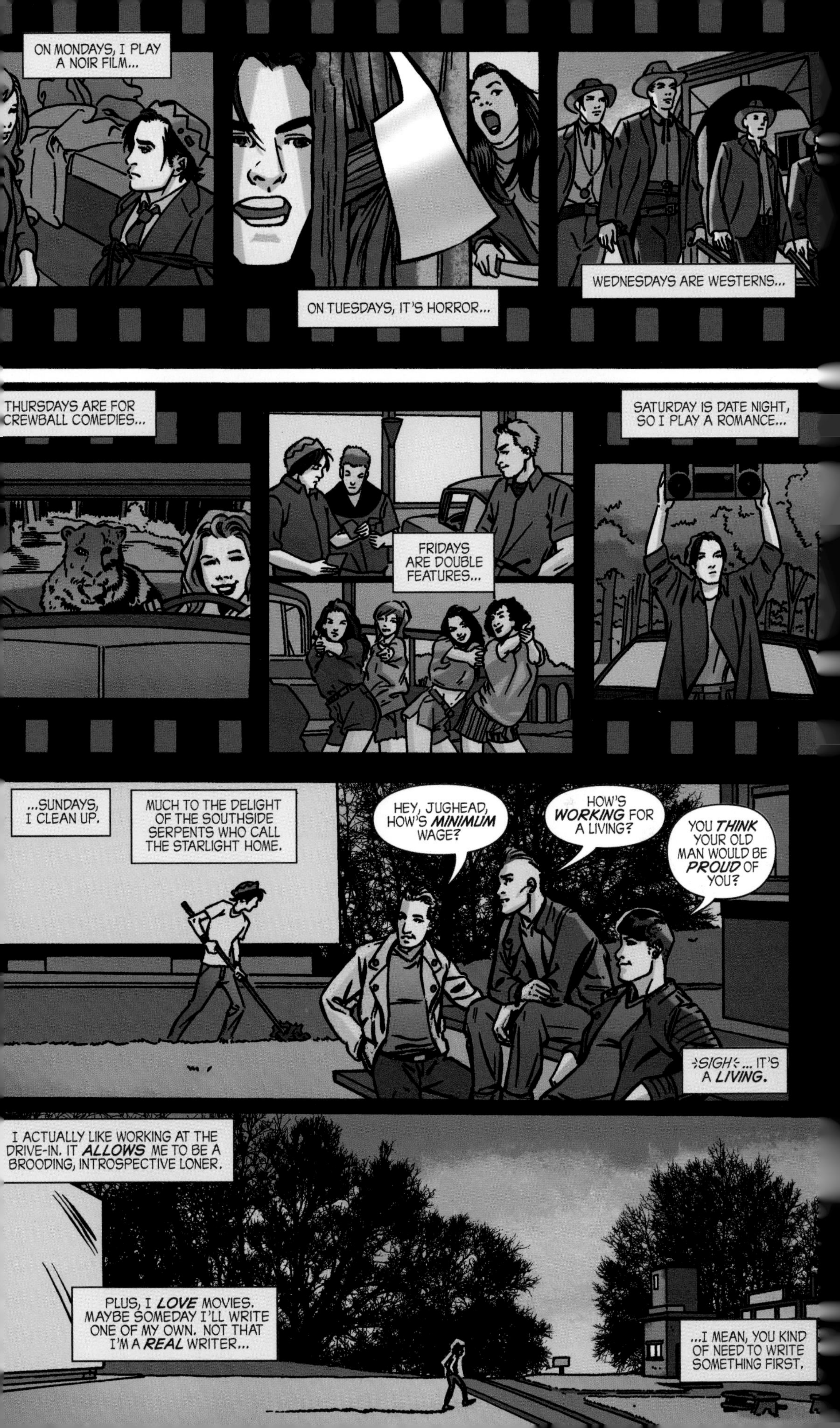
ON MONDAYS, I PLAY A NOIR FILM...
ON TUESDAYS, IT'S HORROR...
WEDNESDAYS ARE WESTERNS...
THURSDAYS ARE FOR CREWBALL COMEDIES...
FRIDAYS ARE DOUBLE FEATURES...
SATURDAY IS DATE NIGHT, SO I PLAY A ROMANCE...
...SUNDAYS, I CLEAN UP.
MUCH TO THE DELIGHT OF THE SOUTHSIDE SERPENTS WHO CALL THE STARLIGHT HOME.
HEY, JUGHEAD, HOW'S MINIMUM WAGE?
HOW'S WORKING FOR A LIVING?
YOU THINK YOUR OLD MAN WOULD BE PROUD OF YOU?
SIGH ... IT'S A LIVING.
I ACTUALLY LIKE WORKING AT THE DRIVE-IN. IT ALLOWS ME TO BE A BROODING, INTROSPECTIVE LONER.
PLUS, I LOVE MOVIES. MAYBE SOMEDAY I'LL WRITE ONE OF MY OWN. NOT THAT I'M A REAL WRITER...
...I MEAN, YOU KIND OF NEED TO WRITE SOMETHING FIRST.

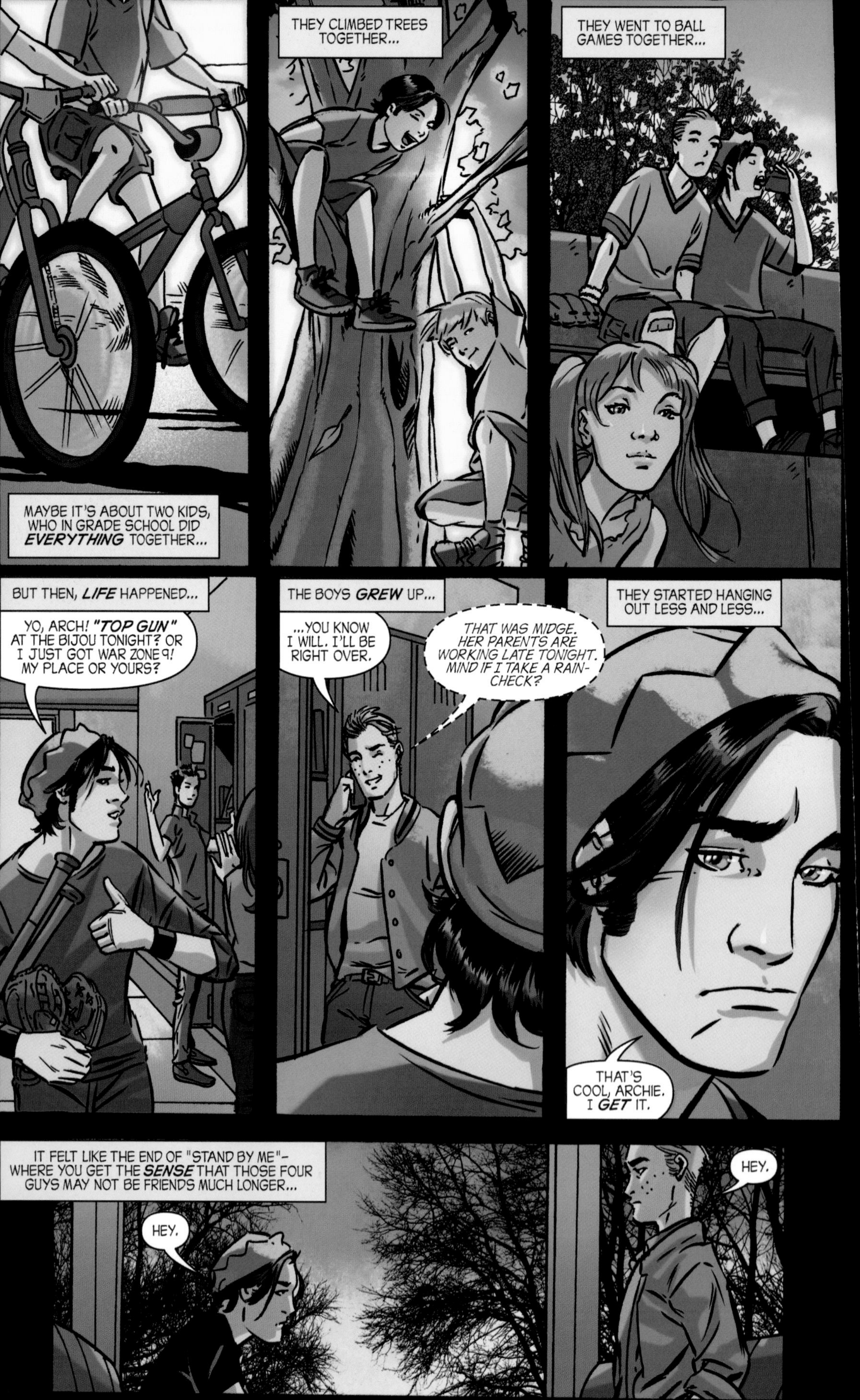
MAYBE IT'S ABOUT TWO KIDS, WHO IN GRADE SCHOOL DID EVERYTHING TOGETHER...
THEY CLIMBED TREES TOGETHER...
THEY WENT TO BALL GAMES TOGETHER...
BUT THEN, LIFE HAPPENED...
YO, ARCH! "TOP GUN" AT THE BIJOU TONIGHT? OR I JUST GOT WAR ZONE 9! MY PLACE OR YOURS?
THE BOYS GREW UP...
...YOU KNOW I WILL. I'LL BE RIGHT OVER.
THAT WAS MIDGE. HER PARENTS ARE WORKING LATE TONIGHT. MIND IF I TAKE A RAIN-CHECK?
THEY STARTED HANGING OUT LESS AND LESS...
THAT'S COOL, ARCHIE. I GET IT.
IT FELT LIKE THE END OF "STAND BY ME"– WHERE YOU GET THE SENSE THAT THOSE FOUR GUYS MAY NOT BE FRIENDS MUCH LONGER...
HEY.
HEY.

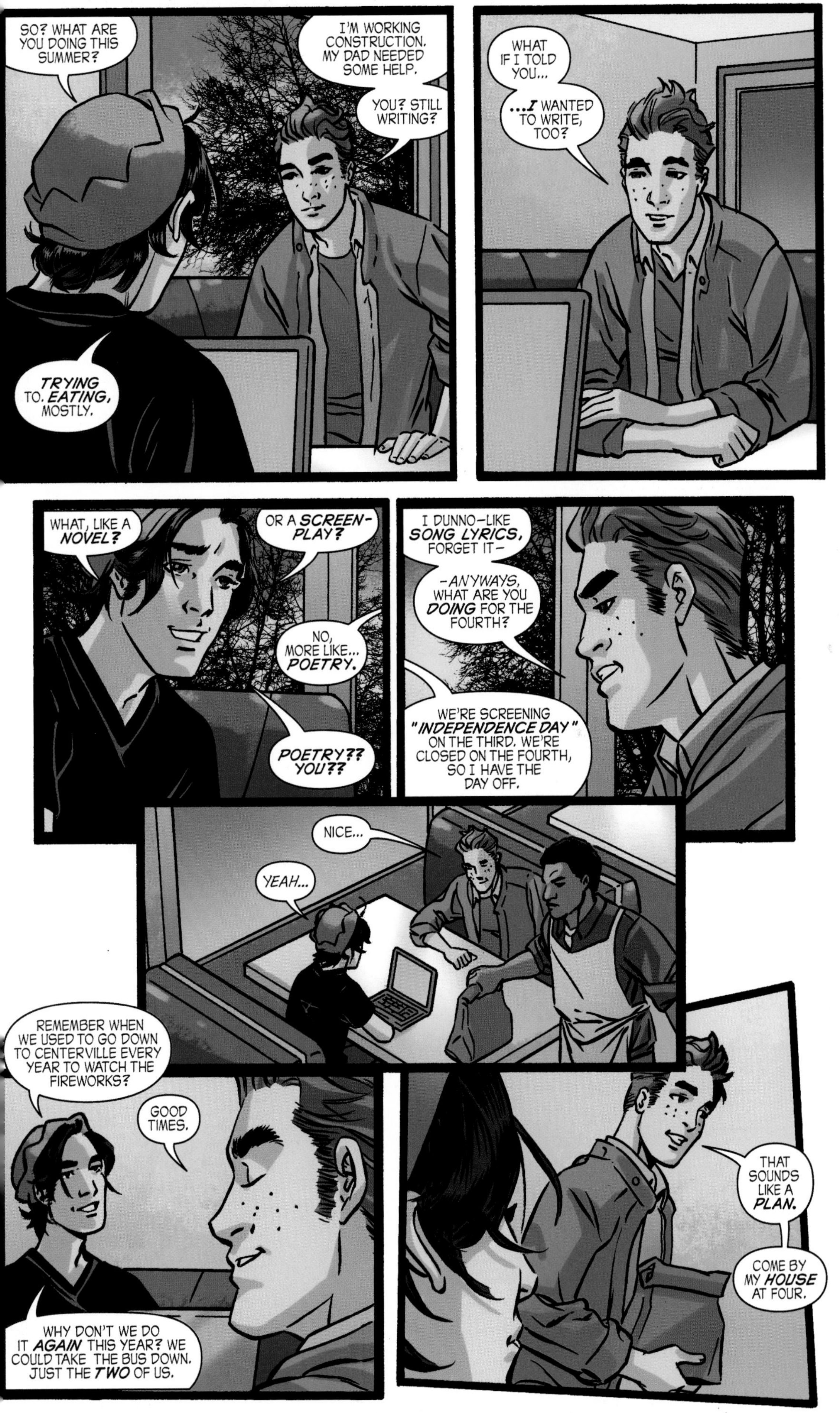
SO? WHAT ARE YOU DOING THIS SUMMER?
I'M WORKING CONSTRUCTION. MY DAD NEEDED SOME HELP.
YOU? STILL WRITING?
TRYING TO. EATING, MOSTLY.
WHAT IF I TOLD YOU...
...I WANTED TO WRITE, TOO?
WHAT, LIKE A NOVEL?
OR A SCREEN-PLAY?
NO, MORE LIKE... POETRY.
POETRY?? YOU??
I DUNNO—LIKE SONG LYRICS, FORGET IT—
—ANYWAYS, WHAT ARE YOU DOING FOR THE FOURTH?
WE'RE SCREENING "INDEPENDENCE DAY" ON THE THIRD. WE'RE CLOSED ON THE FOURTH, SO I HAVE THE DAY OFF.
NICE...
YEAH...
REMEMBER WHEN WE USED TO GO DOWN TO CENTERVILLE EVERY YEAR TO WATCH THE FIREWORKS?
GOOD TIMES.
WHY DON'T WE DO IT AGAIN THIS YEAR? WE COULD TAKE THE BUS DOWN. JUST THE TWO OF US.
THAT SOUNDS LIKE A PLAN.
COME BY MY HOUSE AT FOUR.

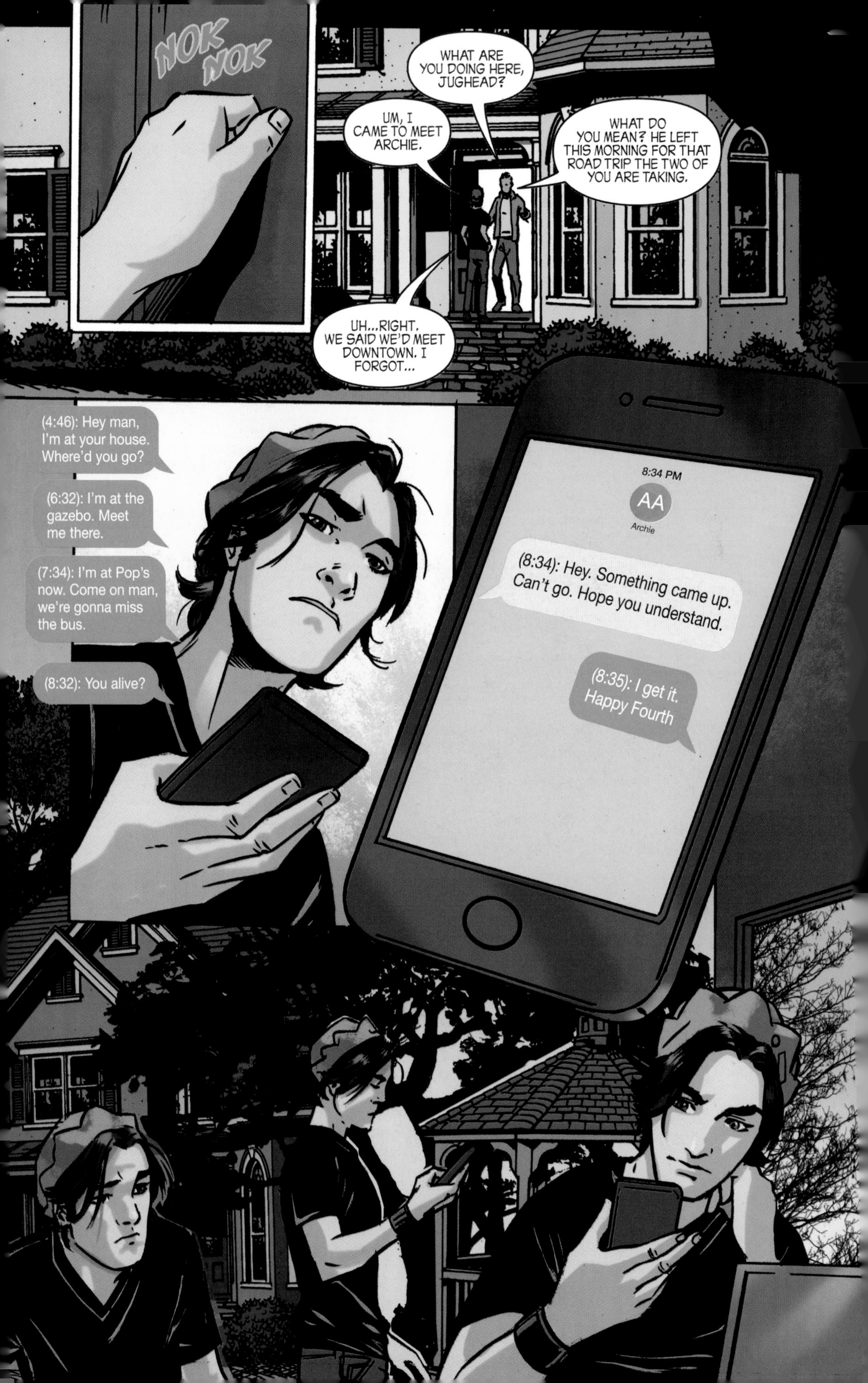
NOK NOK
WHAT ARE YOU DOING HERE, JUGHEAD?
UM, I CAME TO MEET ARCHIE.
WHAT DO YOU MEAN? HE LEFT THIS MORNING FOR THAT ROAD TRIP THE TWO OF YOU ARE TAKING.
UH...RIGHT. WE SAID WE'D MEET DOWNTOWN. I FORGOT...
(4:46): Hey man, I'm at your house. Where'd you go?
(6:32): I'm at the gazebo. Meet me there.
(7:34): I'm at Pop's now. Come on man, we're gonna miss the bus.
(8:32): You alive?
8:34 PM
AA
Archie
(8:34): Hey. Something came up. Can't go. Hope you understand.
(8:35): I get it. Happy Fourth

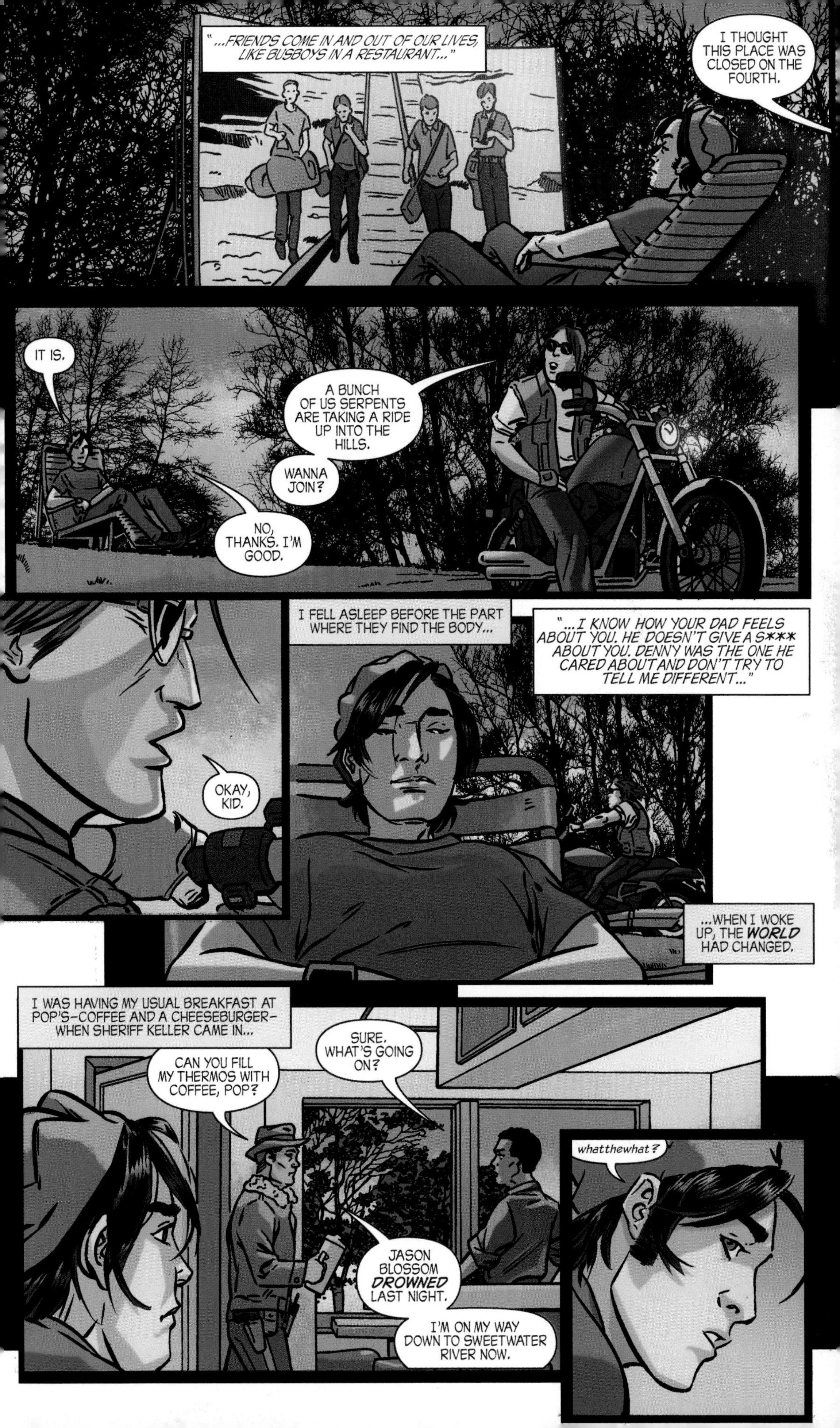
"...FRIENDS COME IN AND OUT OF OUR LIVES, LIKE BUSBOYS IN A RESTAURANT..."
I THOUGHT THIS PLACE WAS CLOSED ON THE FOURTH.
IT IS.
A BUNCH OF US SERPENTS ARE TAKING A RIDE UP INTO THE HILLS.
WANNA JOIN?
NO, THANKS. I'M GOOD.
OKAY, KID.
I FELL ASLEEP BEFORE THE PART WHERE THEY FIND THE BODY...
"...I KNOW HOW YOUR DAD FEELS ABOUT YOU. HE DOESN'T GIVE A S*** ABOUT YOU. DENNY WAS THE ONE HE CARED ABOUT AND DON'T TRY TO TELL ME DIFFERENT..."
...WHEN I WOKE UP, THE WORLD HAD CHANGED.
I WAS HAVING MY USUAL BREAKFAST AT POP'S—COFFEE AND A CHEESEBURGER—WHEN SHERIFF KELLER CAME IN...
CAN YOU FILL MY THERMOS WITH COFFEE, POP?
SURE. WHAT'S GOING ON?
JASON BLOSSOM DROWNED LAST NIGHT.
I'M ON MY WAY DOWN TO SWEETWATER RIVER NOW.
whatthewhat?

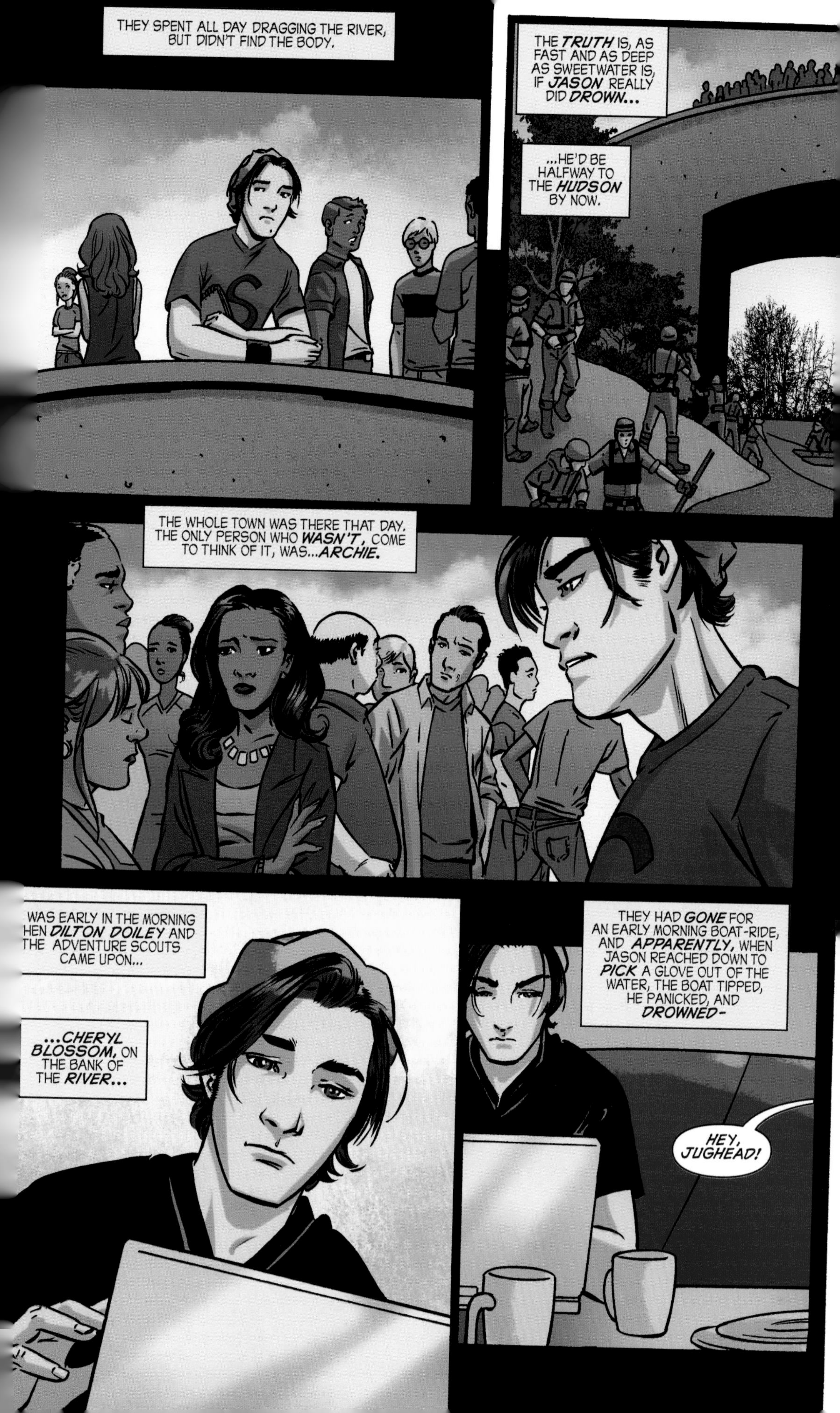
THEY SPENT ALL DAY DRAGGING THE RIVER, BUT DIDN'T FIND THE BODY.
THE TRUTH IS, AS FAST AND AS DEEP AS SWEETWATER IS, IF JASON REALLY DID DROWN...
...HE'D BE HALFWAY TO THE HUDSON BY NOW.
THE WHOLE TOWN WAS THERE THAT DAY. THE ONLY PERSON WHO WASN'T, COME TO THINK OF IT, WAS...ARCHIE.
WAS EARLY IN THE MORNING HEN DILTON DOILEY AND THE ADVENTURE SCOUTS CAME UPON...
...CHERYL BLOSSOM, ON THE BANK OF THE RIVER...
THEY HAD GONE FOR AN EARLY MORNING BOAT-RIDE, AND APPARENTLY, WHEN JASON REACHED DOWN TO PICK A GLOVE OUT OF THE WATER, THE BOAT TIPPED, HE PANICKED, AND DROWNED-
HEY, JUGHEAD!

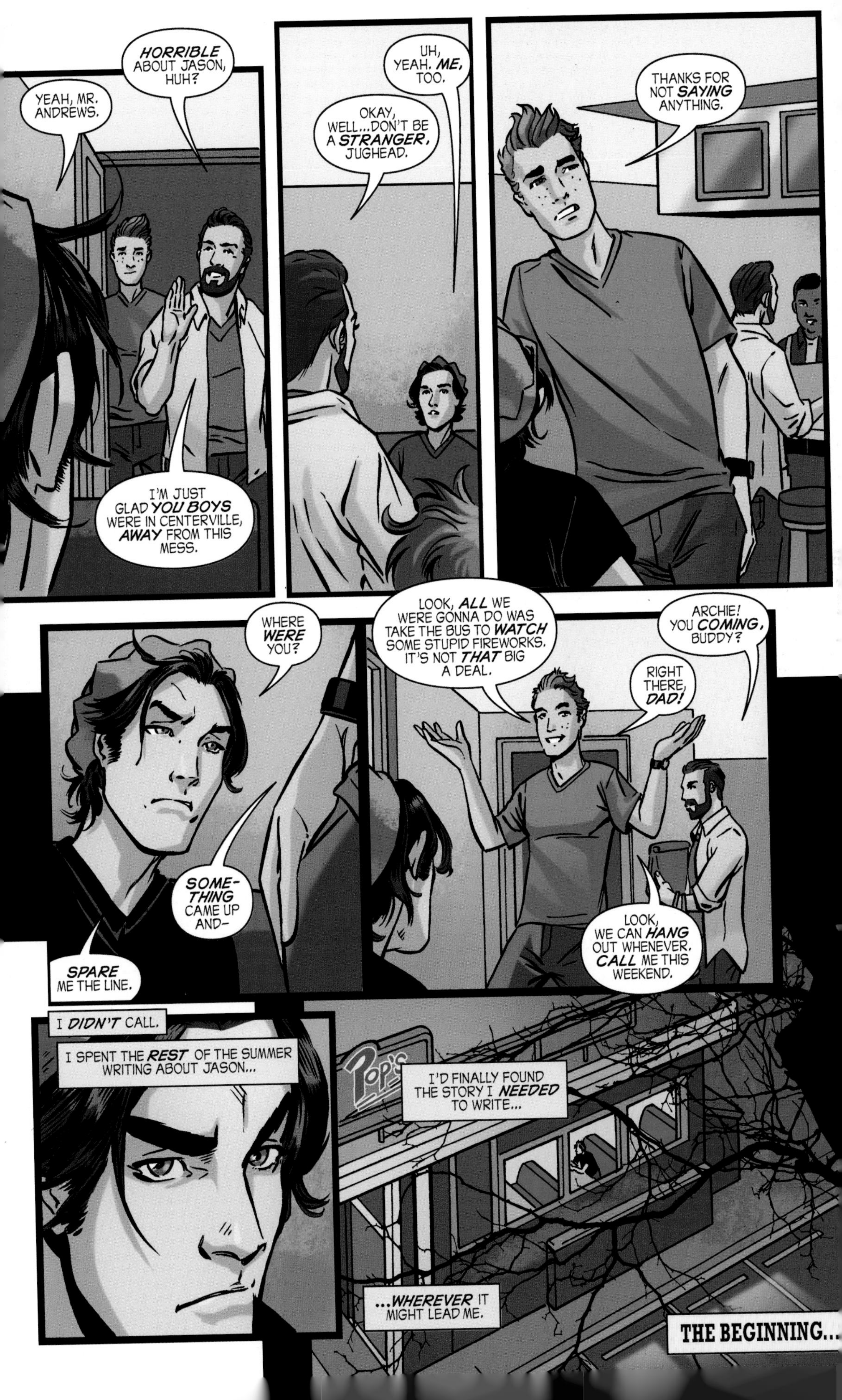
HORRIBLE ABOUT JASON, HUH?
YEAH, MR. ANDREWS.
I'M JUST GLAD YOU BOYS WERE IN CENTERVILLE, AWAY FROM THIS MESS.
UH, YEAH. ME, TOO.
OKAY, WELL...DON'T BE A STRANGER, JUGHEAD.
THANKS FOR NOT SAYING ANYTHING.
WHERE WERE YOU?
SOME-THING CAME UP AND-
SPARE ME THE LINE.
LOOK, ALL WE WERE GONNA DO WAS TAKE THE BUS TO WATCH SOME STUPID FIREWORKS. IT'S NOT THAT BIG A DEAL.
ARCHIE! YOU COMING, BUDDY?
RIGHT THERE, DAD!
LOOK, WE CAN HANG OUT WHENEVER. CALL ME THIS WEEKEND.
I DIDN'T CALL.
I SPENT THE REST OF THE SUMMER WRITING ABOUT JASON...
POP'S
I'D FINALLY FOUND THE STORY I NEEDED TO WRITE...
...WHEREVER IT MIGHT LEAD ME.
THE BEGINNING...

CHAPTER FIVE

BLOODSPORT

WRITER:
WILL EWING

ART:
JOE EISMA

COLORS:
ANDRE SZYMANOWICZ

LETTERS:
JANICE CHIANG

STARRING
ARCHIE ANDREWS

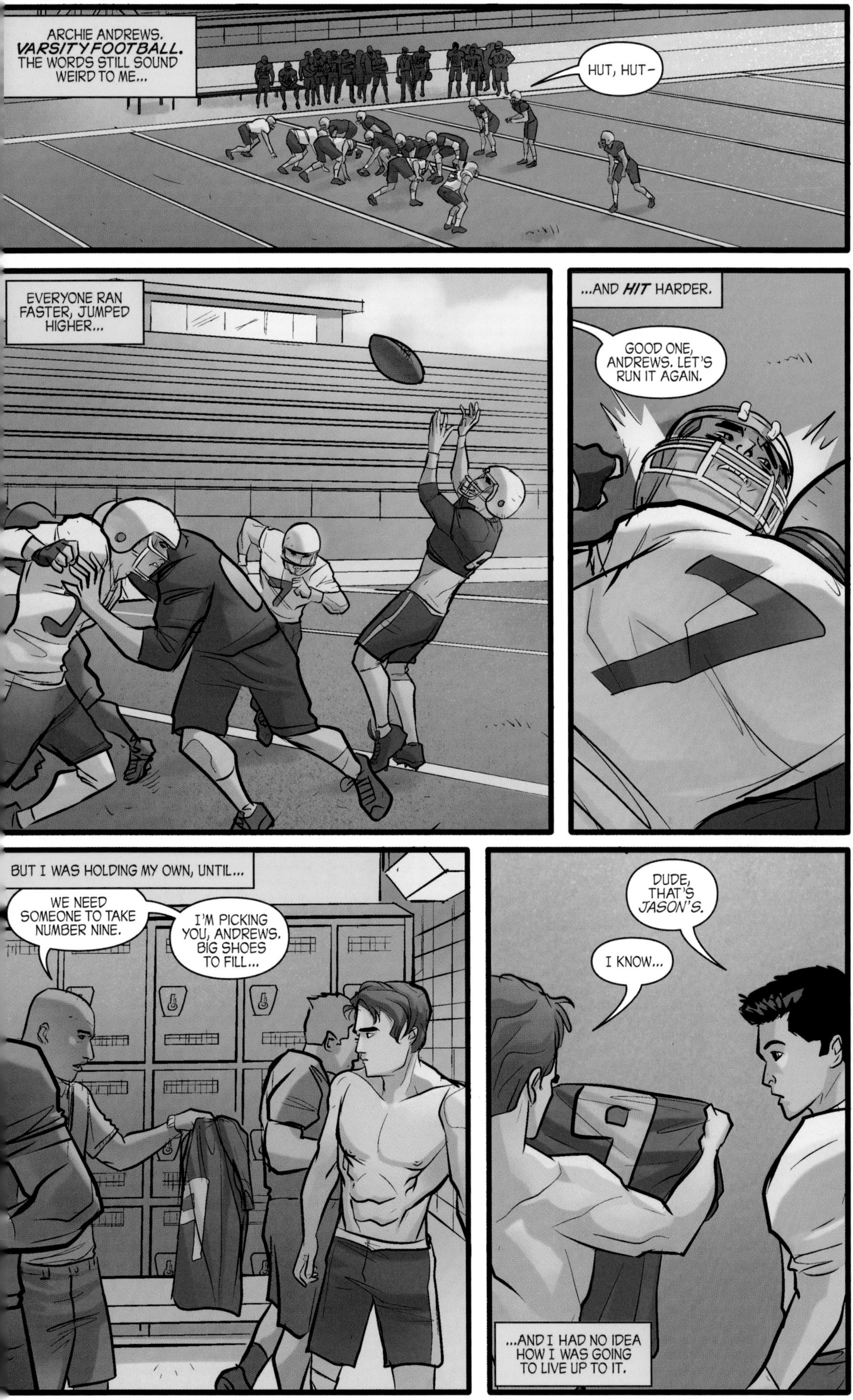
ARCHIE ANDREWS. VARSITY FOOTBALL. THE WORDS STILL SOUND WEIRD TO ME...
HUT, HUT–
EVERYONE RAN FASTER, JUMPED HIGHER...
...AND HIT HARDER.
GOOD ONE, ANDREWS. LET'S RUN IT AGAIN.
BUT I WAS HOLDING MY OWN, UNTIL...
WE NEED SOMEONE TO TAKE NUMBER NINE.
I'M PICKING YOU, ANDREWS. BIG SHOES TO FILL...
DUDE, THAT'S JASON'S.
I KNOW...
...AND I HAD NO IDEA HOW I WAS GOING TO LIVE UP TO IT.

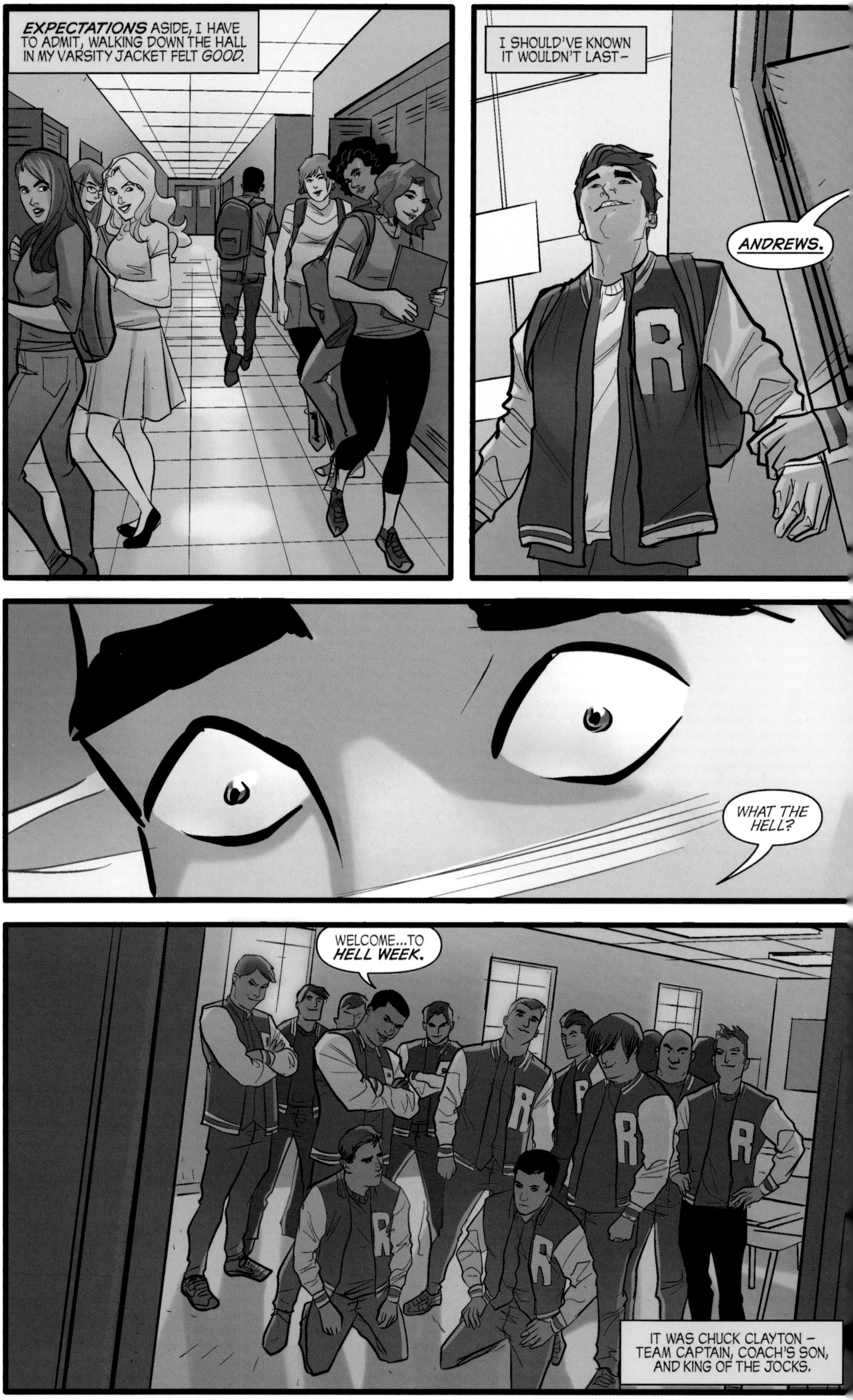
EXPECTATIONS ASIDE, I HAVE TO ADMIT, WALKING DOWN THE HALL IN MY VARSITY JACKET FELT GOOD.
I SHOULD'VE KNOWN IT WOULDN'T LAST–
ANDREWS.
WHAT THE HELL?
WELCOME...TO HELL WEEK.
IT WAS CHUCK CLAYTON – TEAM CAPTAIN, COACH'S SON, AND KING OF THE JOCKS.

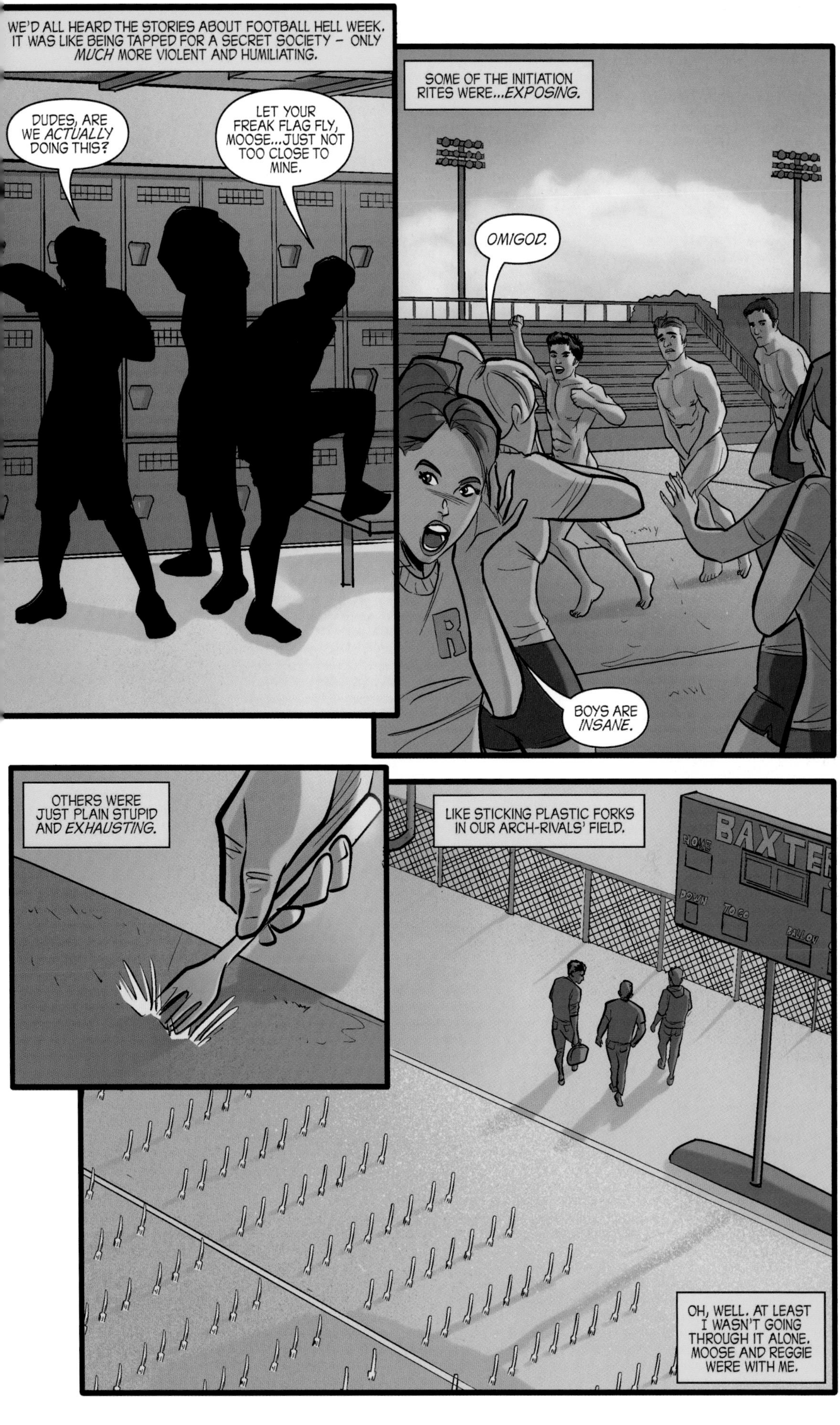
WE'D ALL HEARD THE STORIES ABOUT FOOTBALL HELL WEEK. IT WAS LIKE BEING TAPPED FOR A SECRET SOCIETY – ONLY *MUCH* MORE VIOLENT AND HUMILIATING.
DUDES, ARE WE *ACTUALLY* DOING THIS?
LET YOUR FREAK FLAG FLY, MOOSE...JUST NOT TOO CLOSE TO MINE.
SOME OF THE INITIATION RITES WERE...*EXPOSING.*
OMIGOD.
BOYS ARE *INSANE.*
OTHERS WERE JUST PLAIN STUPID AND *EXHAUSTING.*
LIKE STICKING PLASTIC FORKS IN OUR ARCH-RIVALS' FIELD.
HOME
DOWN
TO GO
OH, WELL. AT LEAST I WASN'T GOING THROUGH IT ALONE. MOOSE AND REGGIE WERE WITH ME.

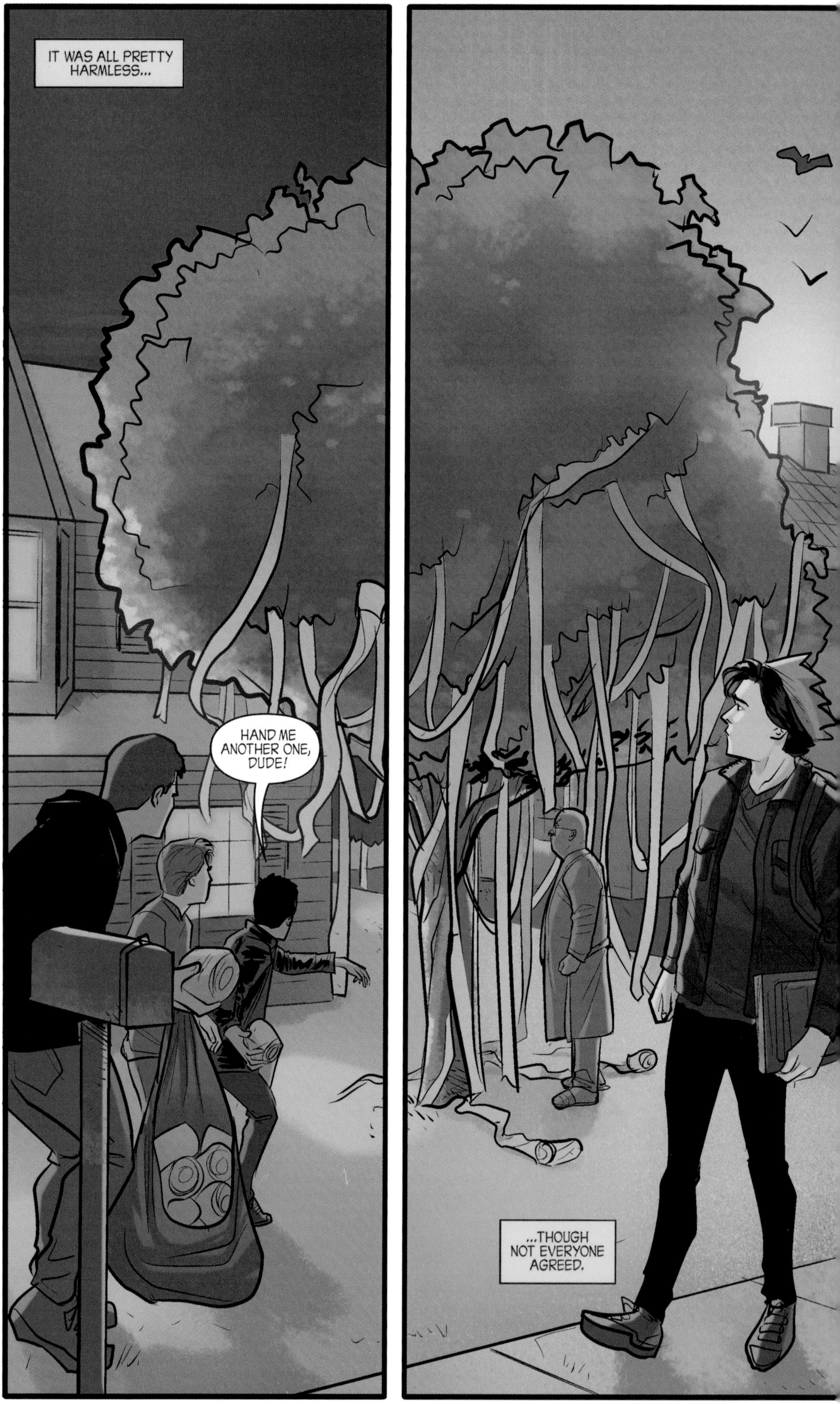
IT WAS ALL PRETTY HARMLESS...
HAND ME ANOTHER ONE, DUDE!
...THOUGH NOT EVERYONE AGREED.

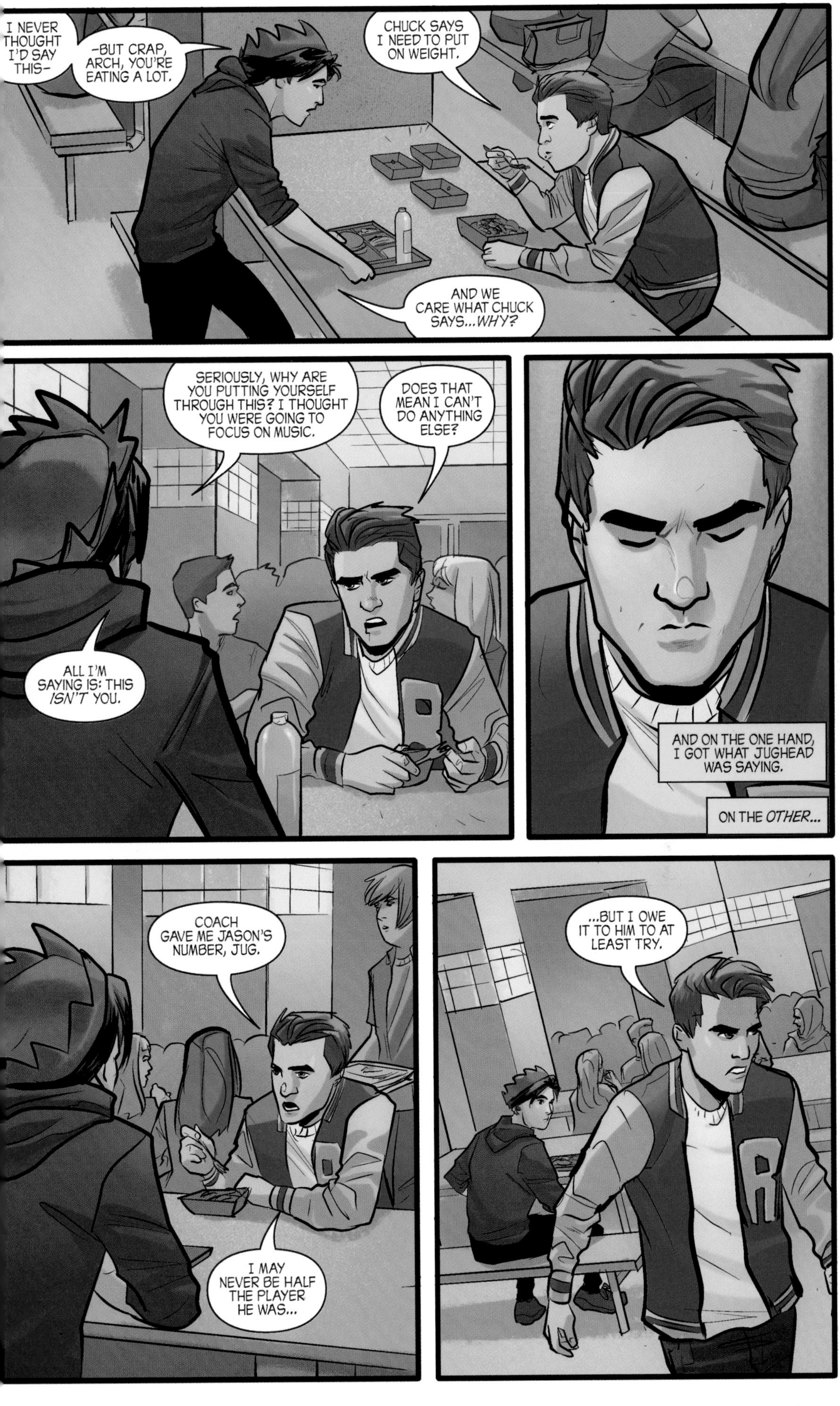
I NEVER THOUGHT I'D SAY THIS–
–BUT CRAP, ARCH, YOU'RE EATING A LOT.
CHUCK SAYS I NEED TO PUT ON WEIGHT.
AND WE CARE WHAT CHUCK SAYS...*WHY?*
SERIOUSLY, WHY ARE YOU PUTTING YOURSELF THROUGH THIS? I THOUGHT YOU WERE GOING TO FOCUS ON MUSIC.
DOES THAT MEAN I CAN'T DO ANYTHING ELSE?
ALL I'M SAYING IS: THIS *ISN'T* YOU.
AND ON THE ONE HAND, I GOT WHAT JUGHEAD WAS SAYING.
ON THE *OTHER*...
COACH GAVE ME JASON'S NUMBER, JUG.
I MAY NEVER BE HALF THE PLAYER HE WAS...
...BUT I OWE IT TO HIM TO AT LEAST TRY.

THAT NIGHT, WE WERE TOLD TO COME TO SCHOOL IN ONLY OUR BATHING SUITS.

GET IN THE BACK. AND FIND SOMETHING TO HOLD ONTO.

WE *ASSUMED* THIS WOULD BE JUST ANOTHER TASK TO EMBARRASS US...

WE WERE WRONG.

YOU'VE PROVED THAT YOU'RE WILLING TO BREAK A FEW RULES. THAT'S A GOOD START. BUT FOOTBALL IS A PHYSICAL GAME. WE NEED TO KNOW YOU'RE TOUGH ENOUGH TO BE A BULLDOG.

THIS IS YOUR FINAL *TEST*:

YOU EACH NEED TO SWIM ACROSS SWEETWATER RIVER AND BACK.

YO, ARE YOU *KIDDING?!*

IT'S AT LEAST 100 YARDS TO THE OTHER SIDE— AND THE WATER'LL BE *FREEZING!*

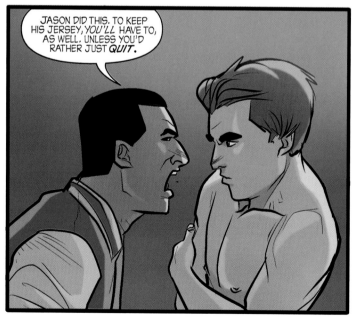

JASON DID THIS. TO KEEP HIS JERSEY, *YOU'LL* HAVE TO, AS WELL. UNLESS YOU'D RATHER JUST *QUIT.*

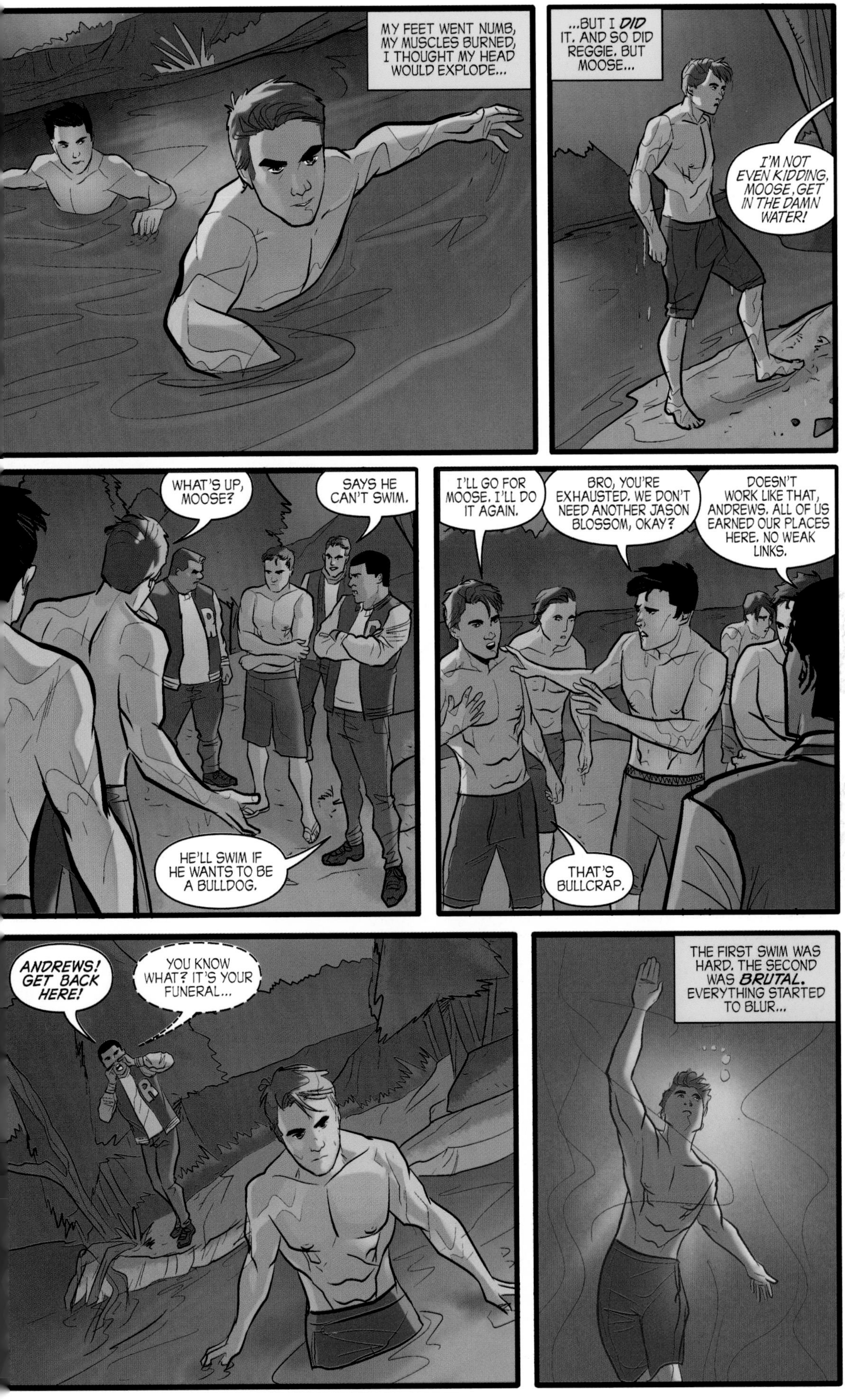
MY FEET WENT NUMB, MY MUSCLES BURNED, I THOUGHT MY HEAD WOULD EXPLODE...
...BUT I DID IT. AND SO DID REGGIE. BUT MOOSE...
I'M NOT EVEN KIDDING, MOOSE, GET IN THE DAMN WATER!
WHAT'S UP, MOOSE?
SAYS HE CAN'T SWIM.
HE'LL SWIM IF HE WANTS TO BE A BULLDOG.
I'LL GO FOR MOOSE. I'LL DO IT AGAIN.
BRO, YOU'RE EXHAUSTED. WE DON'T NEED ANOTHER JASON BLOSSOM, OKAY?
DOESN'T WORK LIKE THAT, ANDREWS. ALL OF US EARNED OUR PLACES HERE. NO WEAK LINKS.
THAT'S BULLCRAP.
ANDREWS! GET BACK HERE!
YOU KNOW WHAT? IT'S YOUR FUNERAL...
THE FIRST SWIM WAS HARD. THE SECOND WAS BRUTAL. EVERYTHING STARTED TO BLUR...

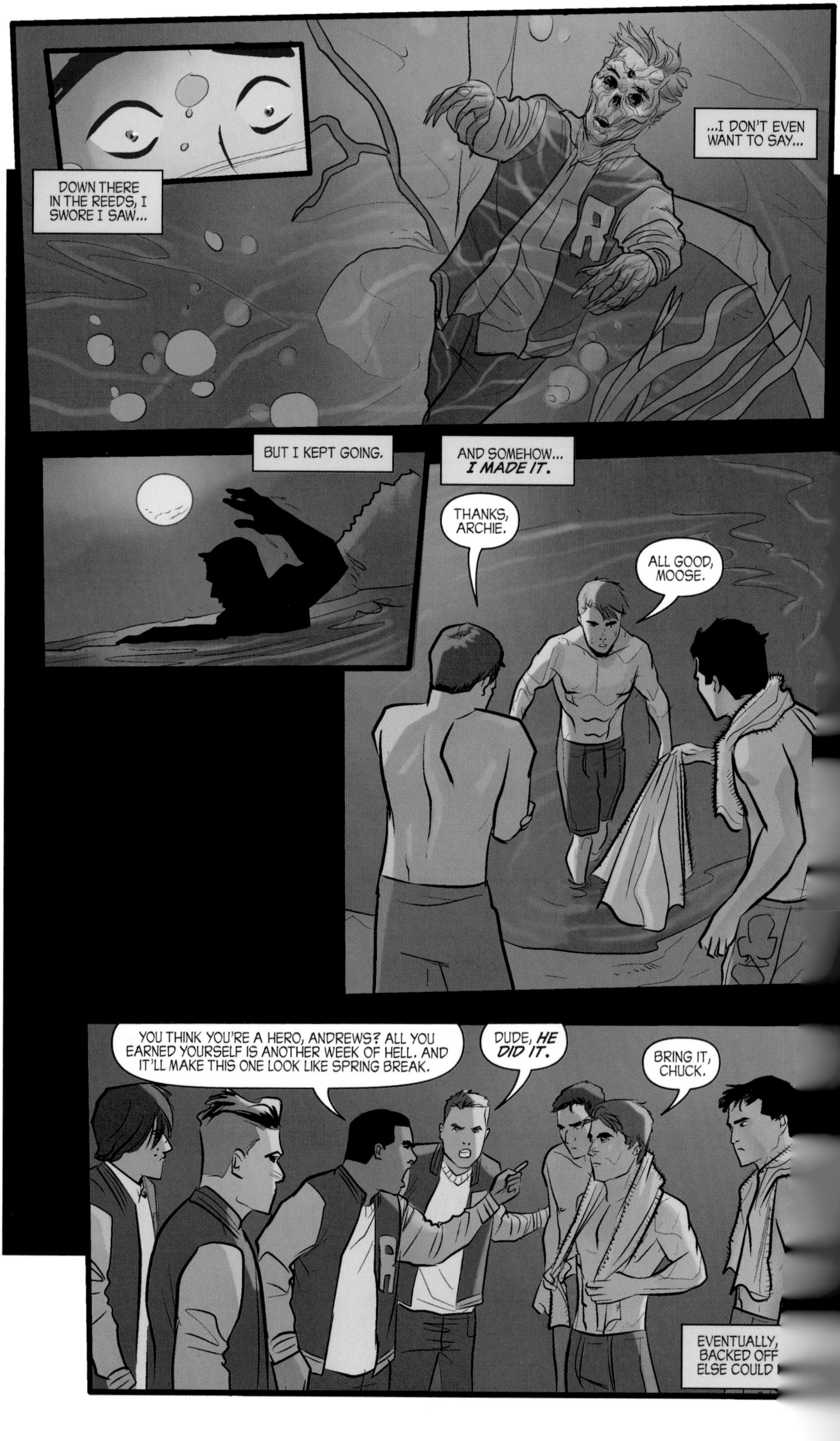
DOWN THERE IN THE REEDS, I SWORE I SAW...
...I DON'T EVEN WANT TO SAY...
BUT I KEPT GOING.
AND SOMEHOW... *I MADE IT.*
THANKS, ARCHIE.
ALL GOOD, MOOSE.
YOU THINK YOU'RE A HERO, ANDREWS? ALL YOU EARNED YOURSELF IS ANOTHER WEEK OF HELL. AND IT'LL MAKE THIS ONE LOOK LIKE SPRING BREAK.
DUDE, *HE DID IT.*
BRING IT, CHUCK.
EVENTUALLY, BACKED OFF ELSE COULD

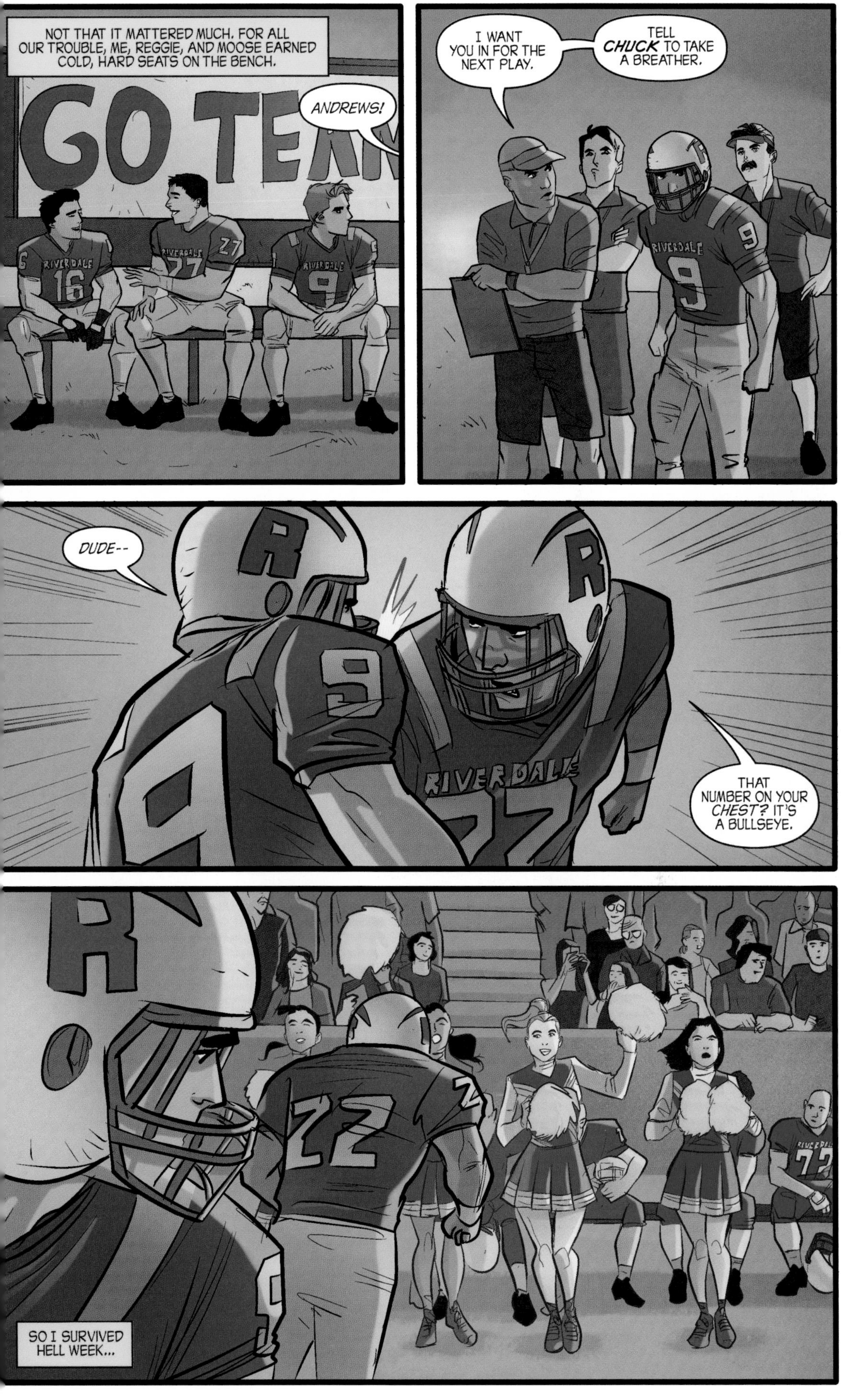
NOT THAT IT MATTERED MUCH. FOR ALL OUR TROUBLE, ME, REGGIE, AND MOOSE EARNED COLD, HARD SEATS ON THE BENCH.
GO TEAM
ANDREWS!
I WANT YOU IN FOR THE NEXT PLAY.
TELL *CHUCK* TO TAKE A BREATHER.
DUDE--
THAT NUMBER ON YOUR *CHEST?* IT'S A BULLSEYE.
SO I SURVIVED HELL WEEK...

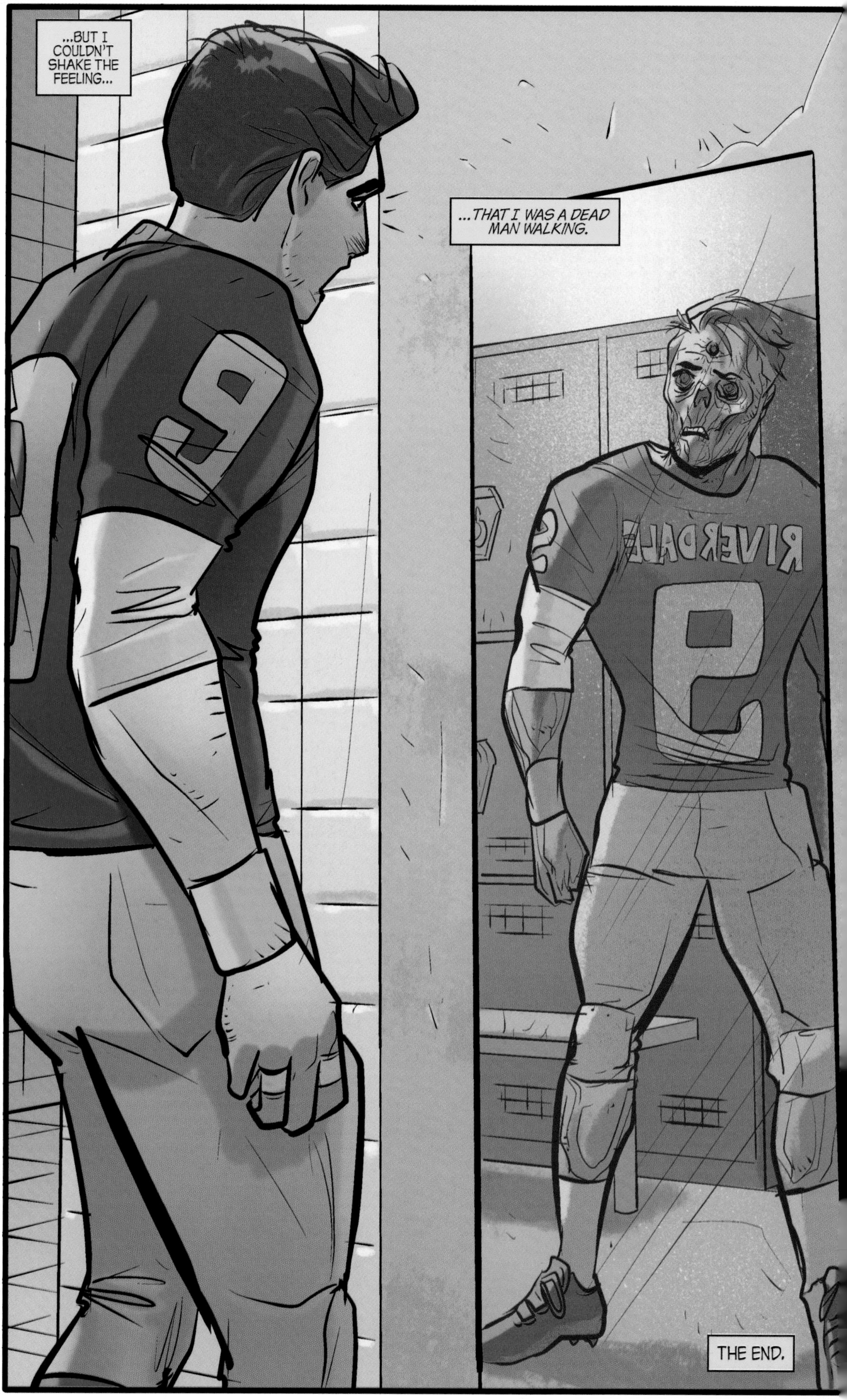
...BUT I COULDN'T SHAKE THE FEELING...
...THAT I WAS A DEAD MAN WALKING.
THE END.

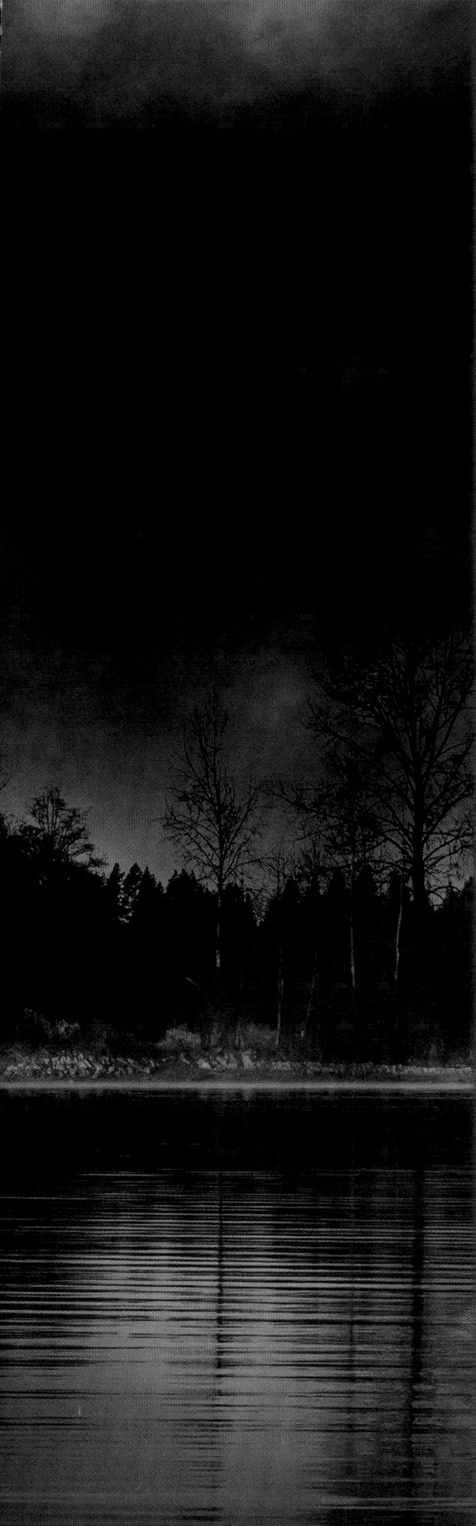

CHAPTER SIX

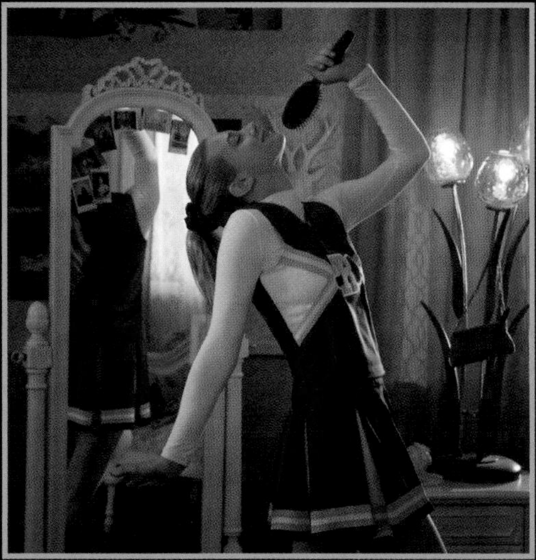

BRING IT ON

WRITER:
MICHAEL GRASSI

ART:
JOE EISMA

COLORS:
ANDRE SZYMANOWICZ

LETTERS:
JOHN WORKMAN

STARRING
BETTY & VERONICA

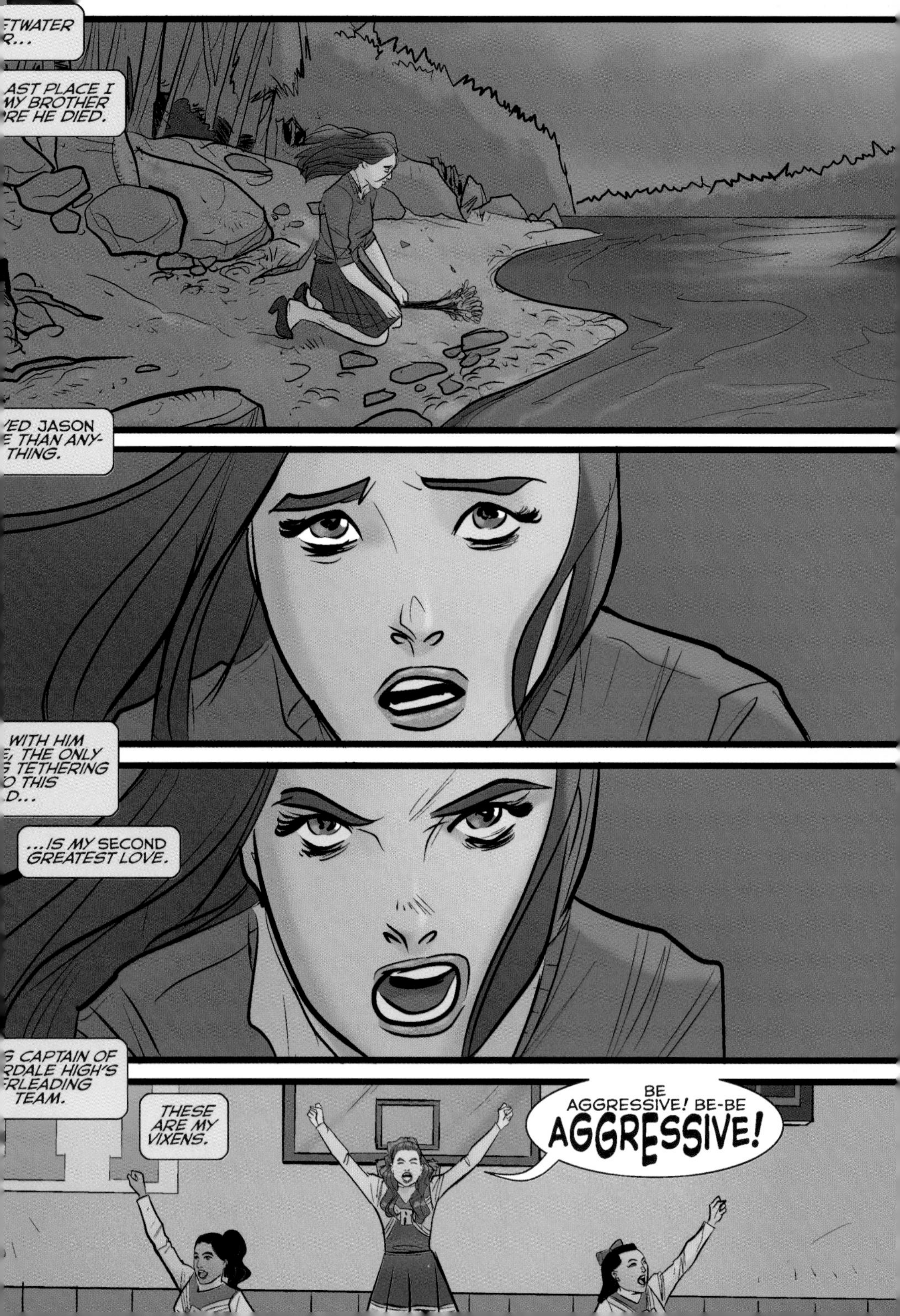

ETWATER R...
AST PLACE I MY BROTHER RE HE DIED.
ED JASON E THAN ANY- THING.
WITH HIM E, THE ONLY G TETHERING O THIS D...
...IS MY SECOND GREATEST LOVE.
G CAPTAIN OF RDALE HIGH'S RLEADING TEAM.
THESE ARE MY VIXENS.
BE AGGRESSIVE! BE-BE AGGRESSIVE!

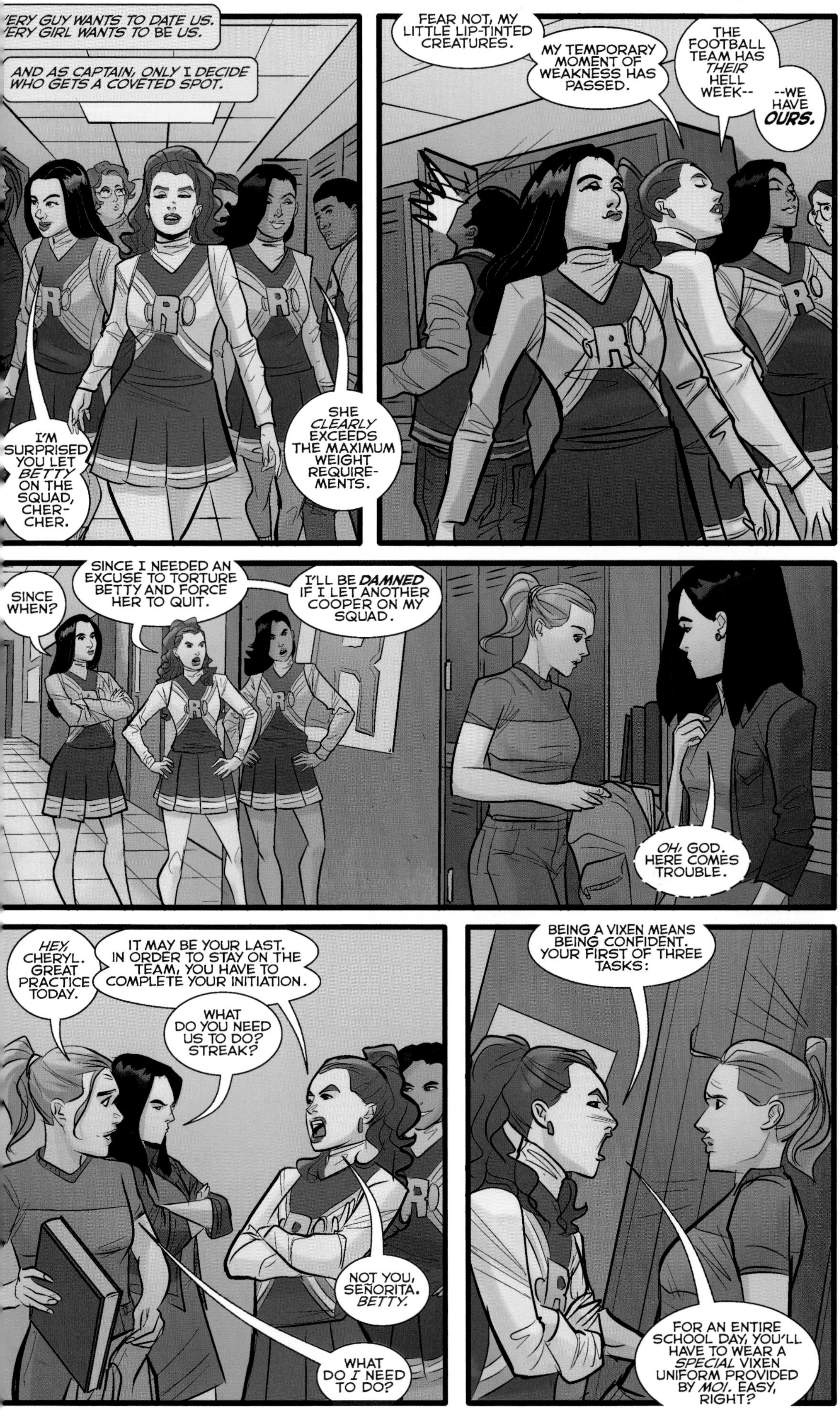
ERY GUY WANTS TO DATE US. ERY GIRL WANTS TO BE US.
AND AS CAPTAIN, ONLY I DECIDE WHO GETS A COVETED SPOT.
I'M SURPRISED YOU LET BETTY ON THE SQUAD, CHER-CHER.
SHE CLEARLY EXCEEDS THE MAXIMUM WEIGHT REQUIRE-MENTS.
FEAR NOT, MY LITTLE LIP-TINTED CREATURES.
MY TEMPORARY MOMENT OF WEAKNESS HAS PASSED.
THE FOOTBALL TEAM HAS THEIR HELL WEEK--
--WE HAVE OURS.
SINCE WHEN?
SINCE I NEEDED AN EXCUSE TO TORTURE BETTY AND FORCE HER TO QUIT.
I'LL BE DAMNED IF I LET ANOTHER COOPER ON MY SQUAD.
OH, GOD. HERE COMES TROUBLE.
HEY, CHERYL. GREAT PRACTICE TODAY.
IT MAY BE YOUR LAST. IN ORDER TO STAY ON THE TEAM, YOU HAVE TO COMPLETE YOUR INITIATION.
WHAT DO YOU NEED US TO DO? STREAK?
NOT YOU, SEÑORITA. BETTY.
WHAT DO I NEED TO DO?
BEING A VIXEN MEANS BEING CONFIDENT. YOUR FIRST OF THREE TASKS:
FOR AN ENTIRE SCHOOL DAY, YOU'LL HAVE TO WEAR A SPECIAL VIXEN UNIFORM PROVIDED BY MOI. EASY, RIGHT?

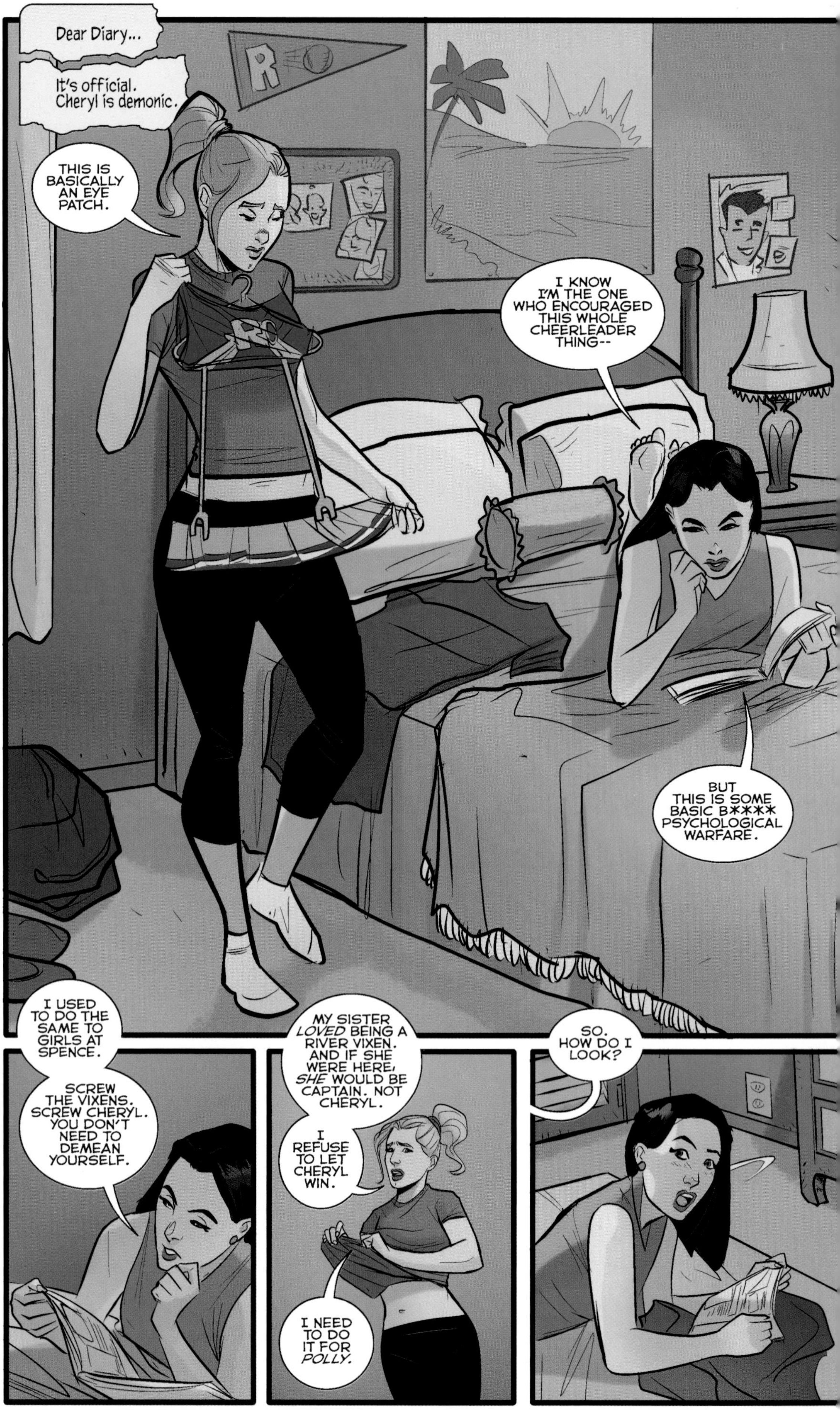

Dear Diary...
It's official. Cheryl is demonic.
THIS IS BASICALLY AN EYE PATCH.
I KNOW I'M THE ONE WHO ENCOURAGED THIS WHOLE CHEERLEADER THING--
BUT THIS IS SOME BASIC B**** PSYCHOLOGICAL WARFARE.
I USED TO DO THE SAME TO GIRLS AT SPENCE.
SCREW THE VIXENS. SCREW CHERYL. YOU DON'T NEED TO DEMEAN YOURSELF.
MY SISTER *LOVED* BEING A RIVER VIXEN. AND IF SHE WERE HERE, *SHE* WOULD BE CAPTAIN. NOT CHERYL.
I REFUSE TO LET CHERYL WIN.
I NEED TO DO IT FOR *POLLY*.
SO. HOW DO I LOOK?

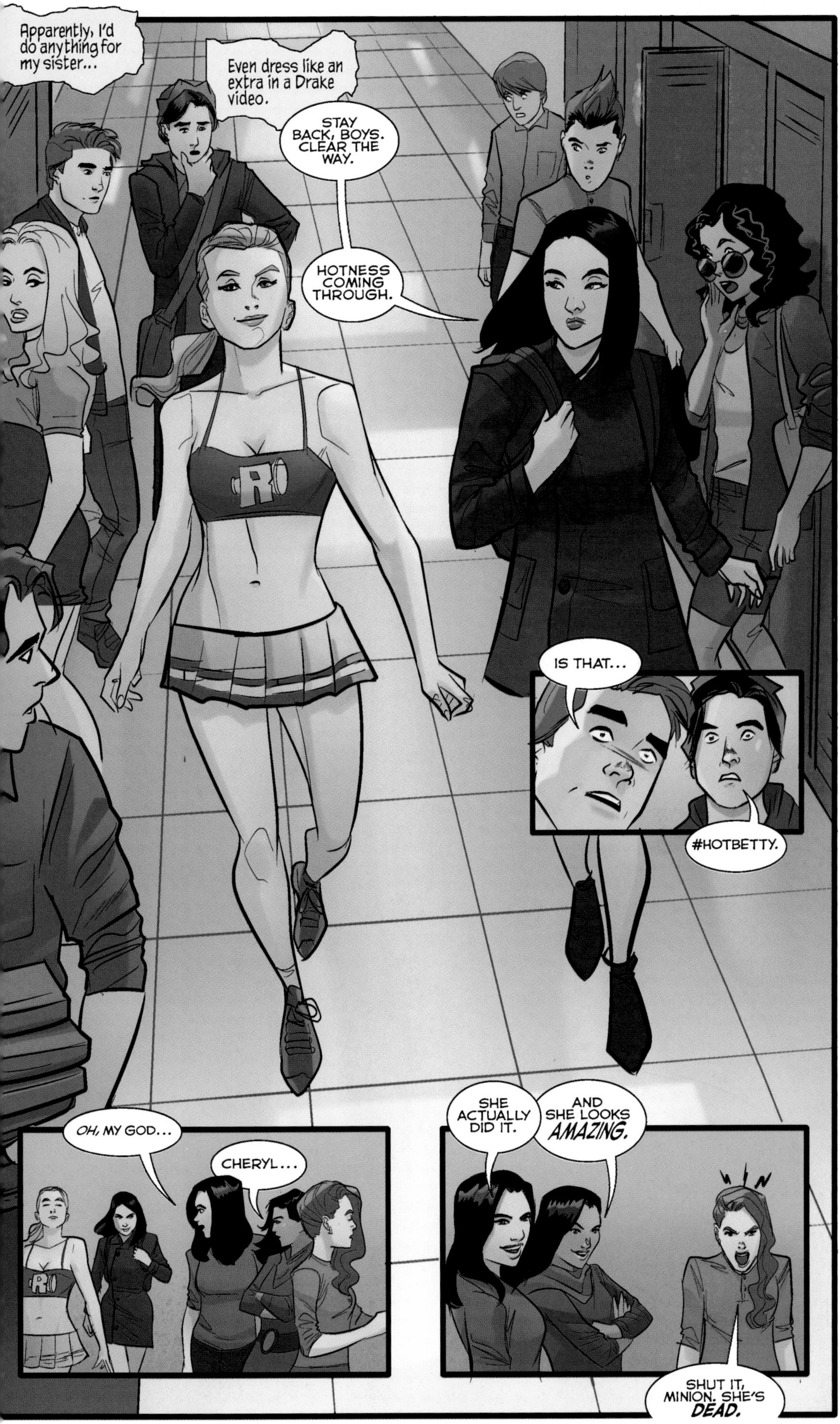
Apparently, I'd do anything for my sister...
Even dress like an extra in a Drake video.
STAY BACK, BOYS. CLEAR THE WAY.
HOTNESS COMING THROUGH.
IS THAT...
#HOTBETTY.
OH, MY GOD...
CHERYL...
SHE ACTUALLY DID IT.
AND SHE LOOKS *AMAZING.*
SHUT IT, MINION. SHE'S *DEAD.*

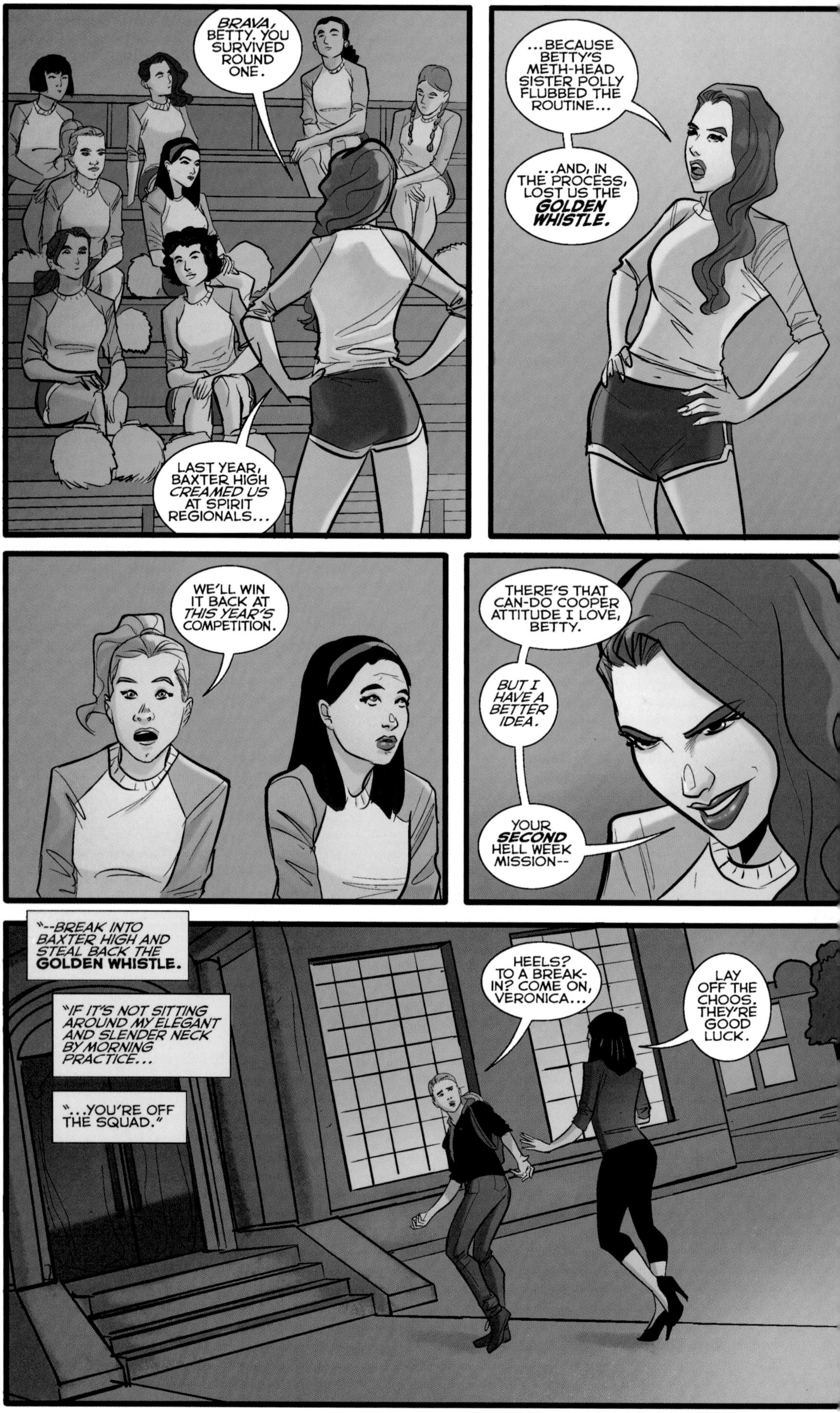
BRAVA, BETTY. YOU SURVIVED ROUND ONE.
LAST YEAR, BAXTER HIGH CREAMED US AT SPIRIT REGIONALS...
...BECAUSE BETTY'S METH-HEAD SISTER POLLY FLUBBED THE ROUTINE...
...AND, IN THE PROCESS, LOST US THE GOLDEN WHISTLE.
WE'LL WIN IT BACK AT THIS YEAR'S COMPETITION.
THERE'S THAT CAN-DO COOPER ATTITUDE I LOVE, BETTY.
BUT I HAVE A BETTER IDEA.
YOUR SECOND HELL WEEK MISSION--
"--BREAK INTO BAXTER HIGH AND STEAL BACK THE GOLDEN WHISTLE.
"IF IT'S NOT SITTING AROUND MY ELEGANT AND SLENDER NECK BY MORNING PRACTICE...
"...YOU'RE OFF THE SQUAD."
HEELS? TO A BREAK-IN? COME ON, VERONICA...
LAY OFF THE CHOOS. THEY'RE GOOD LUCK.

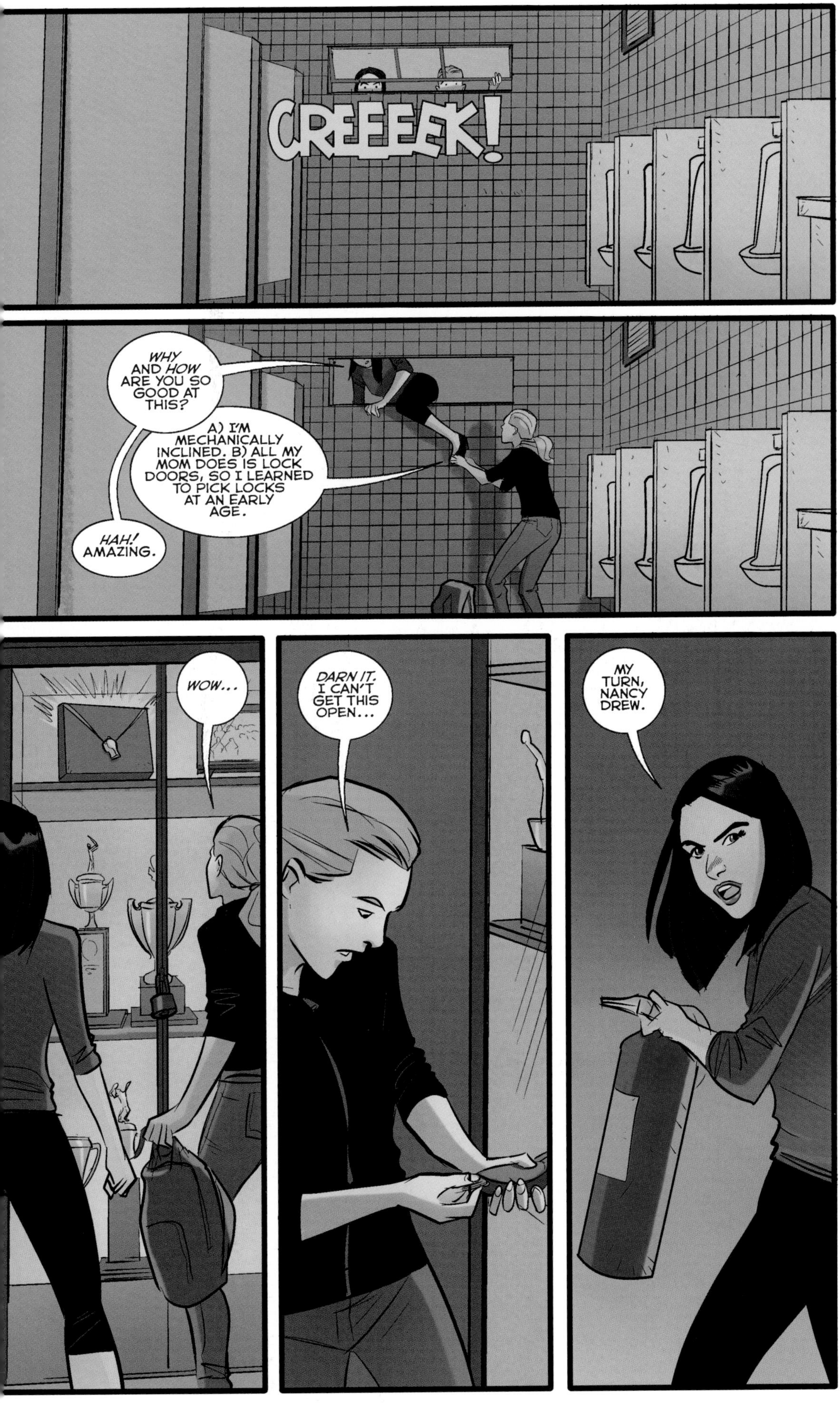
CREEEEK!
WHY AND HOW ARE YOU SO GOOD AT THIS?
A) I'M MECHANICALLY INCLINED. B) ALL MY MOM DOES IS LOCK DOORS, SO I LEARNED TO PICK LOCKS AT AN EARLY AGE.
HAH! AMAZING.
WOW...
DARN IT. I CAN'T GET THIS OPEN...
MY TURN, NANCY DREW.

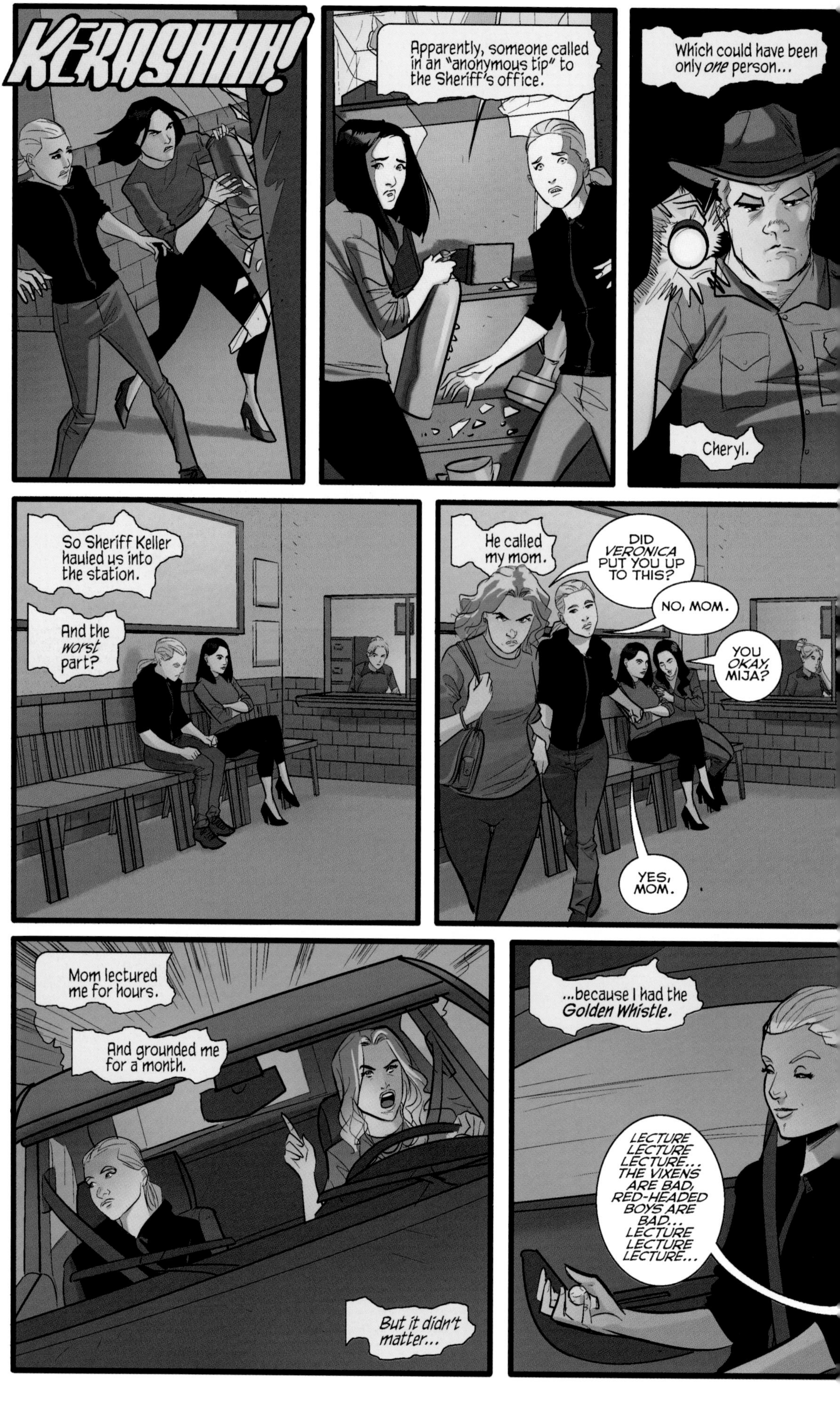
KERASHHH!
Apparently, someone called in an "anonymous tip" to the Sheriff's office.
Which could have been only *one* person...
Cheryl.
So Sheriff Keller hauled us into the station.
And the *worst* part?
He called my mom.
DID *VERONICA* PUT YOU UP TO THIS?
NO, MOM.
YOU *OKAY*, MIJA?
YES, MOM.
Mom lectured me for hours.
And grounded me for a month.
But it didn't matter...
...because I had the *Golden Whistle.*
LECTURE LECTURE LECTURE... THE VIXENS ARE BAD, RED-HEADED BOYS ARE BAD... LECTURE LECTURE LECTURE...

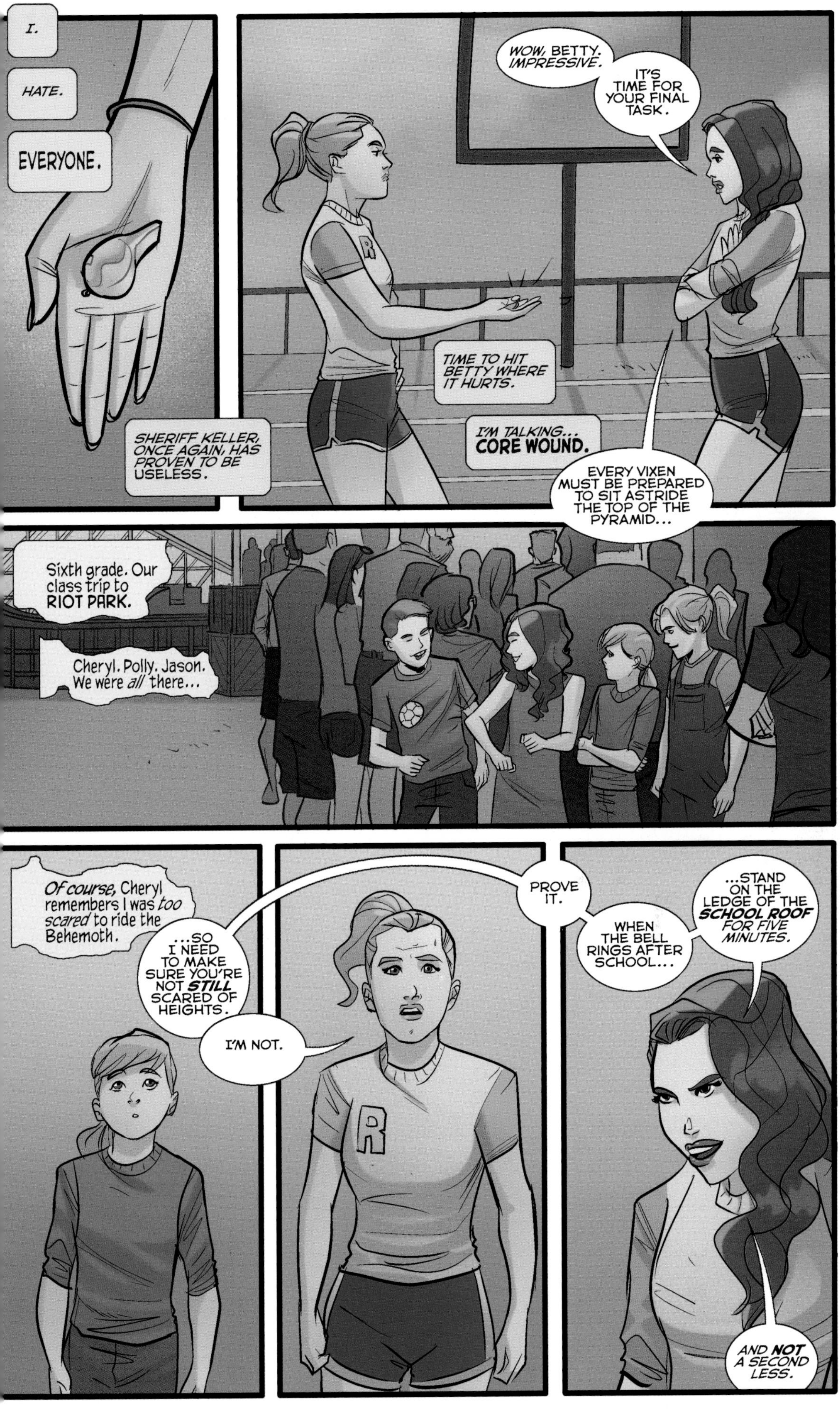

I.
HATE.
EVERYONE.
WOW, BETTY. IMPRESSIVE.
IT'S TIME FOR YOUR FINAL TASK.
TIME TO HIT BETTY WHERE IT HURTS.
I'M TALKING... CORE WOUND.
SHERIFF KELLER, ONCE AGAIN, HAS PROVEN TO BE USELESS.
EVERY VIXEN MUST BE PREPARED TO SIT ASTRIDE THE TOP OF THE PYRAMID...
Sixth grade. Our class trip to RIOT PARK.
Cheryl. Polly. Jason. We were all there...
Of course, Cheryl remembers I was too scared to ride the Behemoth.
...SO I NEED TO MAKE SURE YOU'RE NOT STILL SCARED OF HEIGHTS.
I'M NOT.
PROVE IT.
WHEN THE BELL RINGS AFTER SCHOOL...
...STAND ON THE LEDGE OF THE SCHOOL ROOF FOR FIVE MINUTES.
AND NOT A SECOND LESS.

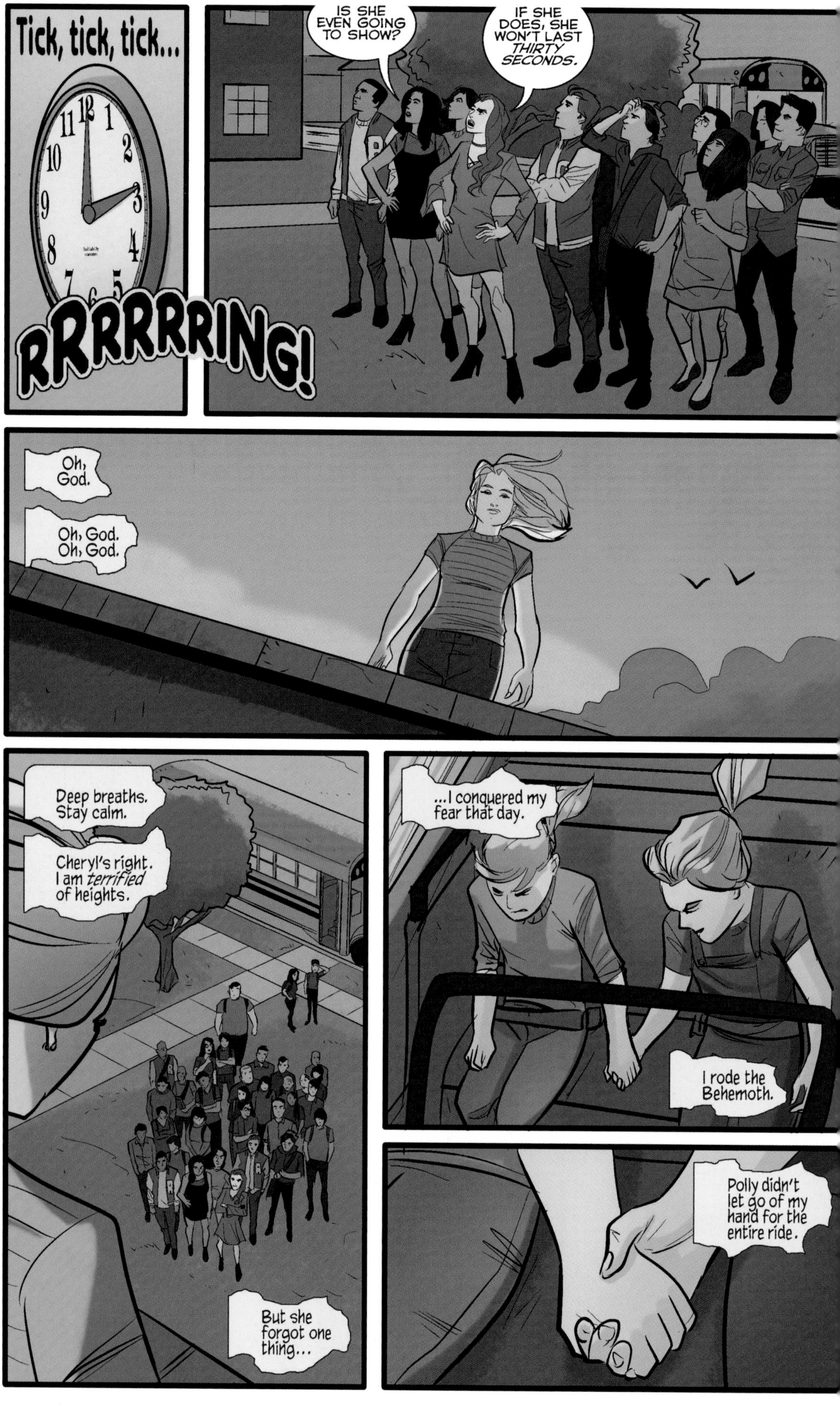
Tick, tick, tick...
RRRRRRING!
IS SHE EVEN GOING TO SHOW?
IF SHE DOES, SHE WON'T LAST *THIRTY SECONDS.*
Oh, God.
Oh, God. Oh, God.
Deep breaths. Stay calm.
Cheryl's right. I am *terrified* of heights.
But she forgot one thing...
...I conquered my fear that day.
I rode the Behemoth.
Polly didn't let go of my hand for the entire ride.

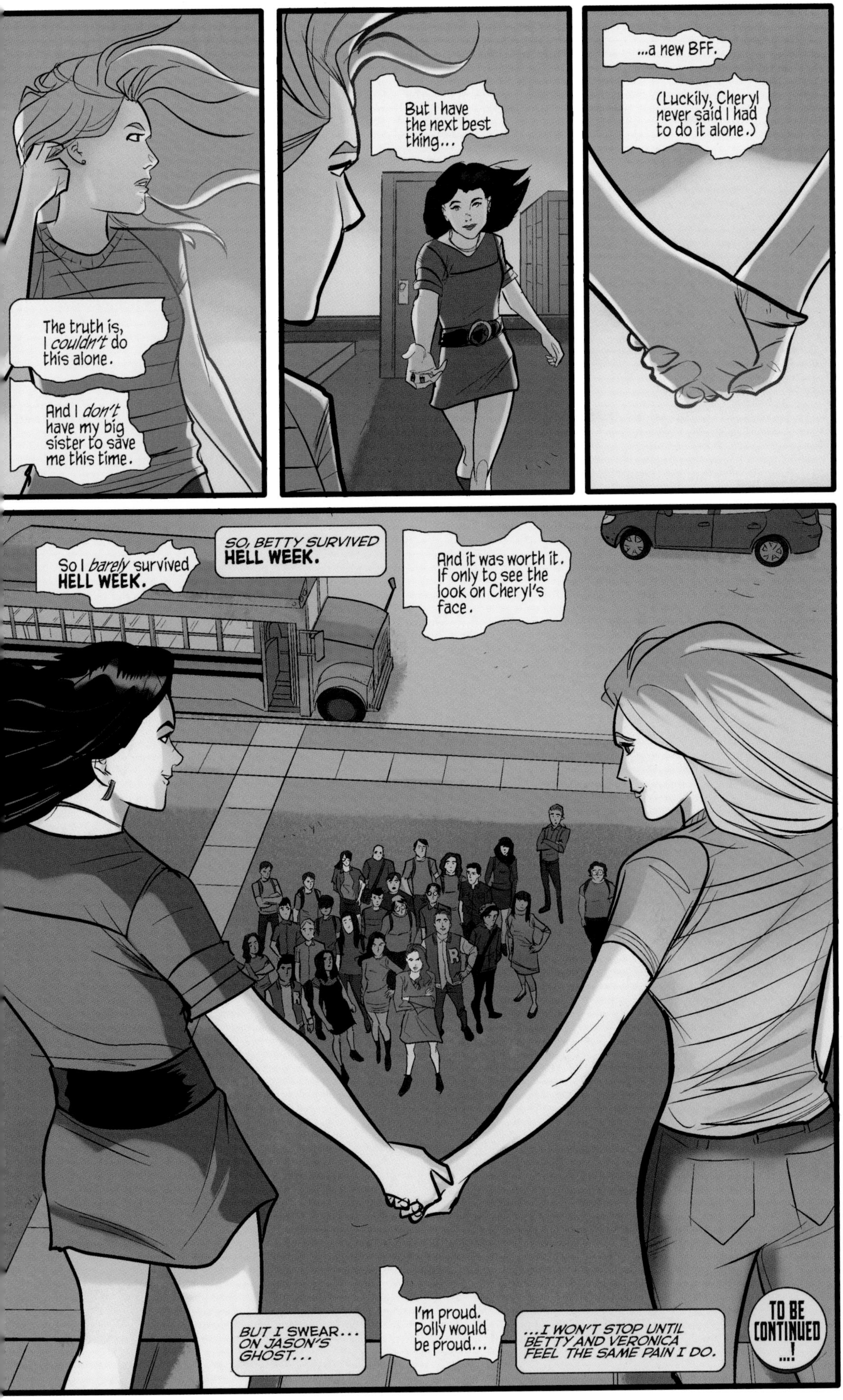
The truth is, I couldn't do this alone.
And I don't have my big sister to save me this time.
But I have the next best thing...
...a new BFF.
(Luckily, Cheryl never said I had to do it alone.)
So I barely survived HELL WEEK.
SO, BETTY SURVIVED HELL WEEK.
And it was worth it. If only to see the look on Cheryl's face.
BUT I SWEAR... ON JASON'S GHOST...
I'm proud. Polly would be proud...
...I WON'T STOP UNTIL BETTY AND VERONICA FEEL THE SAME PAIN I DO.
TO BE CONTINUED...!

CHAPTER SEVEN

THE BREAKFAST CLUB

WRITERS:
GREG MURRAY
DANIEL KING

ART:
JOE EISMA
THOMAS PITILLI

COLORS:
ANDRE SZYMANOWICZ

LETTERS:
JOHN WORKMAN

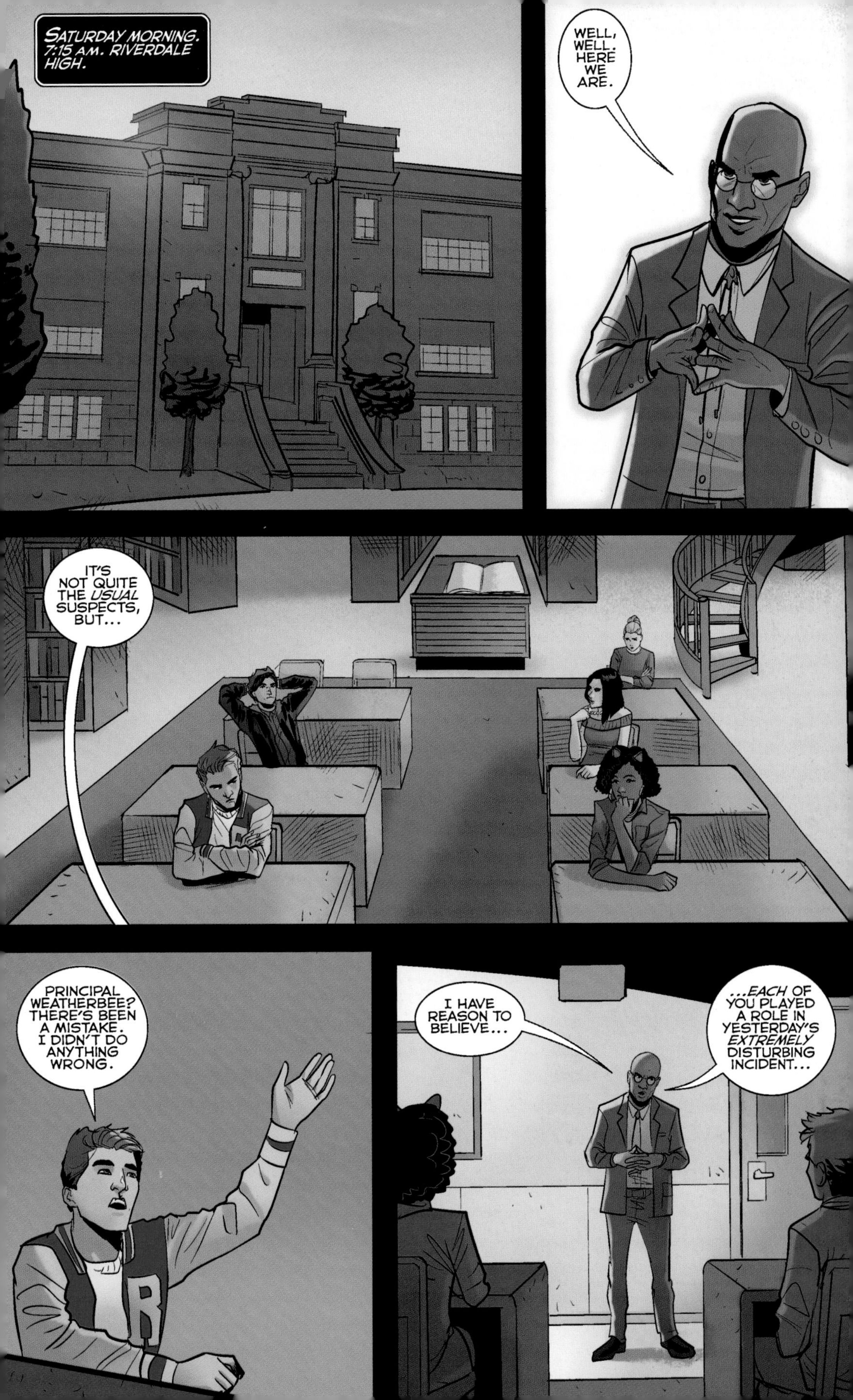
SATURDAY MORNING. 7:15 AM. RIVERDALE HIGH.
WELL, WELL. HERE WE ARE.
IT'S NOT QUITE THE *USUAL* SUSPECTS, BUT...
PRINCIPAL WEATHERBEE? THERE'S BEEN A MISTAKE. I DIDN'T DO ANYTHING WRONG.
I HAVE REASON TO BELIEVE...
...*EACH* OF YOU PLAYED A ROLE IN YESTERDAY'S *EXTREMELY* DISTURBING INCIDENT...

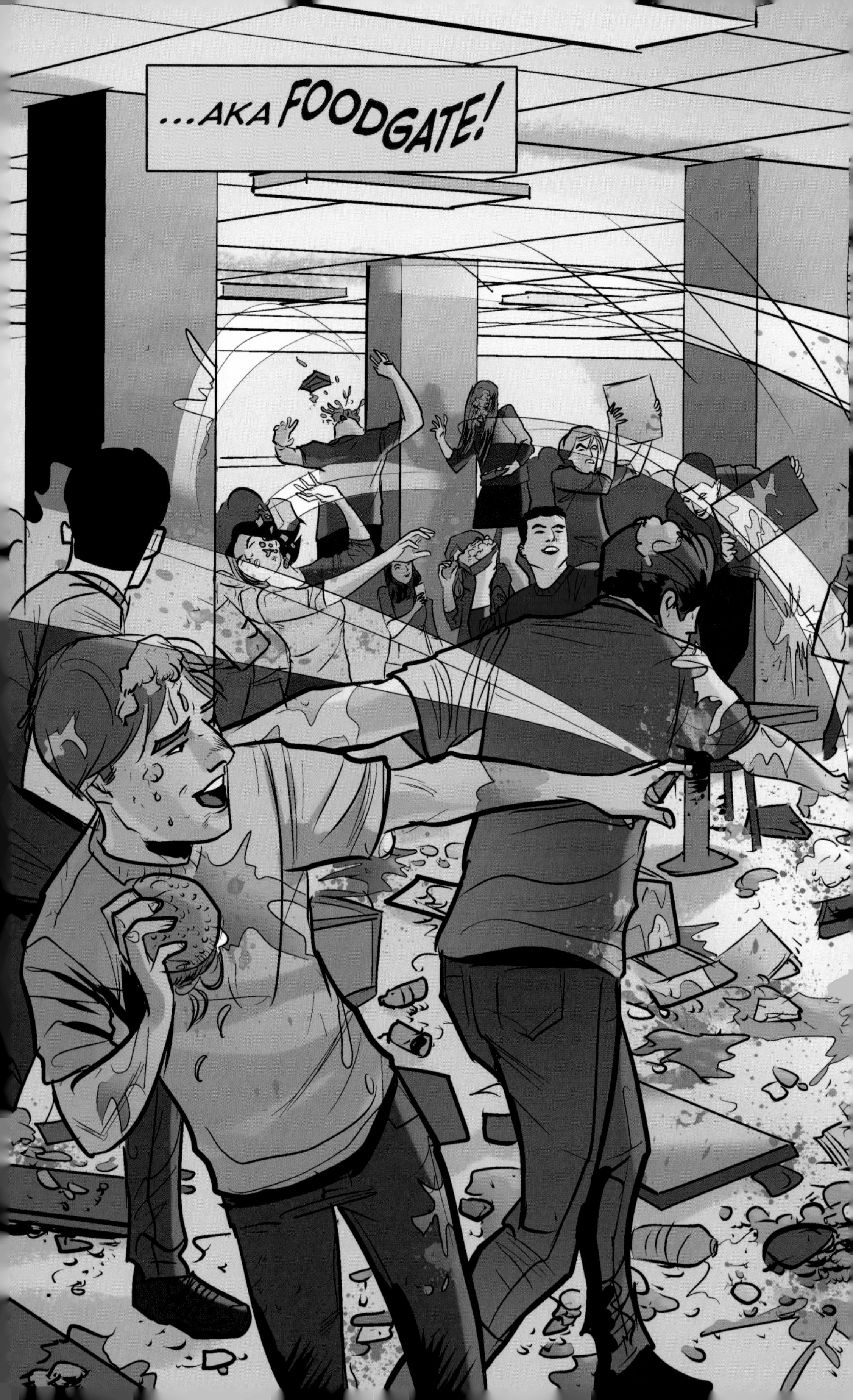
...AKA FOODGATE!

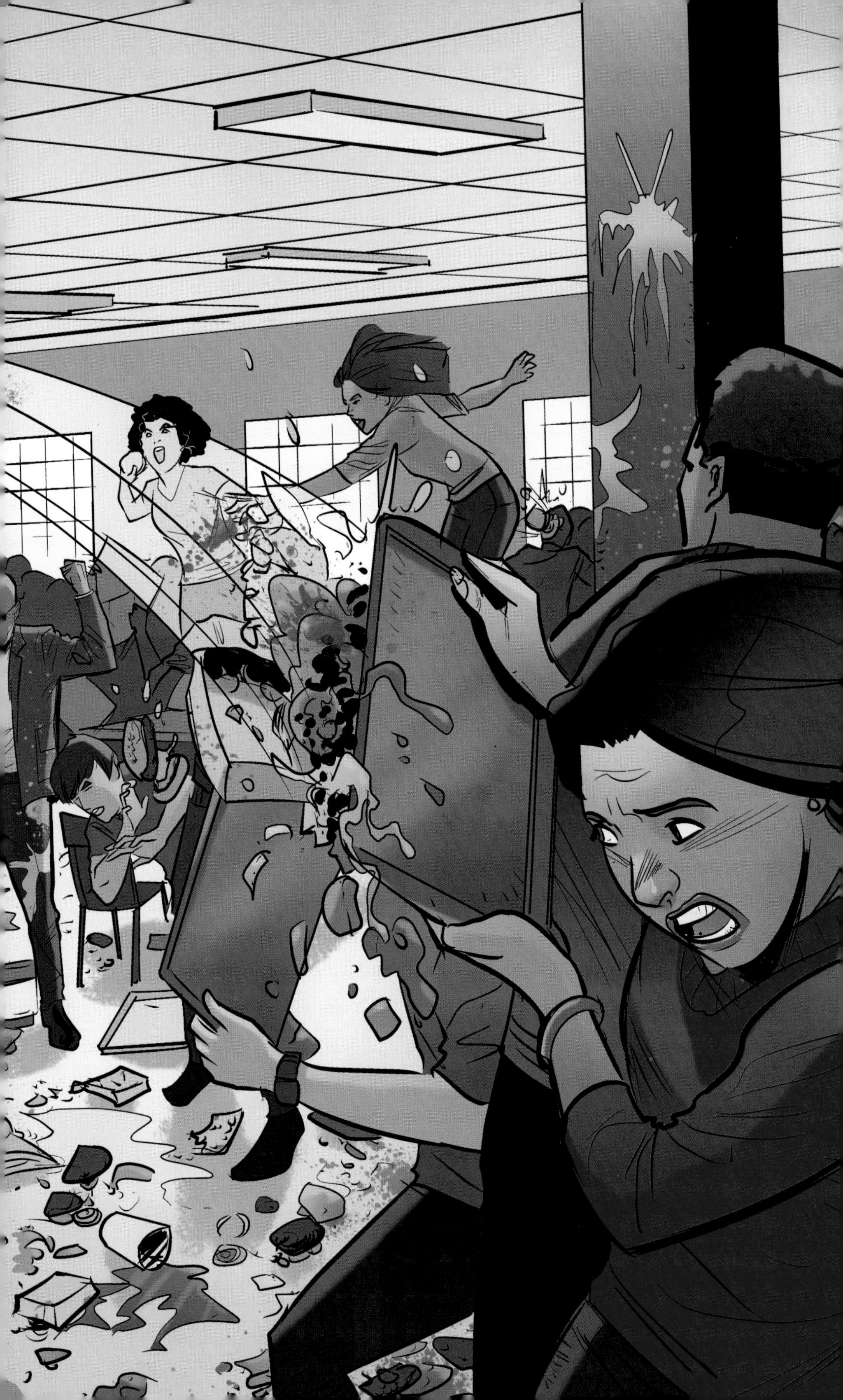

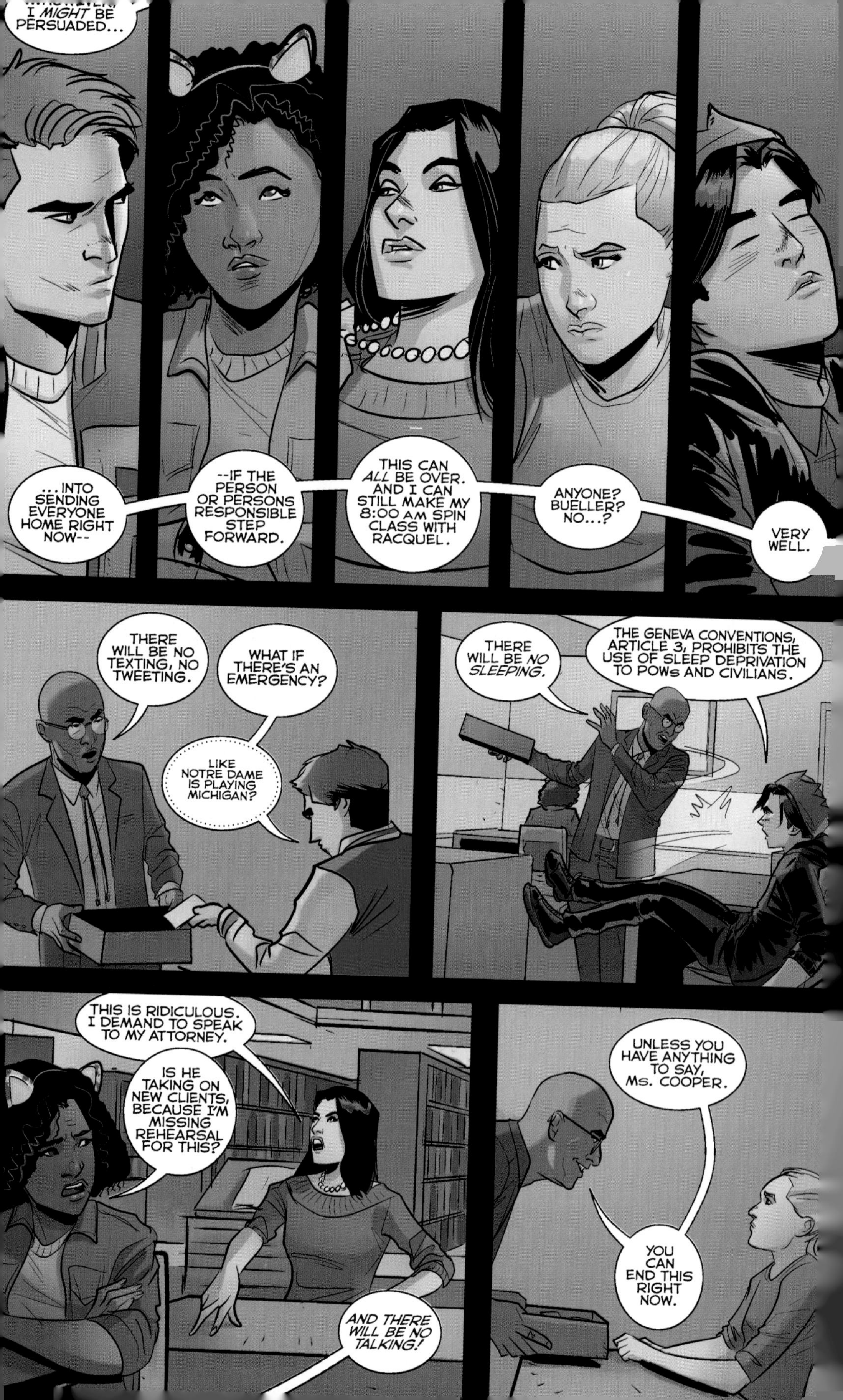
I MIGHT BE PERSUADED...
...INTO SENDING EVERYONE HOME RIGHT NOW--
--IF THE PERSON OR PERSONS RESPONSIBLE STEP FORWARD.
THIS CAN ALL BE OVER. AND I CAN STILL MAKE MY 8:00 AM SPIN CLASS WITH RACQUEL.
ANYONE? BUELLER? NO...?
VERY WELL.
THERE WILL BE NO TEXTING, NO TWEETING.
WHAT IF THERE'S AN EMERGENCY?
LIKE NOTRE DAME IS PLAYING MICHIGAN?
THERE WILL BE NO SLEEPING.
THE GENEVA CONVENTIONS, ARTICLE 3, PROHIBITS THE USE OF SLEEP DEPRIVATION TO POWs AND CIVILIANS.
THIS IS RIDICULOUS. I DEMAND TO SPEAK TO MY ATTORNEY.
IS HE TAKING ON NEW CLIENTS, BECAUSE I'M MISSING REHEARSAL FOR THIS?
AND THERE WILL BE NO TALKING!
UNLESS YOU HAVE ANYTHING TO SAY, Ms. COOPER.
YOU CAN END THIS RIGHT NOW.

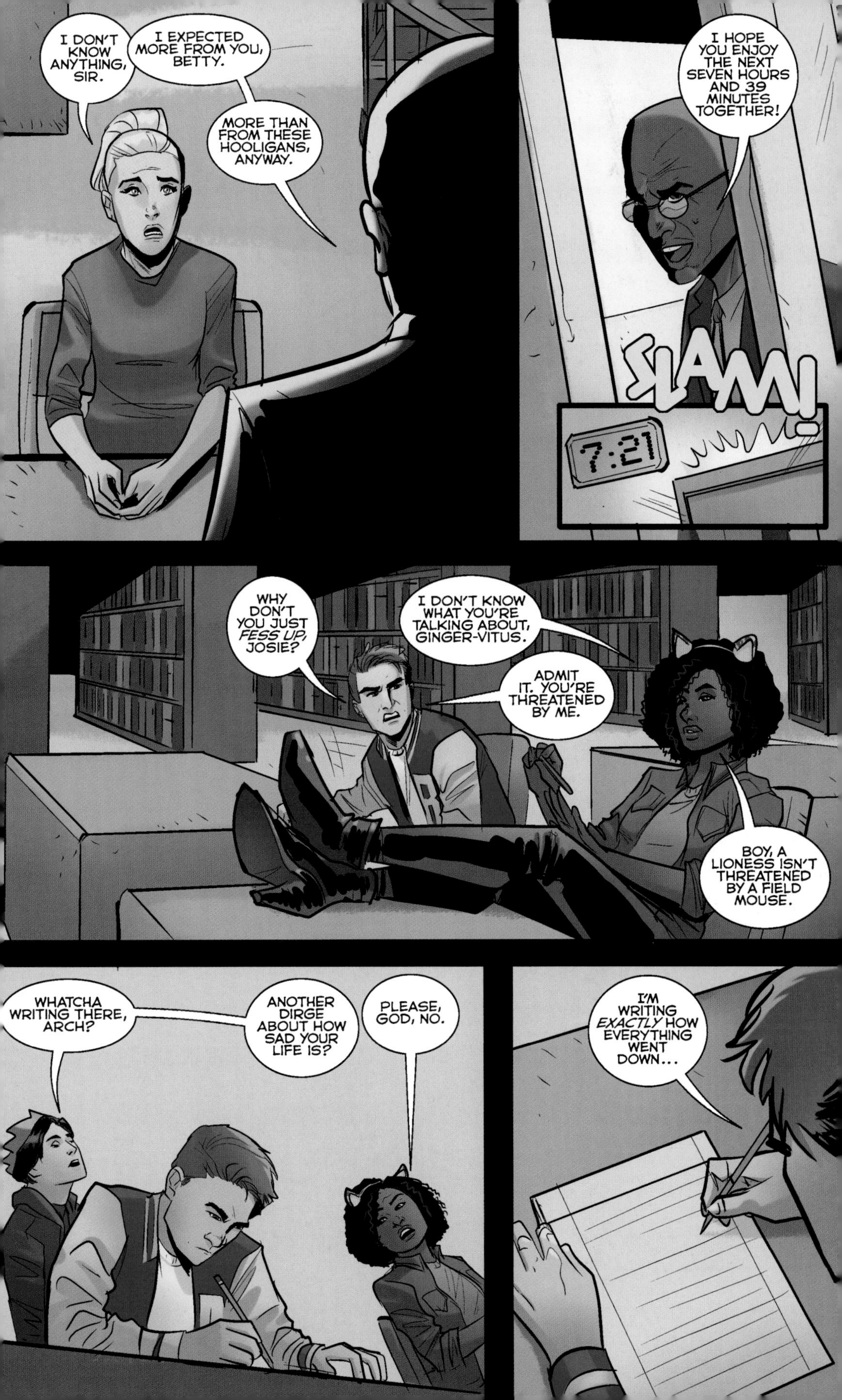

I DON'T KNOW ANYTHING, SIR.
I EXPECTED MORE FROM YOU, BETTY.
MORE THAN FROM THESE HOOLIGANS, ANYWAY.
I HOPE YOU ENJOY THE NEXT SEVEN HOURS AND 39 MINUTES TOGETHER!
SLAM!
7:21
WHY DON'T YOU JUST *FESS UP,* JOSIE?
I DON'T KNOW WHAT YOU'RE TALKING ABOUT, GINGER-VITUS.
ADMIT IT. YOU'RE THREATENED BY ME.
BOY, A LIONESS ISN'T THREATENED BY A FIELD MOUSE.
WHATCHA WRITING THERE, ARCH?
ANOTHER DIRGE ABOUT HOW SAD YOUR LIFE IS?
PLEASE, GOD, NO.
I'M WRITING *EXACTLY* HOW EVERYTHING WENT DOWN...

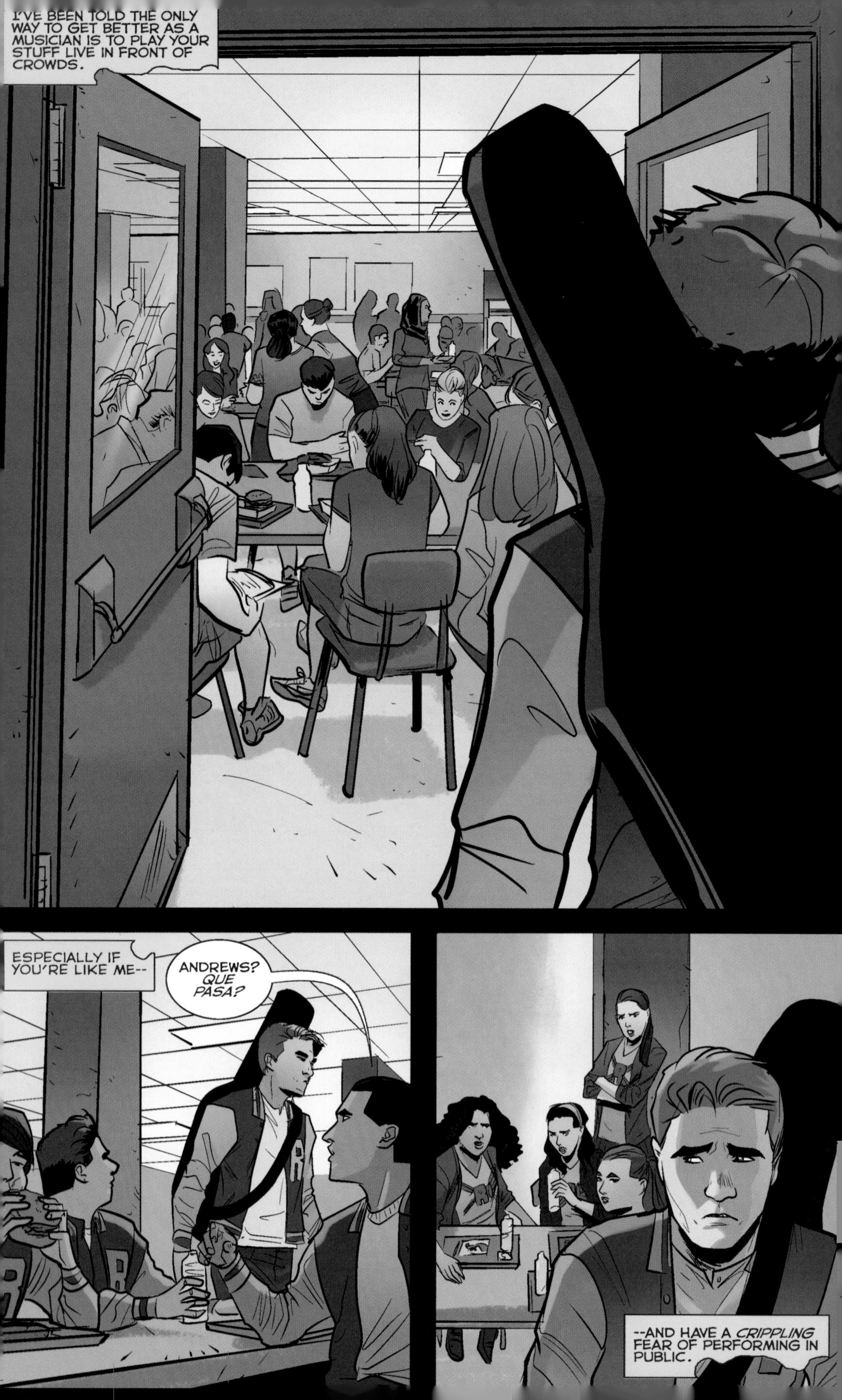
I'VE BEEN TOLD THE ONLY WAY TO GET BETTER AS A MUSICIAN IS TO PLAY YOUR STUFF LIVE IN FRONT OF CROWDS.
ESPECIALLY IF YOU'RE LIKE ME--
ANDREWS? *QUE PASA?*
--AND HAVE A *CRIPPLING* FEAR OF PERFORMING IN PUBLIC.

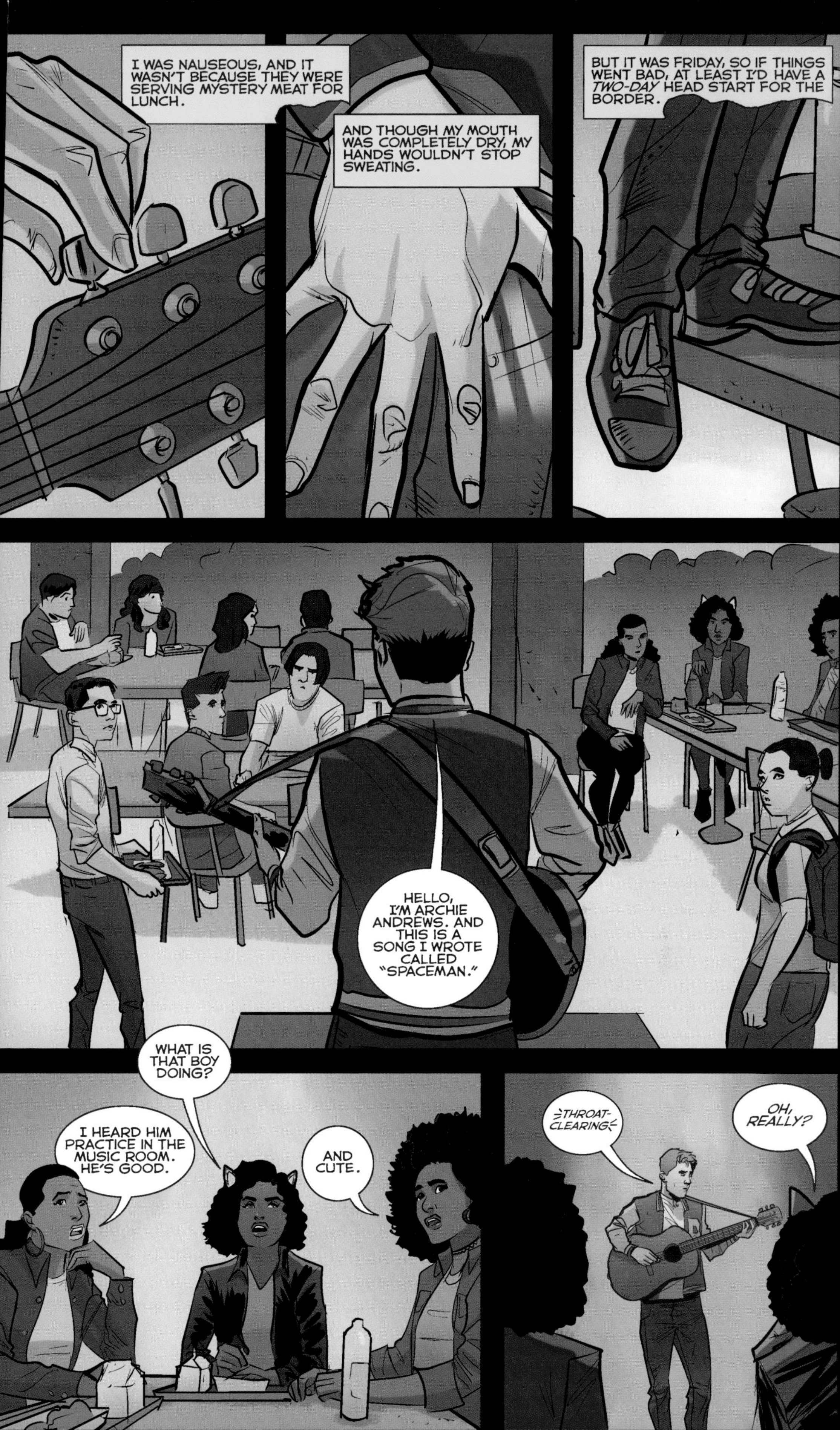
I WAS NAUSEOUS, AND IT WASN'T BECAUSE THEY WERE SERVING MYSTERY MEAT FOR LUNCH.
AND THOUGH MY MOUTH WAS COMPLETELY DRY, MY HANDS WOULDN'T STOP SWEATING.
BUT IT WAS FRIDAY, SO IF THINGS WENT BAD, AT LEAST I'D HAVE A *TWO-DAY* HEAD START FOR THE BORDER.
HELLO, I'M ARCHIE ANDREWS. AND THIS IS A SONG I WROTE CALLED "SPACEMAN."
WHAT IS THAT BOY DOING?
I HEARD HIM PRACTICE IN THE MUSIC ROOM. HE'S GOOD.
AND CUTE.
THROAT-CLEARING
OH, REALLY?

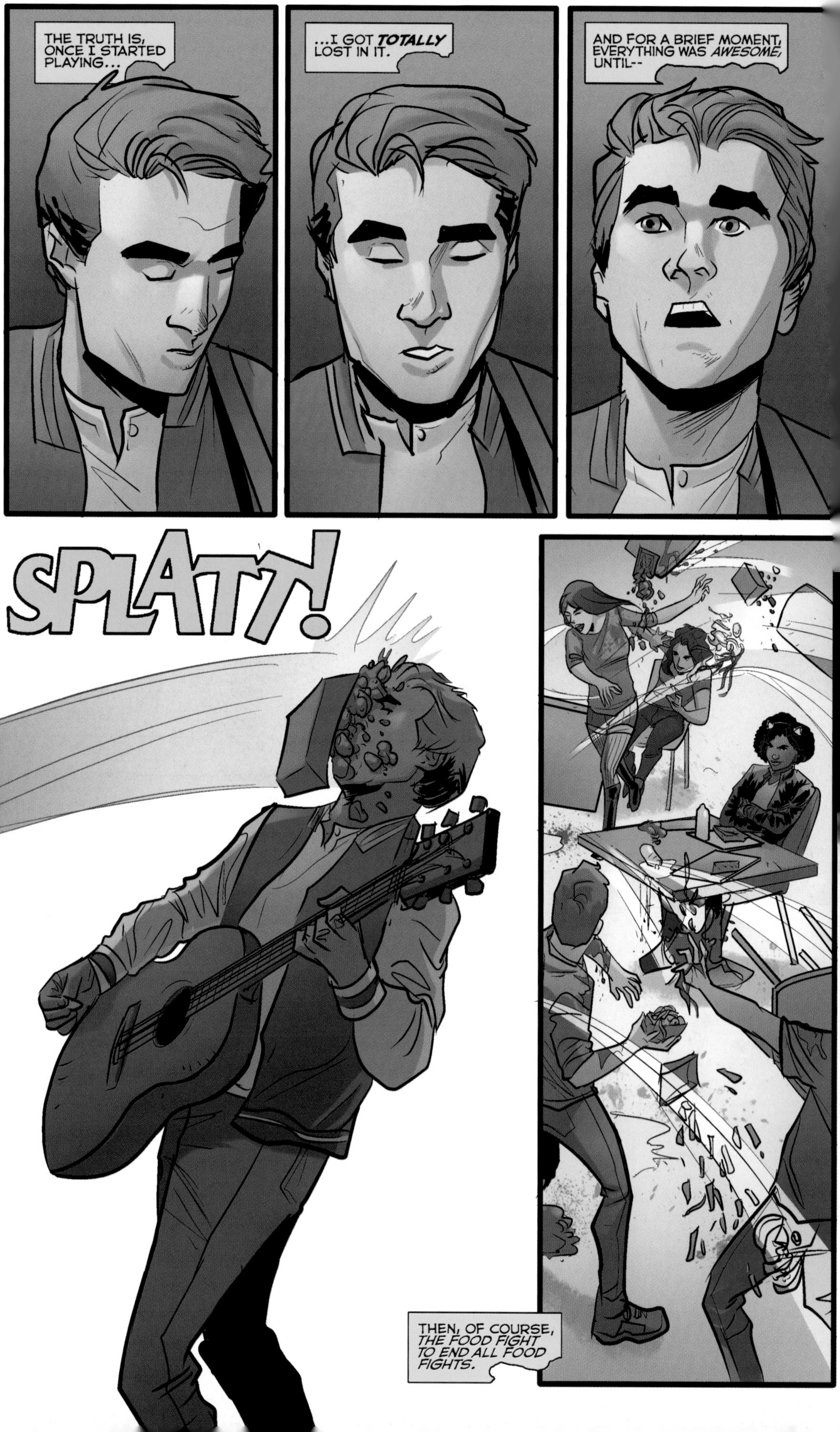
THE TRUTH IS, ONCE I STARTED PLAYING...
...I GOT *TOTALLY* LOST IN IT.
AND FOR A BRIEF MOMENT, EVERYTHING WAS *AWESOME*, UNTIL--
SPLATT!
THEN, OF COURSE, *THE FOOD FIGHT TO END ALL FOOD FIGHTS.*

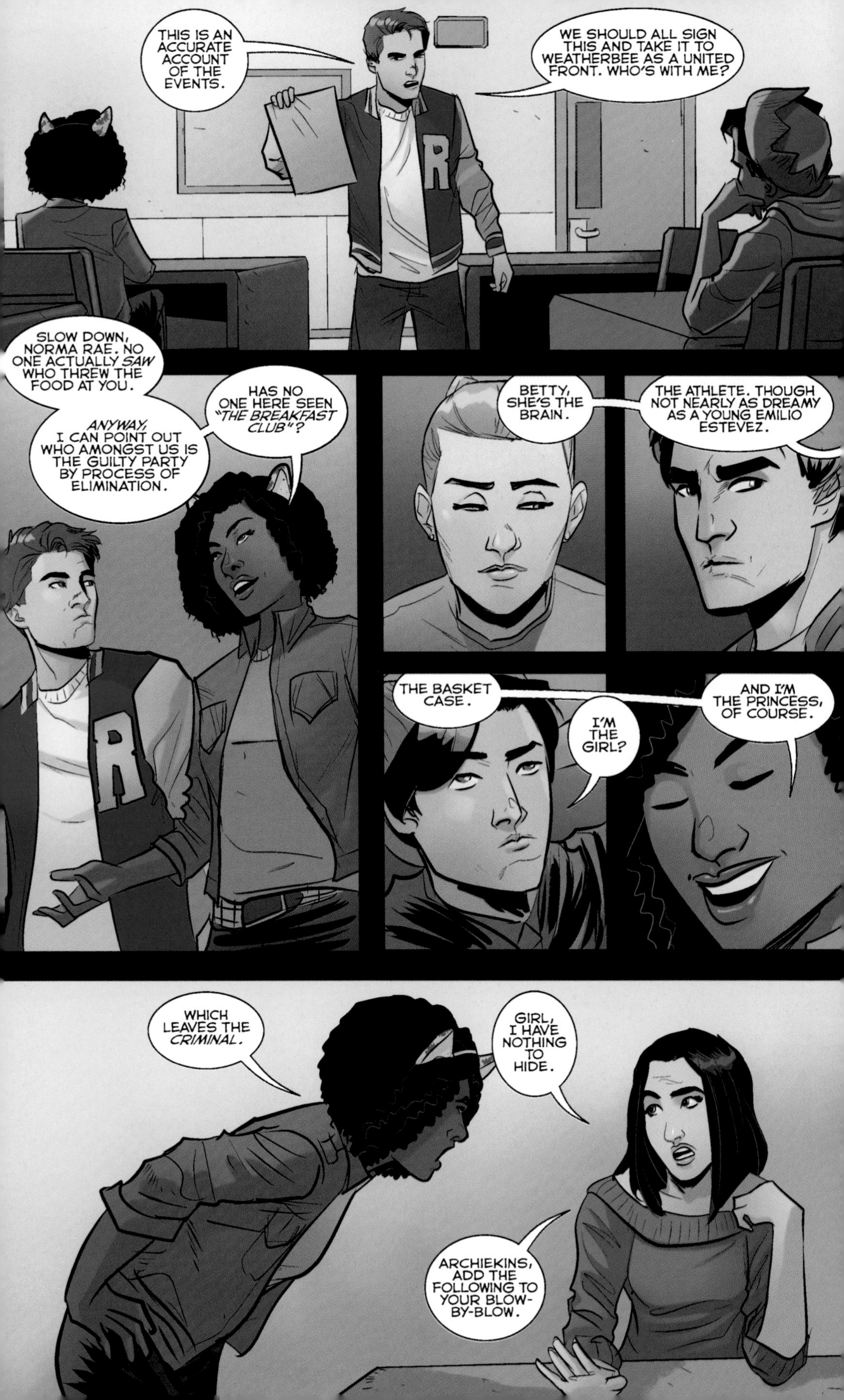
THIS IS AN ACCURATE ACCOUNT OF THE EVENTS.
WE SHOULD ALL SIGN THIS AND TAKE IT TO WEATHERBEE AS A UNITED FRONT. WHO'S WITH ME?
SLOW DOWN, NORMA RAE. NO ONE ACTUALLY *SAW* WHO THREW THE FOOD AT YOU.
ANYWAY, I CAN POINT OUT WHO AMONGST US IS THE GUILTY PARTY BY PROCESS OF ELIMINATION.
HAS NO ONE HERE SEEN *"THE BREAKFAST CLUB"*?
BETTY, SHE'S THE BRAIN.
THE ATHLETE. THOUGH NOT NEARLY AS DREAMY AS A YOUNG EMILIO ESTEVEZ.
THE BASKET CASE.
I'M THE GIRL?
AND I'M THE PRINCESS, OF COURSE.
WHICH LEAVES THE *CRIMINAL.*
GIRL, I HAVE NOTHING TO HIDE.
ARCHIEKINS, ADD THE FOLLOWING TO YOUR BLOW-BY-BLOW.

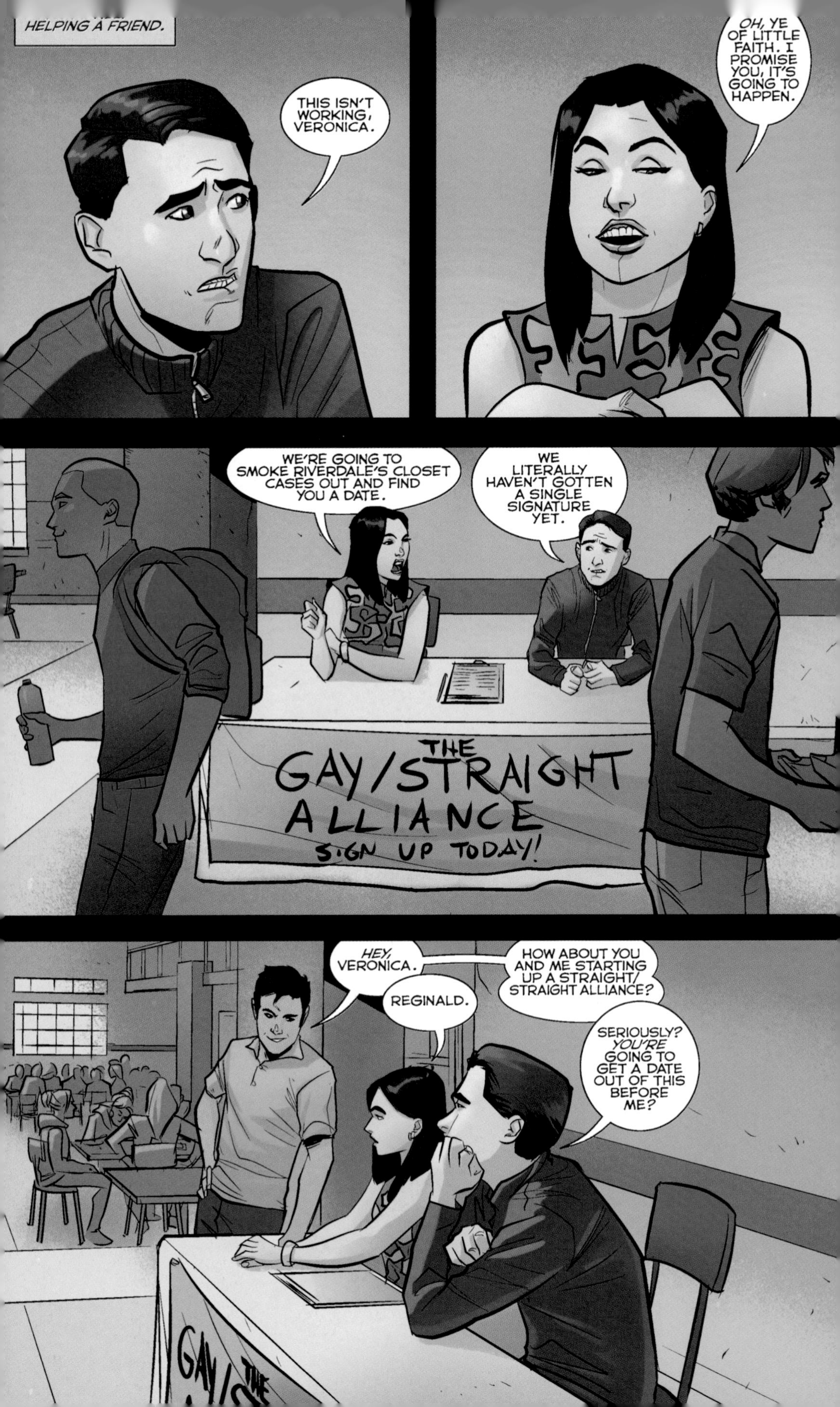
HELPING A FRIEND.
THIS ISN'T WORKING, VERONICA.
OH, YE OF LITTLE FAITH. I PROMISE YOU, IT'S GOING TO HAPPEN.
WE'RE GOING TO SMOKE RIVERDALE'S CLOSET CASES OUT AND FIND YOU A DATE.
WE LITERALLY HAVEN'T GOTTEN A SINGLE SIGNATURE YET.
THE GAY/STRAIGHT ALLIANCE SIGN UP TODAY!
HEY, VERONICA.
REGINALD.
HOW ABOUT YOU AND ME STARTING UP A STRAIGHT/ STRAIGHT ALLIANCE?
SERIOUSLY? YOU'RE GOING TO GET A DATE OUT OF THIS BEFORE ME?

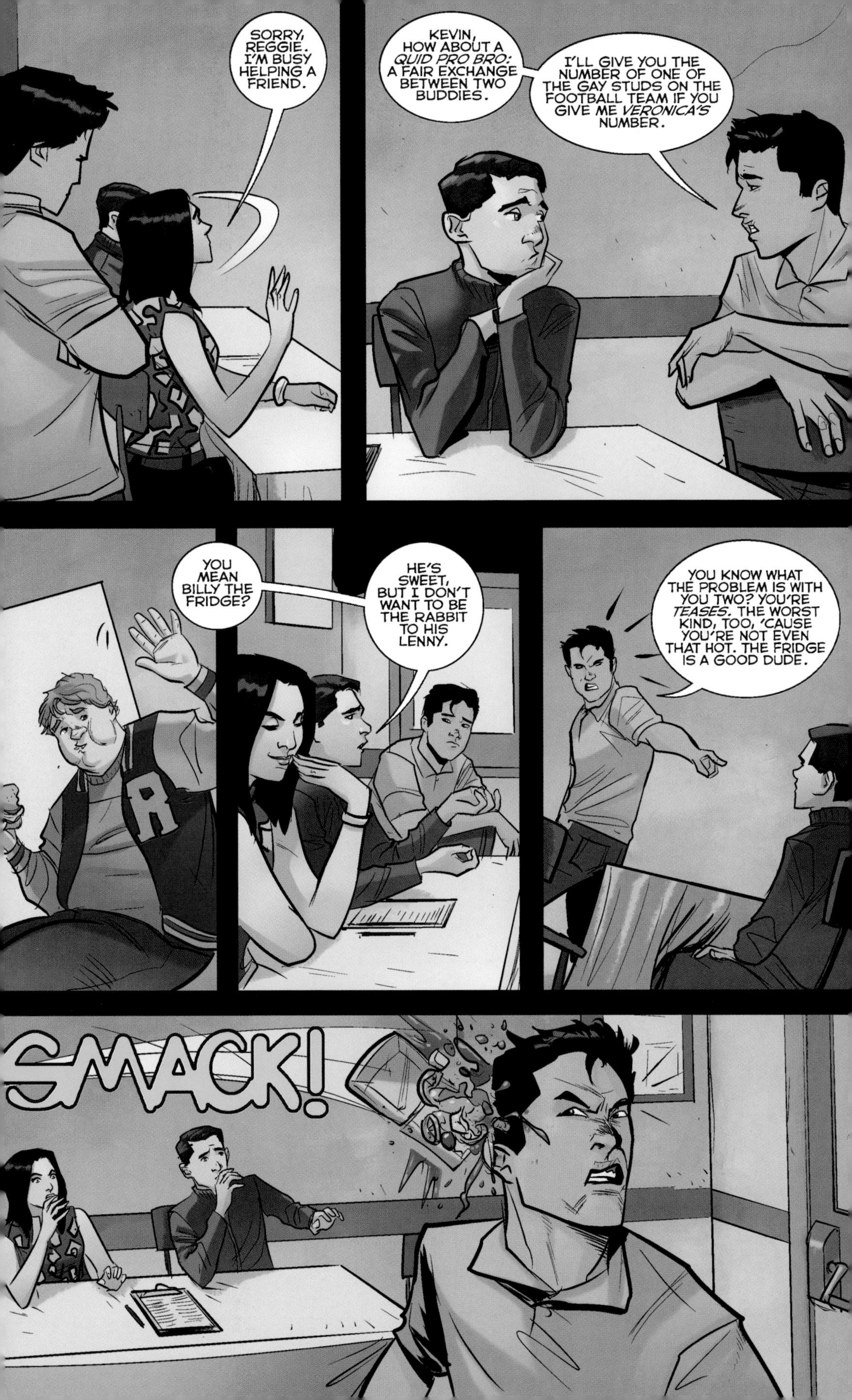
SORRY, REGGIE. I'M BUSY HELPING A FRIEND.
KEVIN, HOW ABOUT A *QUID PRO BRO:* A FAIR EXCHANGE BETWEEN TWO BUDDIES.
I'LL GIVE YOU THE NUMBER OF ONE OF THE GAY STUDS ON THE FOOTBALL TEAM IF YOU GIVE ME *VERONICA'S* NUMBER.
YOU MEAN BILLY THE FRIDGE?
HE'S SWEET, BUT I DON'T WANT TO BE THE RABBIT TO HIS LENNY.
YOU KNOW WHAT THE PROBLEM IS WITH YOU TWO? YOU'RE *TEASES.* THE WORST KIND, TOO, 'CAUSE YOU'RE NOT EVEN THAT HOT. THE FRIDGE IS A GOOD DUDE.
SMACK!

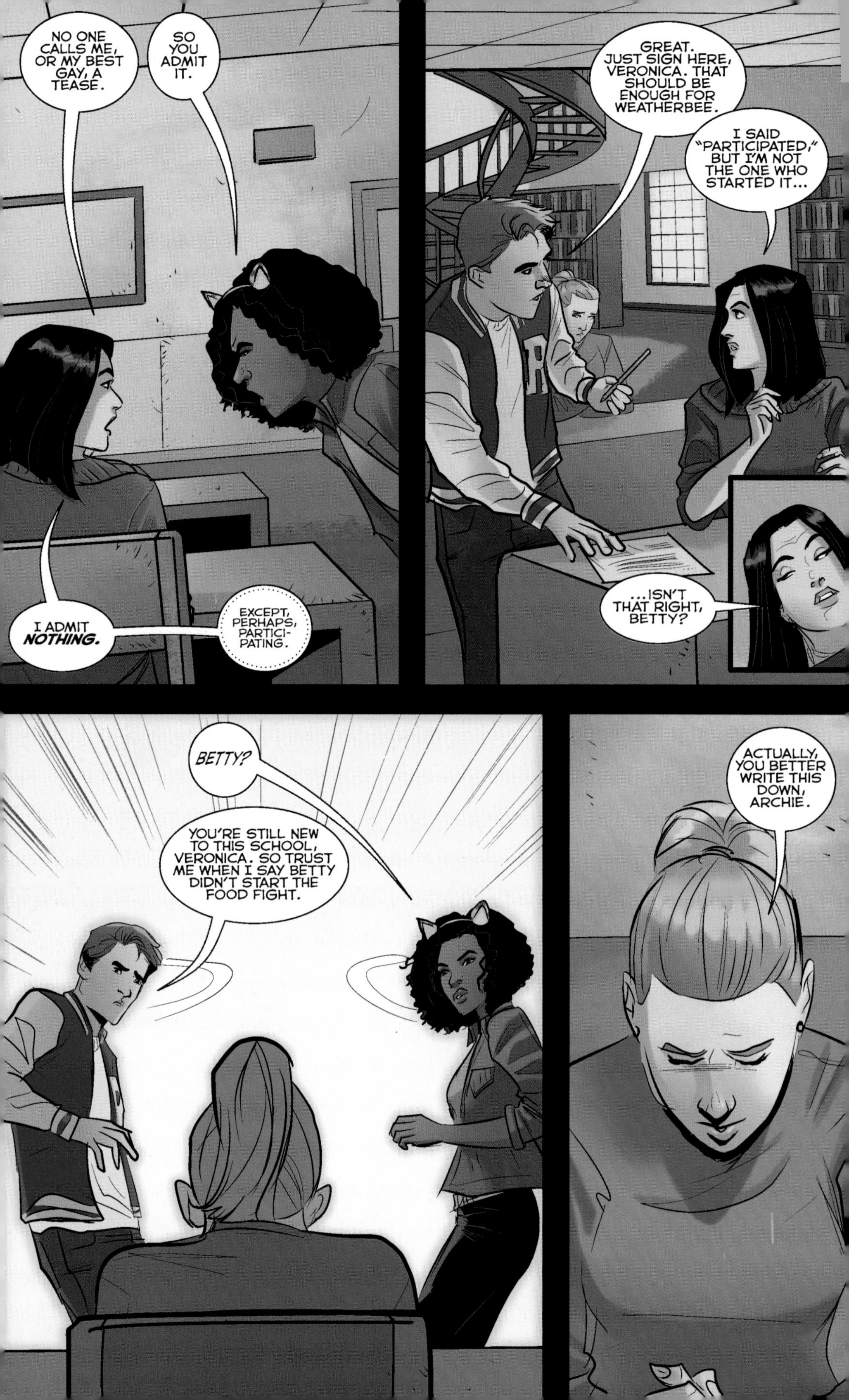
NO ONE CALLS ME, OR MY BEST GAY, A TEASE.
SO YOU ADMIT IT.
I ADMIT ***NOTHING.***
EXCEPT, PERHAPS, PARTICI-PATING.
GREAT. JUST SIGN HERE, VERONICA. THAT SHOULD BE ENOUGH FOR WEATHERBEE.
I SAID "PARTICIPATED," BUT I'M NOT THE ONE WHO STARTED IT...
...ISN'T THAT RIGHT, BETTY?
BETTY?
YOU'RE STILL NEW TO THIS SCHOOL, VERONICA. SO TRUST ME WHEN I SAY BETTY DIDN'T START THE FOOD FIGHT.
ACTUALLY, YOU BETTER WRITE THIS DOWN, ARCHIE.

WITH EVERYTHING GOING ON THIS YEAR, I DON'T GET TOO MANY MOMENTS FOR MYSELF.

I'M EITHER LEARNING NEW ROUTINES FOR THE RIVER VIXENS...

...WRITING AND EDITING STORIES FOR *THE BLUE AND GOLD*...

...OR ACTING AS PRINCIPAL WEATHERBEE'S PERSONAL ASSISTANT...

--ONE *MORE* THING, MS. COOPER, I'M HOPING YOU'LL ONCE AGAIN CHAIR THE HOME-COMING DANCE.

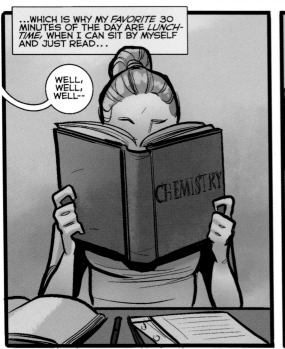

...WHICH IS WHY MY *FAVORITE* 30 MINUTES OF THE DAY ARE *LUNCH-TIME,* WHEN I CAN SIT BY MYSELF AND JUST READ...

WELL, WELL, WELL--

CHEMISTRY

--WHAT DO WE HAVE HERE?

CHEMISTRY

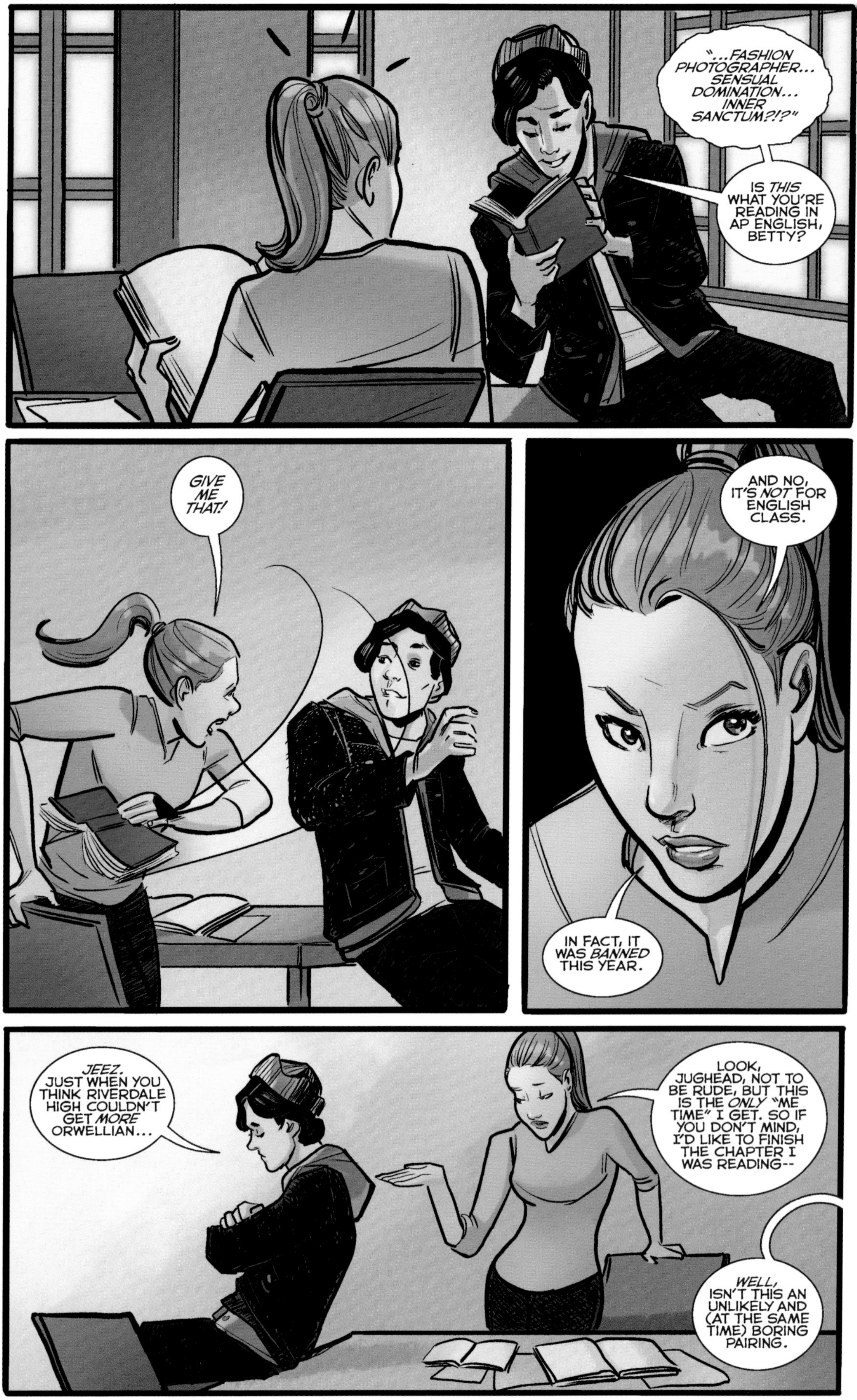
"...FASHION PHOTOGRAPHER... SENSUAL DOMINATION... INNER SANCTUM?!?"
IS THIS WHAT YOU'RE READING IN AP ENGLISH, BETTY?
GIVE ME THAT!
AND NO, IT'S NOT FOR ENGLISH CLASS.
IN FACT, IT WAS BANNED THIS YEAR.
JEEZ. JUST WHEN YOU THINK RIVERDALE HIGH COULDN'T GET MORE ORWELLIAN...
LOOK, JUGHEAD, NOT TO BE RUDE, BUT THIS IS THE ONLY "ME TIME" I GET. SO IF YOU DON'T MIND, I'D LIKE TO FINISH THE CHAPTER I WAS READING--
WELL, ISN'T THIS AN UNLIKELY AND (AT THE SAME TIME) BORING PAIRING.

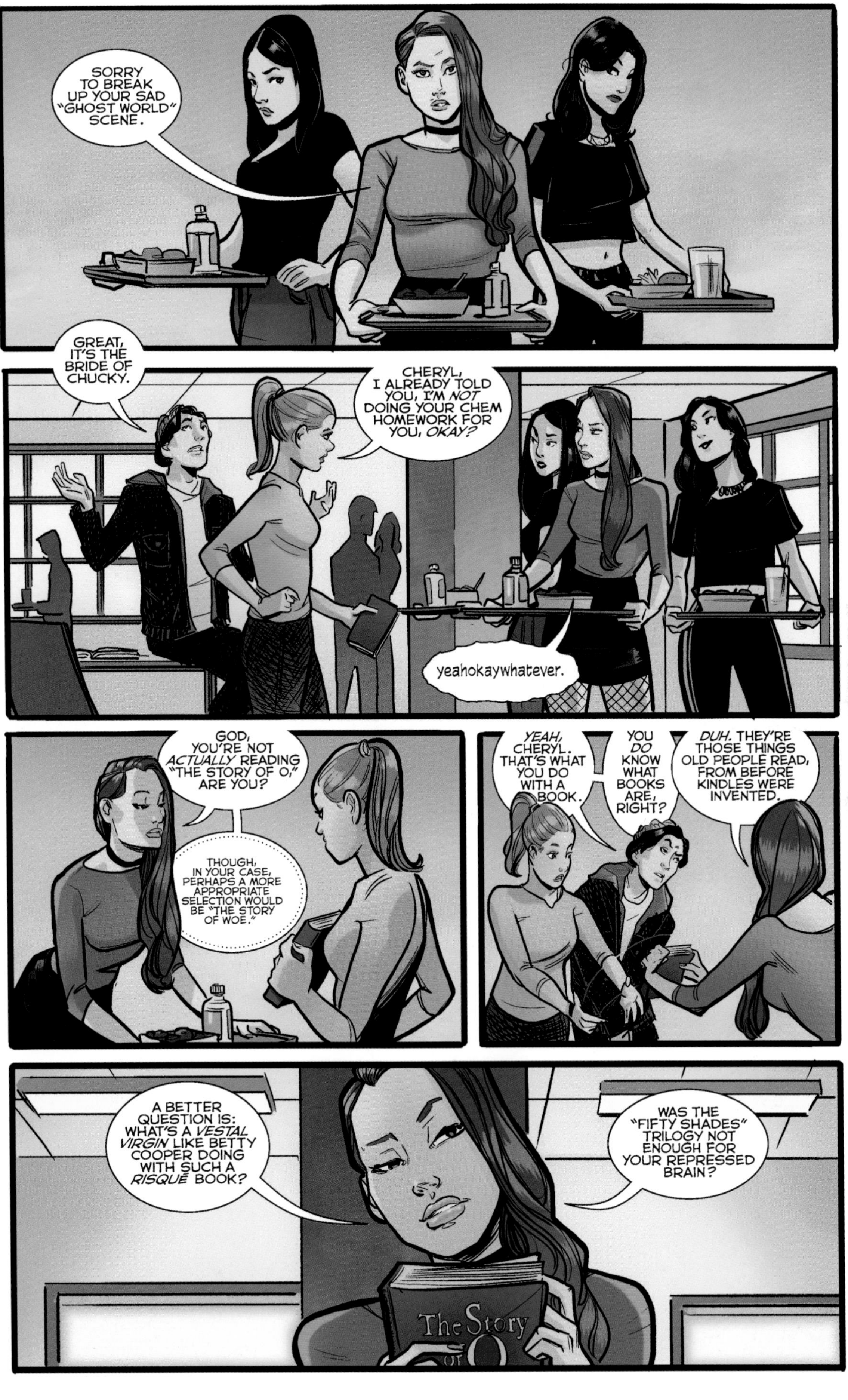
SORRY TO BREAK UP YOUR SAD "GHOST WORLD" SCENE.
GREAT, IT'S THE BRIDE OF CHUCKY.
CHERYL, I ALREADY TOLD YOU, I'M NOT DOING YOUR CHEM HOMEWORK FOR YOU, OKAY?
yeahokaywhatever.
GOD, YOU'RE NOT ACTUALLY READING "THE STORY OF O," ARE YOU?
THOUGH, IN YOUR CASE, PERHAPS A MORE APPROPRIATE SELECTION WOULD BE "THE STORY OF WOE."
YEAH, CHERYL. THAT'S WHAT YOU DO WITH A BOOK.
YOU DO KNOW WHAT BOOKS ARE, RIGHT?
DUH. THEY'RE THOSE THINGS OLD PEOPLE READ, FROM BEFORE KINDLES WERE INVENTED.
A BETTER QUESTION IS: WHAT'S A VESTAL VIRGIN LIKE BETTY COOPER DOING WITH SUCH A RISQUE BOOK?
WAS THE "FIFTY SHADES" TRILOGY NOT ENOUGH FOR YOUR REPRESSED BRAIN?
The Story of O

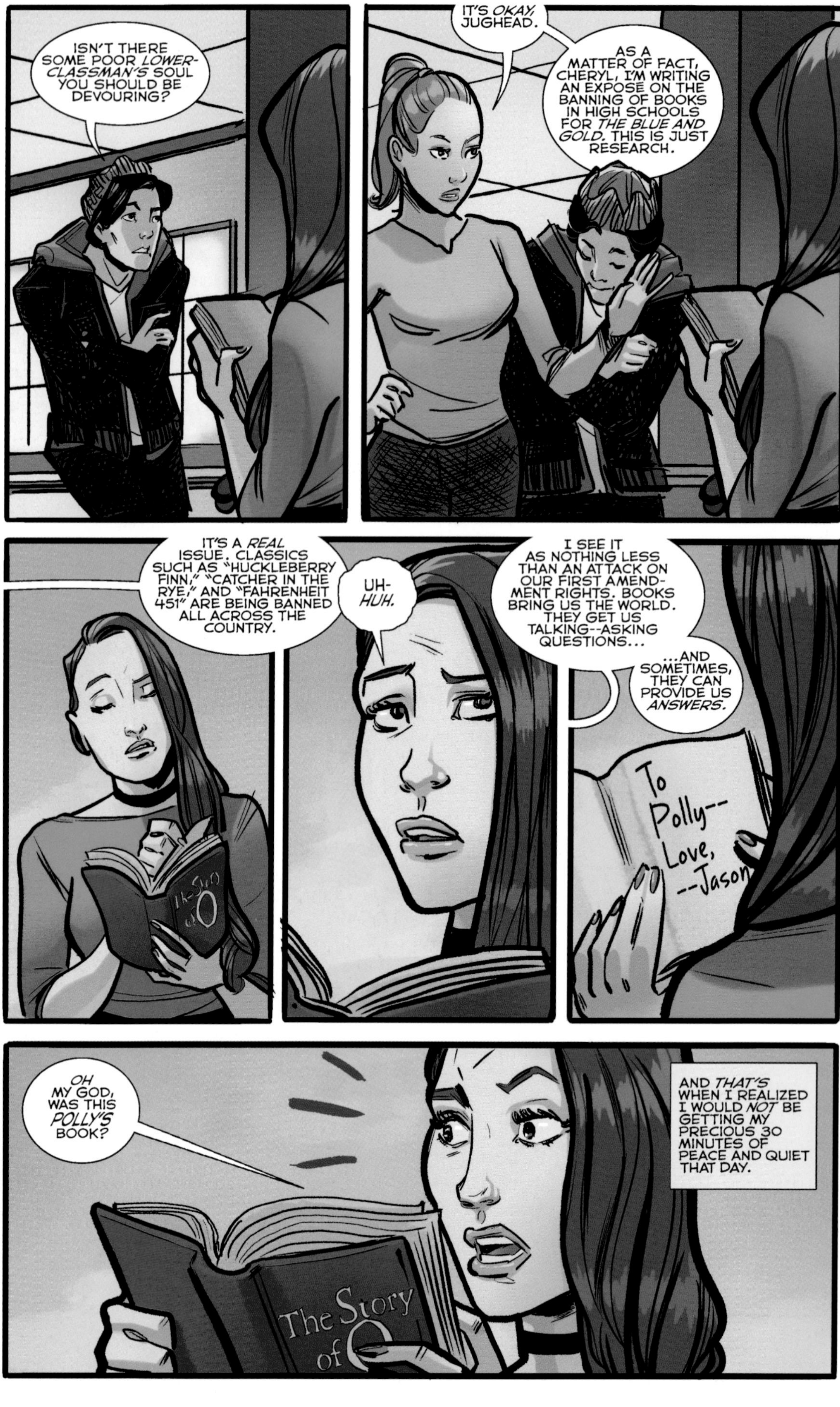

ISN'T THERE SOME POOR *LOWER-CLASSMAN'S* SOUL YOU SHOULD BE DEVOURING?
IT'S *OKAY,* JUGHEAD.
AS A MATTER OF FACT, CHERYL, I'M WRITING AN EXPOSÉ ON THE BANNING OF BOOKS IN HIGH SCHOOLS FOR *THE BLUE AND GOLD.* THIS IS JUST RESEARCH.
IT'S A *REAL* ISSUE. CLASSICS SUCH AS "HUCKLEBERRY FINN," "CATCHER IN THE RYE," AND "FAHRENHEIT 451" ARE BEING BANNED ALL ACROSS THE COUNTRY.
The Story of O
UH-*HUH.*
I SEE IT AS NOTHING LESS THAN AN ATTACK ON OUR FIRST AMENDMENT RIGHTS. BOOKS BRING US THE WORLD. THEY GET US TALKING--ASKING QUESTIONS...
...AND SOMETIMES, THEY CAN PROVIDE US *ANSWERS.*
To Polly-- Love, --Jason
OH MY GOD, WAS THIS *POLLY'S* BOOK?
AND *THAT'S* WHEN I REALIZED I WOULD *NOT* BE GETTING MY PRECIOUS 30 MINUTES OF PEACE AND QUIET THAT DAY.
The Story of O

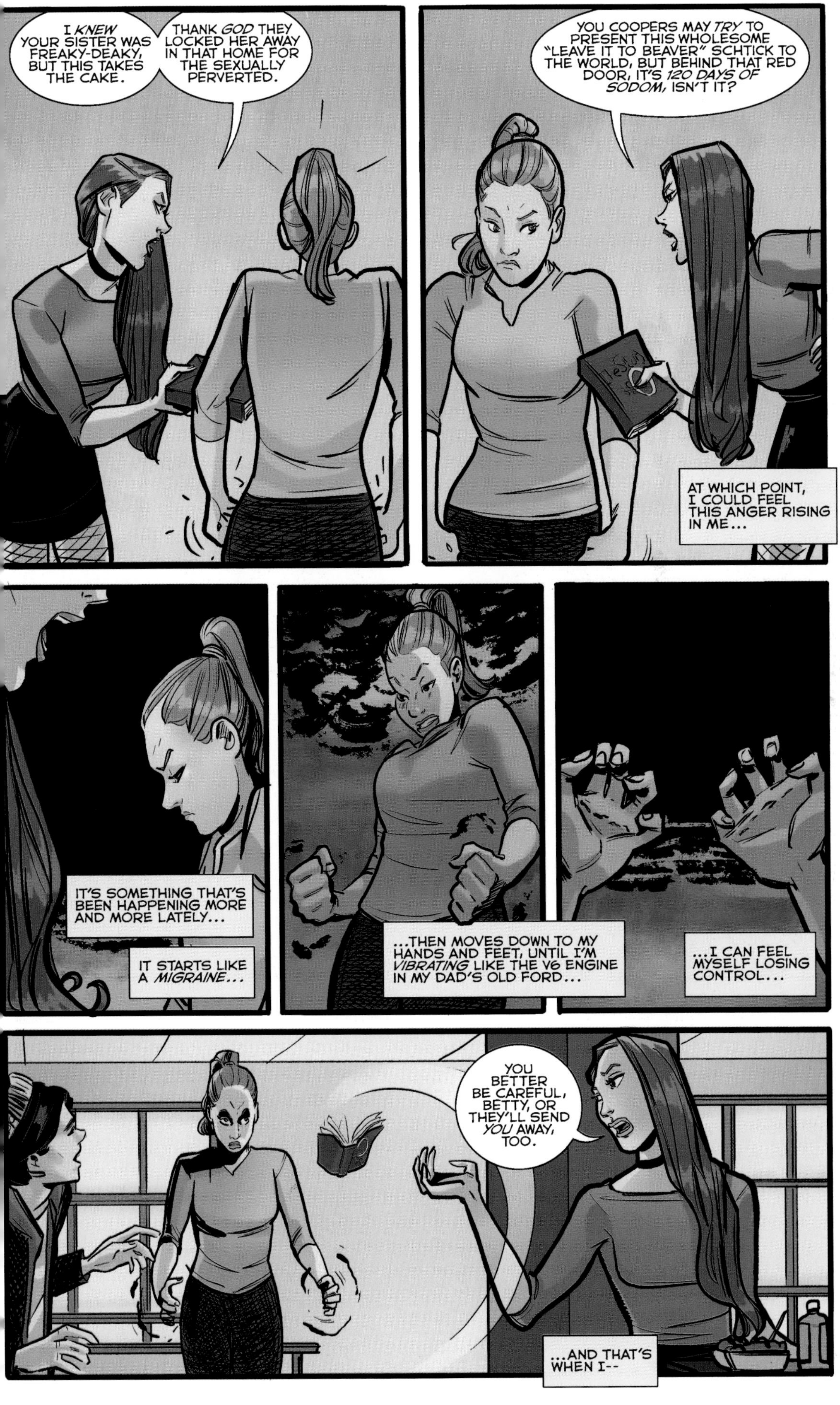
I KNEW YOUR SISTER WAS FREAKY-DEAKY, BUT THIS TAKES THE CAKE.
THANK GOD THEY LOCKED HER AWAY IN THAT HOME FOR THE SEXUALLY PERVERTED.
YOU COOPERS MAY TRY TO PRESENT THIS WHOLESOME "LEAVE IT TO BEAVER" SCHTICK TO THE WORLD, BUT BEHIND THAT RED DOOR, IT'S 120 DAYS OF SODOM, ISN'T IT?
AT WHICH POINT, I COULD FEEL THIS ANGER RISING IN ME...
IT'S SOMETHING THAT'S BEEN HAPPENING MORE AND MORE LATELY...
IT STARTS LIKE A MIGRAINE...
...THEN MOVES DOWN TO MY HANDS AND FEET, UNTIL I'M VIBRATING LIKE THE V6 ENGINE IN MY DAD'S OLD FORD...
...I CAN FEEL MYSELF LOSING CONTROL...
YOU BETTER BE CAREFUL, BETTY, OR THEY'LL SEND YOU AWAY, TOO.
...AND THAT'S WHEN I--

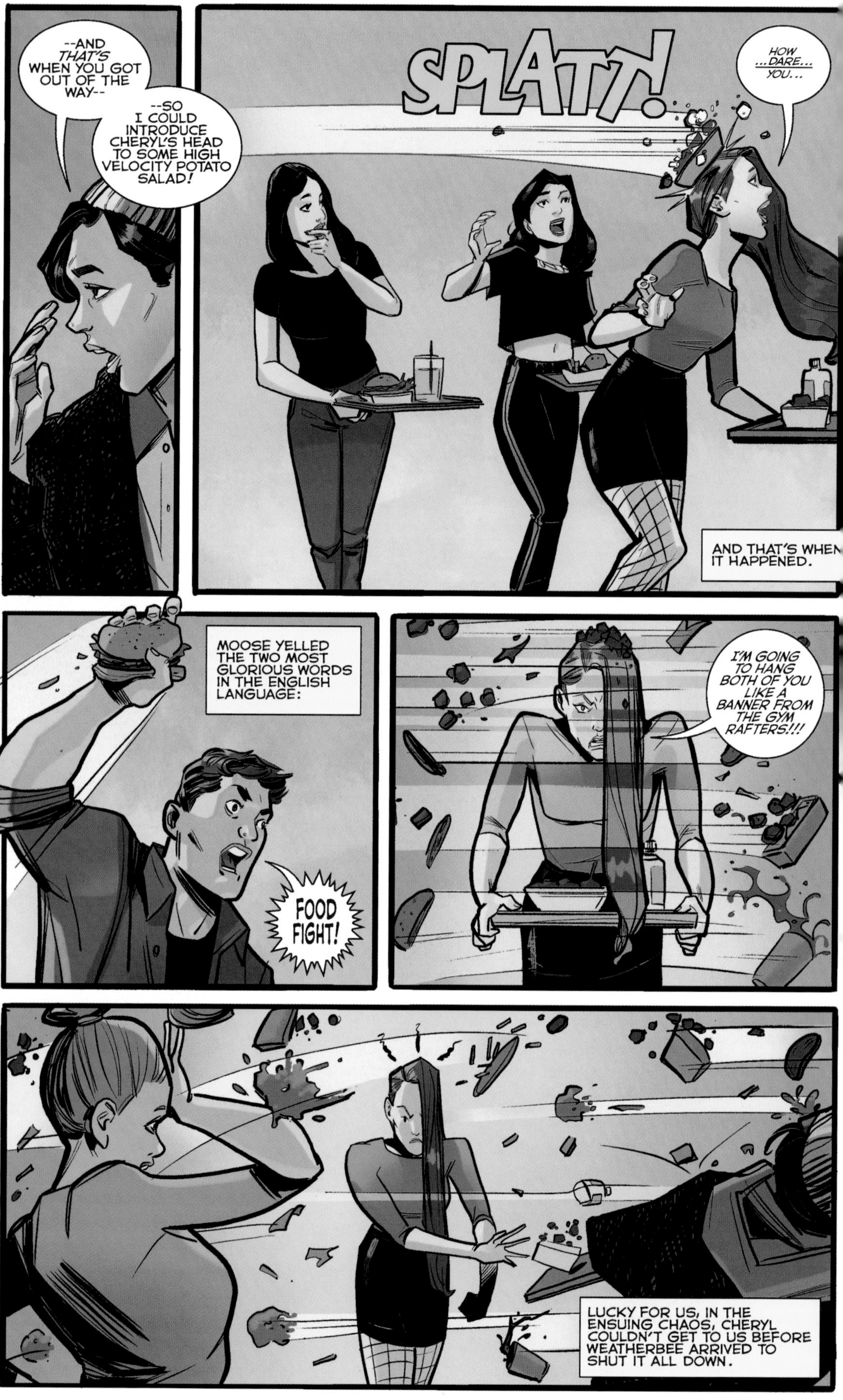
--AND THAT'S WHEN YOU GOT OUT OF THE WAY--
--SO I COULD INTRODUCE CHERYL'S HEAD TO SOME HIGH VELOCITY POTATO SALAD!
SPLATT!
HOW ...DARE... YOU...
AND THAT'S WHEN IT HAPPENED.
MOOSE YELLED THE TWO MOST GLORIOUS WORDS IN THE ENGLISH LANGUAGE:
FOOD FIGHT!
I'M GOING TO HANG BOTH OF YOU LIKE A BANNER FROM THE GYM RAFTERS!!!
LUCKY FOR US, IN THE ENSUING CHAOS, CHERYL COULDN'T GET TO US BEFORE WEATHERBEE ARRIVED TO SHUT IT ALL DOWN.

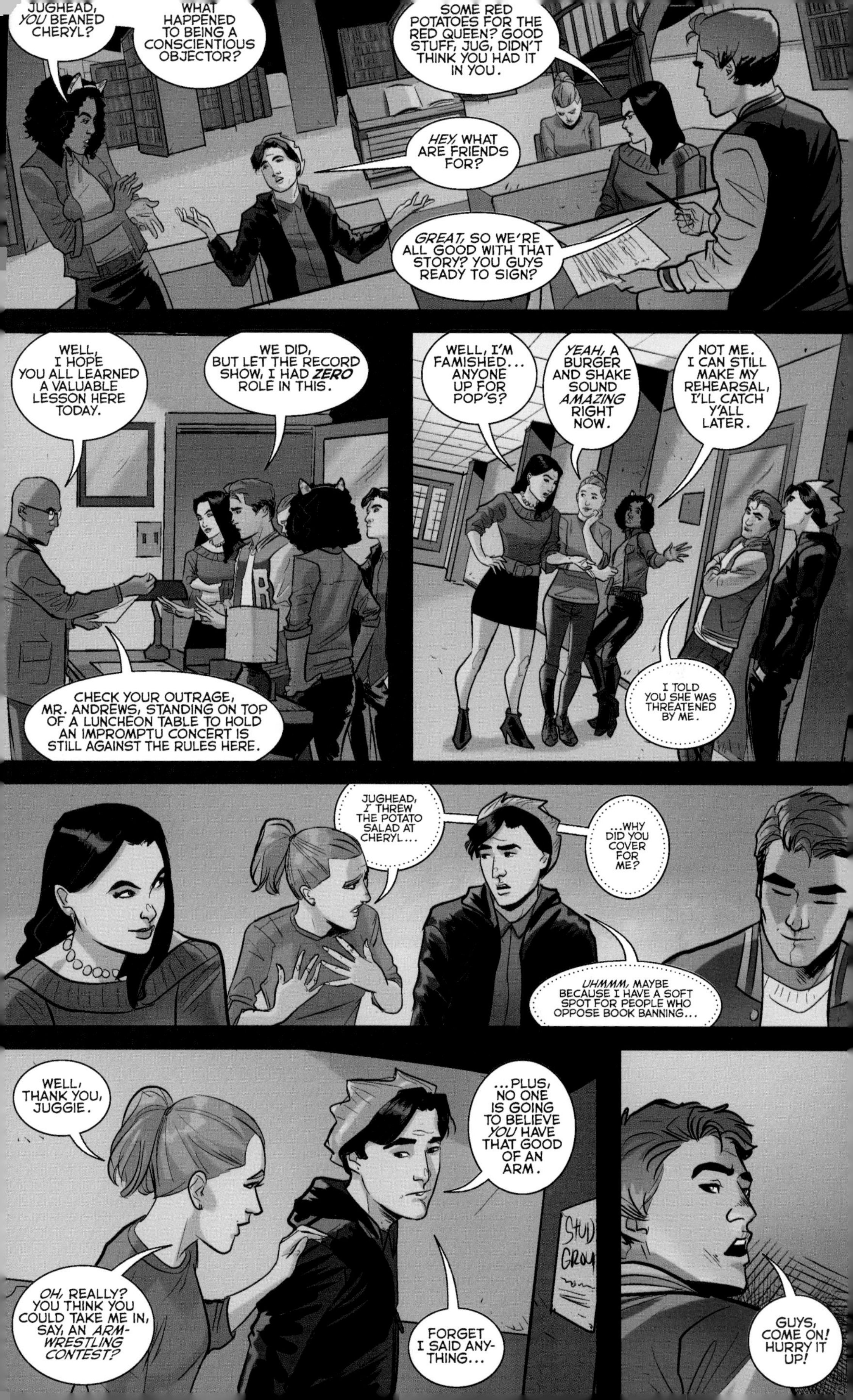
JUGHEAD, *YOU* BEANED CHERYL?
WHAT HAPPENED TO BEING A CONSCIENTIOUS OBJECTOR?
SOME RED POTATOES FOR THE RED QUEEN? GOOD STUFF, JUG, DIDN'T THINK *YOU* HAD IT IN YOU.
HEY, WHAT ARE FRIENDS FOR?
GREAT, SO WE'RE ALL GOOD WITH THAT STORY? YOU GUYS READY TO SIGN?
WELL, I HOPE YOU ALL LEARNED A VALUABLE LESSON HERE TODAY.
WE DID, BUT LET THE RECORD SHOW, I HAD *ZERO* ROLE IN THIS.
CHECK YOUR OUTRAGE, MR. ANDREWS, STANDING ON TOP OF A LUNCHEON TABLE TO HOLD AN IMPROMPTU CONCERT IS STILL AGAINST THE RULES HERE.
WELL, I'M FAMISHED... ANYONE UP FOR POP'S?
YEAH, A BURGER AND SHAKE SOUND *AMAZING* RIGHT NOW.
NOT ME. I CAN STILL MAKE MY REHEARSAL, I'LL CATCH Y'ALL LATER.
I TOLD YOU SHE WAS THREATENED BY ME.
JUGHEAD, *I* THREW THE POTATO SALAD AT CHERYL...
...WHY DID YOU COVER FOR ME?
UHMMM, MAYBE BECAUSE I HAVE A SOFT SPOT FOR PEOPLE WHO OPPOSE BOOK BANNING...
WELL, THANK YOU, JUGGIE.
...PLUS, NO ONE IS GOING TO BELIEVE *YOU* HAVE THAT GOOD OF AN ARM.
OH, REALLY? YOU THINK YOU COULD TAKE ME IN, SAY, AN *ARM-WRESTLING CONTEST?*
FORGET I SAID ANY-THING...
STUDY GROUP
GUYS, COME ON! HURRY IT UP!

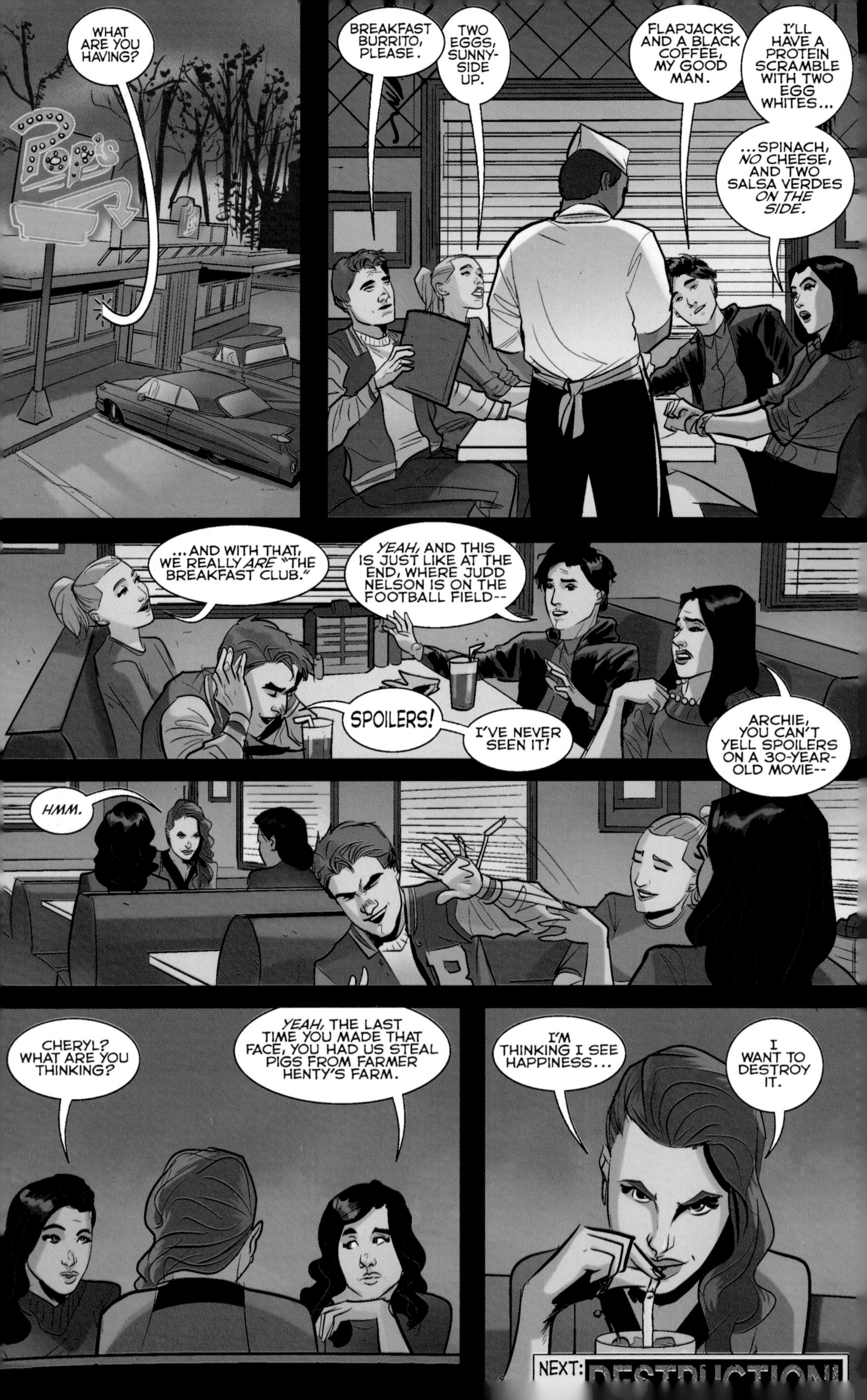
WHAT ARE YOU HAVING?
BREAKFAST BURRITO, PLEASE.
TWO EGGS, SUNNY-SIDE UP.
FLAPJACKS AND A BLACK COFFEE, MY GOOD MAN.
I'LL HAVE A PROTEIN SCRAMBLE WITH TWO EGG WHITES...
...SPINACH, *NO* CHEESE, AND TWO SALSA VERDES *ON THE SIDE.*
...AND WITH THAT, WE REALLY *ARE* "THE BREAKFAST CLUB."
YEAH, AND THIS IS JUST LIKE AT THE END, WHERE JUDD NELSON IS ON THE FOOTBALL FIELD--
SPOILERS!
I'VE NEVER SEEN IT!
ARCHIE, YOU CAN'T YELL SPOILERS ON A 30-YEAR-OLD MOVIE--
HMM.
CHERYL? WHAT ARE YOU THINKING?
YEAH, THE LAST TIME YOU MADE THAT FACE, YOU HAD US STEAL PIGS FROM FARMER HENTY'S FARM.
I'M THINKING I SEE HAPPINESS...
I WANT TO DESTROY IT.
NEXT:

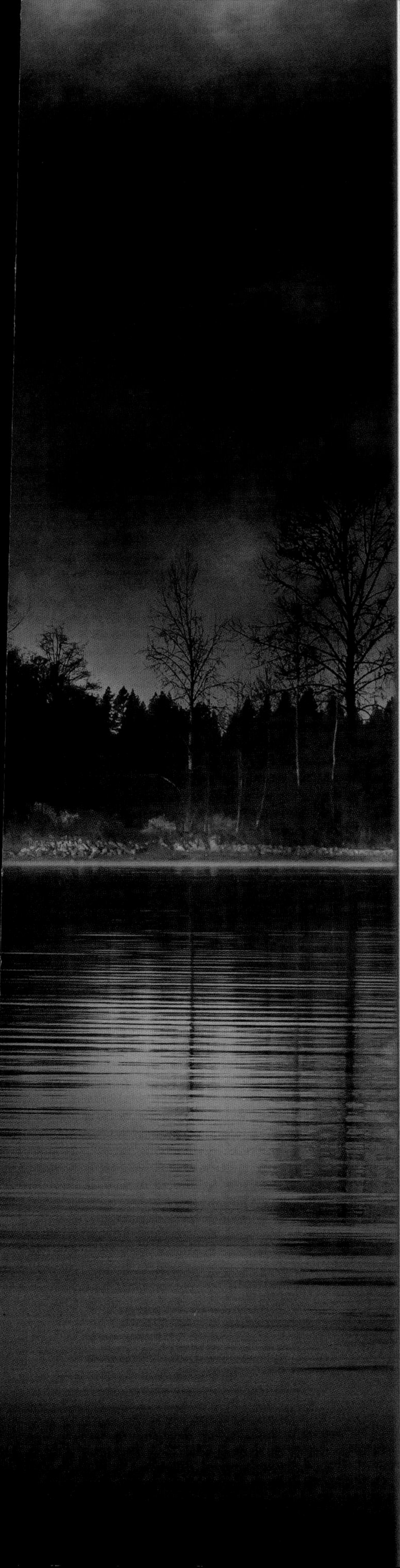

CHAPTER EIGHT

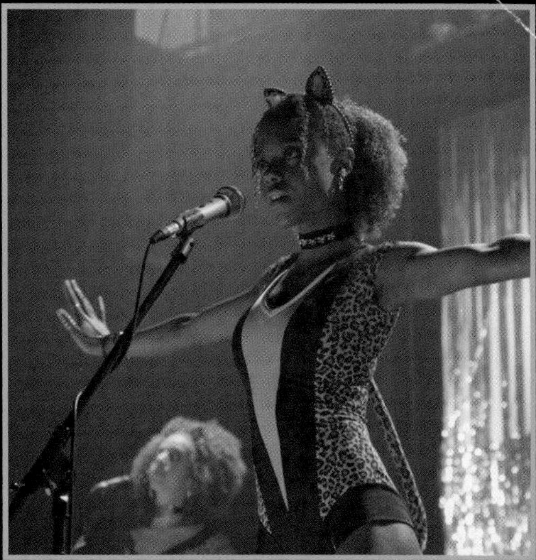

WILD THINGS

WRITER:
JAMES DEWILLE

ART:
JOE EISMA

COLORS:
ANDRE SZYMANOWICZ

LETTERS:
JANICE CHIANG

STARRING
JOSIE AND THE PUSSYCATS

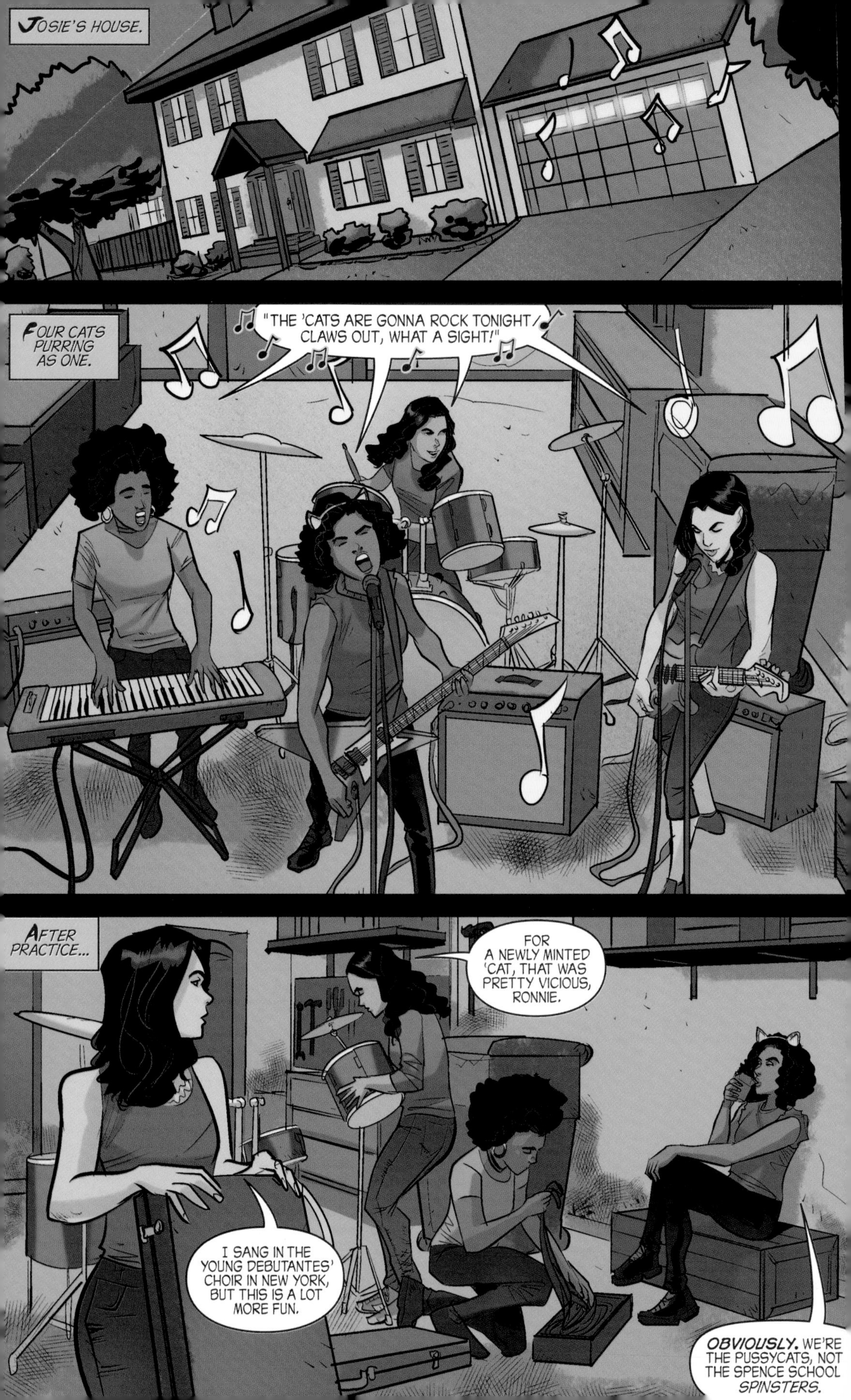
JOSIE'S HOUSE.
FOUR CATS PURRING AS ONE.
"THE 'CATS ARE GONNA ROCK TONIGHT/ CLAWS OUT, WHAT A SIGHT!"
AFTER PRACTICE...
FOR A NEWLY MINTED 'CAT, THAT WAS PRETTY VICIOUS, RONNIE.
I SANG IN THE YOUNG DEBUTANTES' CHOIR IN NEW YORK, BUT THIS IS A LOT MORE FUN.
OBVIOUSLY. WE'RE THE PUSSYCATS, NOT THE SPENCE SCHOOL SPINSTERS.

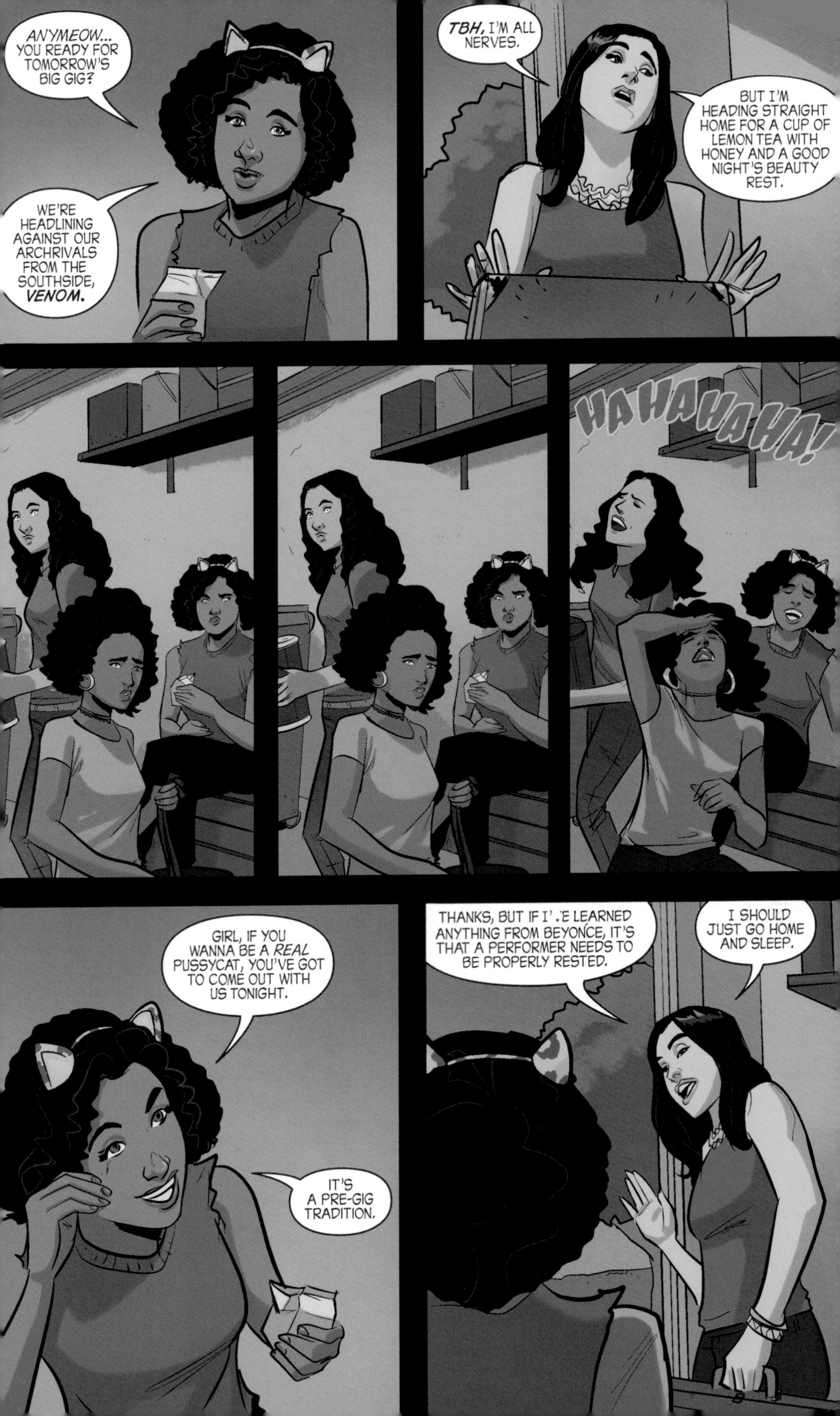

ANYMEOW... YOU READY FOR TOMORROW'S BIG GIG?
WE'RE HEADLINING AGAINST OUR ARCHRIVALS FROM THE SOUTHSIDE, ***VENOM.***
TBH, I'M ALL NERVES.
BUT I'M HEADING STRAIGHT HOME FOR A CUP OF LEMON TEA WITH HONEY AND A GOOD NIGHT'S BEAUTY REST.
HAHAHAHA!
GIRL, IF YOU WANNA BE A *REAL* PUSSYCAT, YOU'VE GOT TO COME OUT WITH US TONIGHT.
IT'S A PRE-GIG TRADITION.
THANKS, BUT IF I'VE LEARNED ANYTHING FROM BEYONCE, IT'S THAT A PERFORMER NEEDS TO BE PROPERLY RESTED.
I SHOULD JUST GO HOME AND SLEEP.

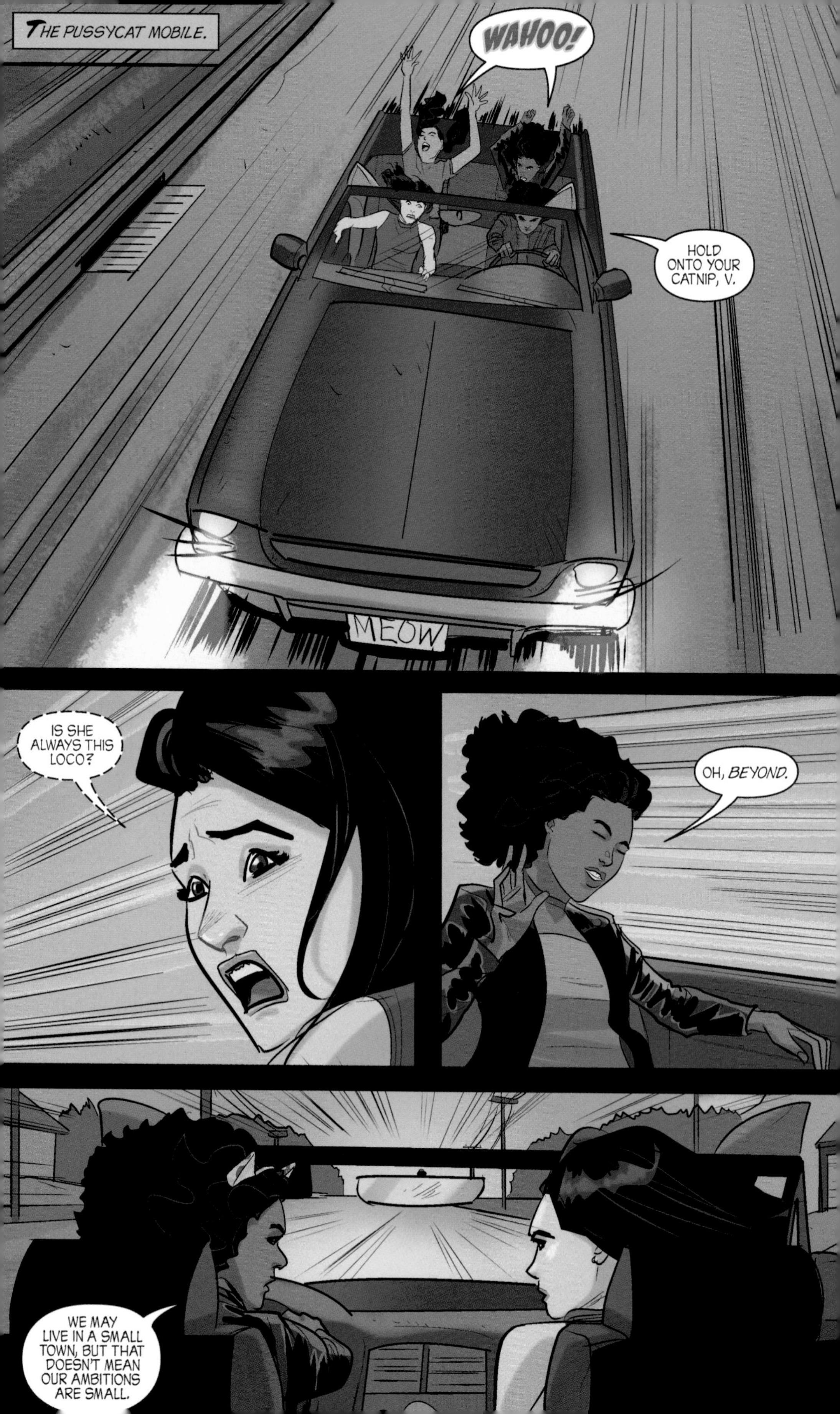
THE PUSSYCAT MOBILE.
WAHOO!
HOLD ONTO YOUR CATNIP, V.
MEOW
IS SHE ALWAYS THIS LOCO?
OH, *BEYOND.*
WE MAY LIVE IN A SMALL TOWN, BUT THAT DOESN'T MEAN OUR AMBITIONS ARE SMALL.

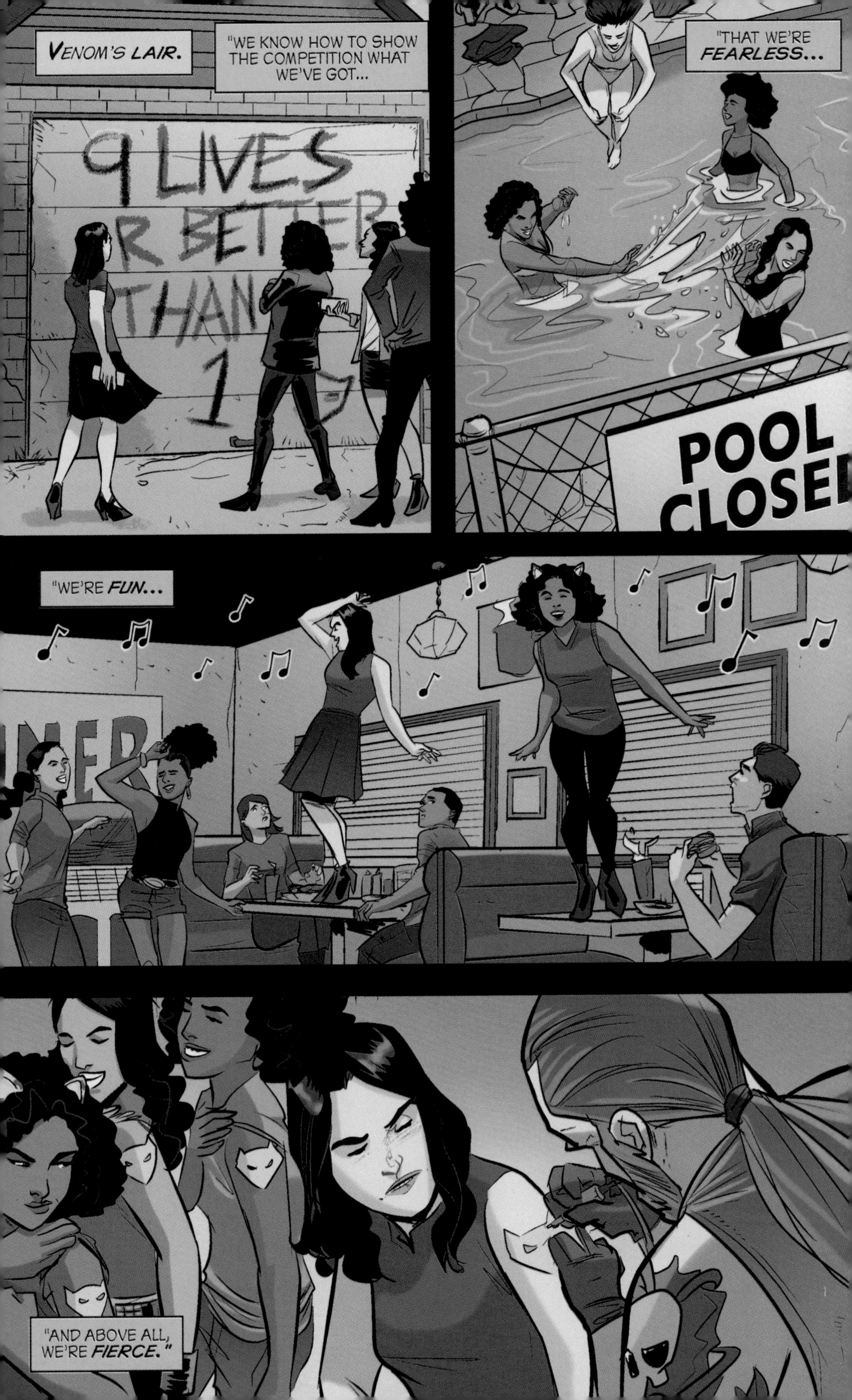
VENOM'S LAIR.
"WE KNOW HOW TO SHOW THE COMPETITION WHAT WE'VE GOT...
9 LIVES R BETTER THAN 1
"THAT WE'RE FEARLESS...
POOL CLOSED
"WE'RE FUN...
"AND ABOVE ALL, WE'RE FIERCE."

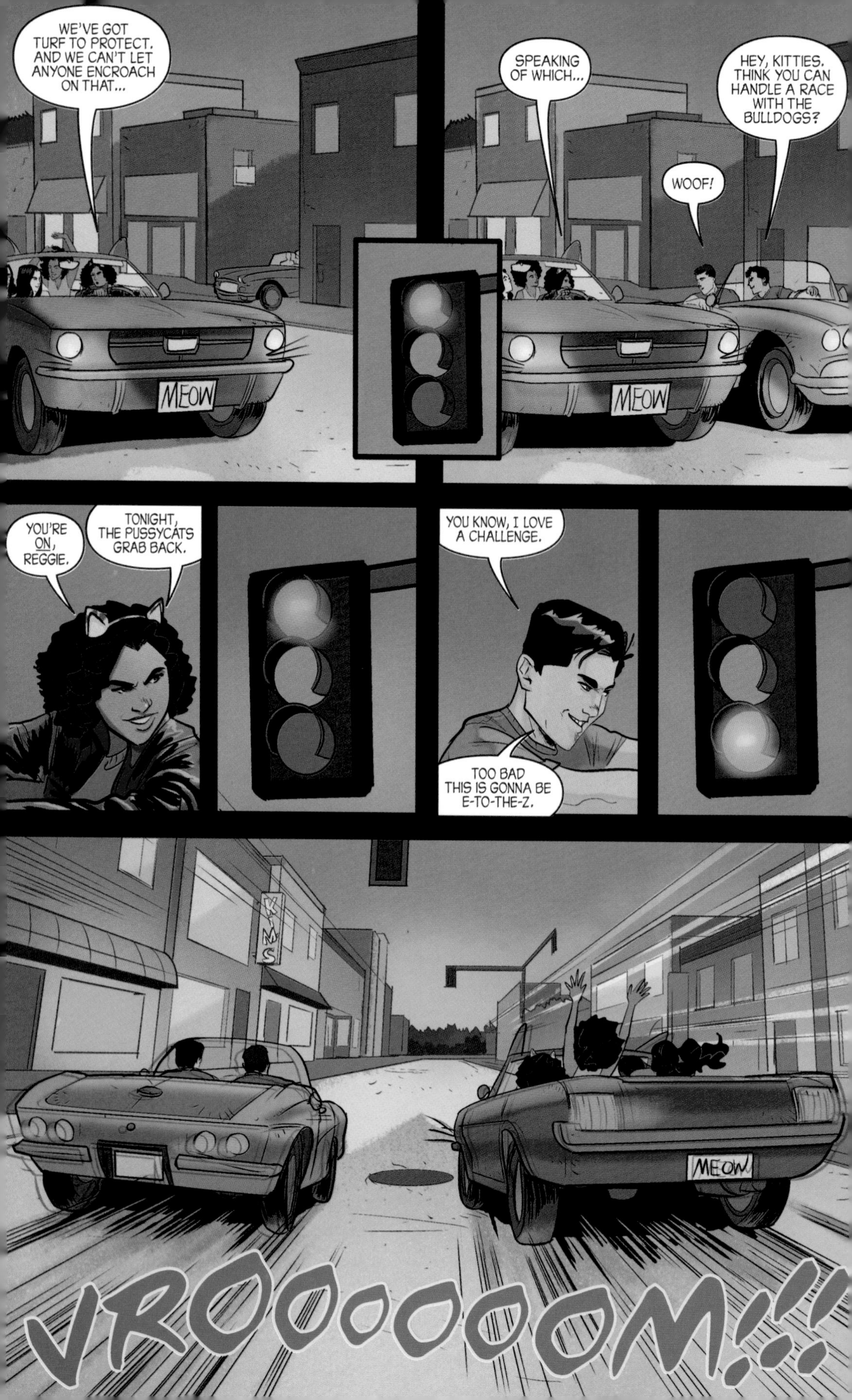
WE'VE GOT TURF TO PROTECT. AND WE CAN'T LET ANYONE ENCROACH ON THAT...
MEOW
SPEAKING OF WHICH...
HEY, KITTIES. THINK YOU CAN HANDLE A RACE WITH THE BULLDOGS?
WOOF!
MEOW
YOU'RE ON, REGGIE.
TONIGHT, THE PUSSYCATS GRAB BACK.
YOU KNOW, I LOVE A CHALLENGE.
TOO BAD THIS IS GONNA BE E-TO-THE-Z.
KIMS
MEOW
VROOOOOOM!!!

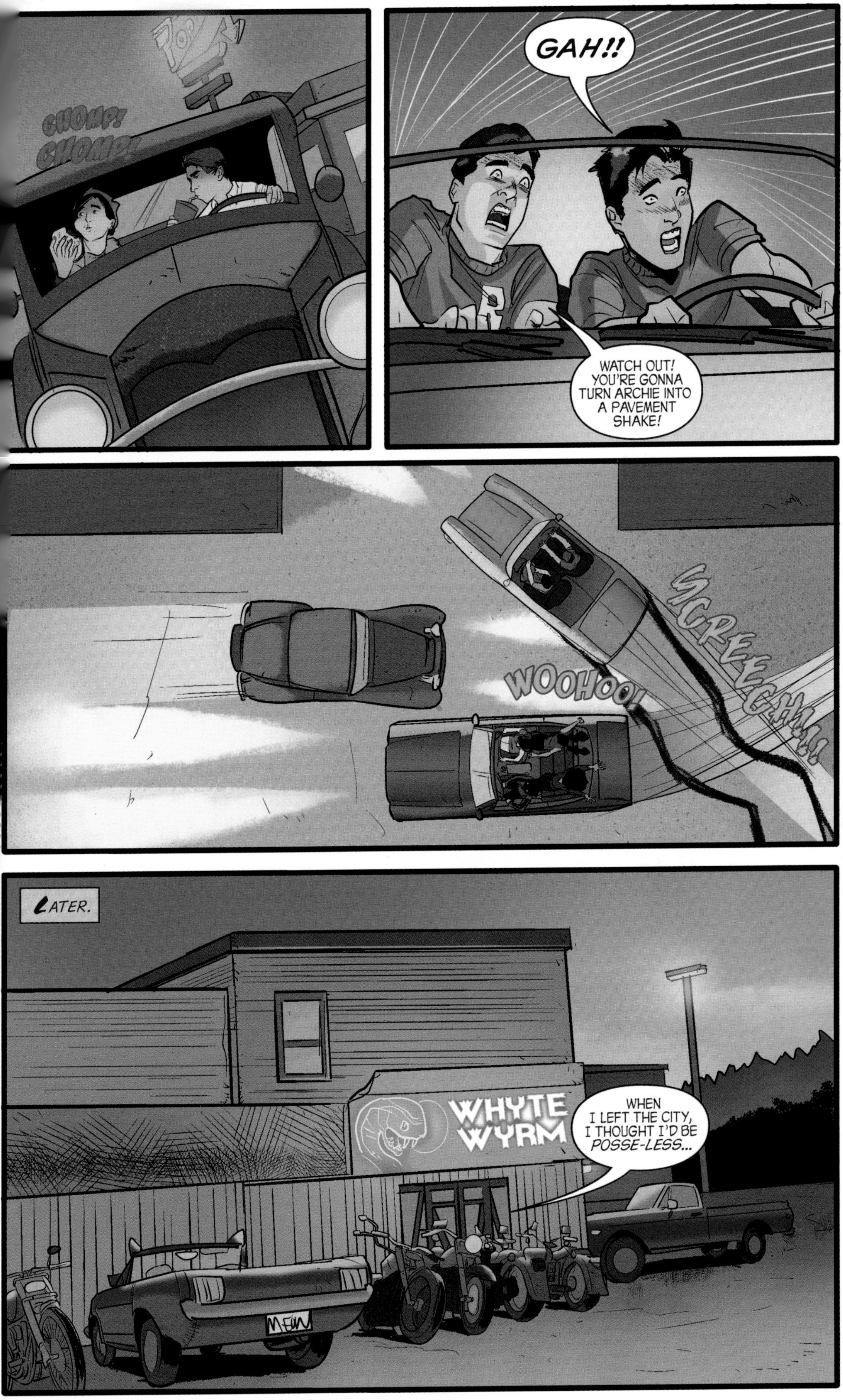
CHOMP!
CHOMP!
GAH!!
WATCH OUT! YOU'RE GONNA TURN ARCHIE INTO A PAVEMENT SHAKE!
SCREECH!!!
WOOHOO!
LATER.
WHYTE WYRM
WHEN I LEFT THE CITY, I THOUGHT I'D BE POSSE-LESS...
MEOW

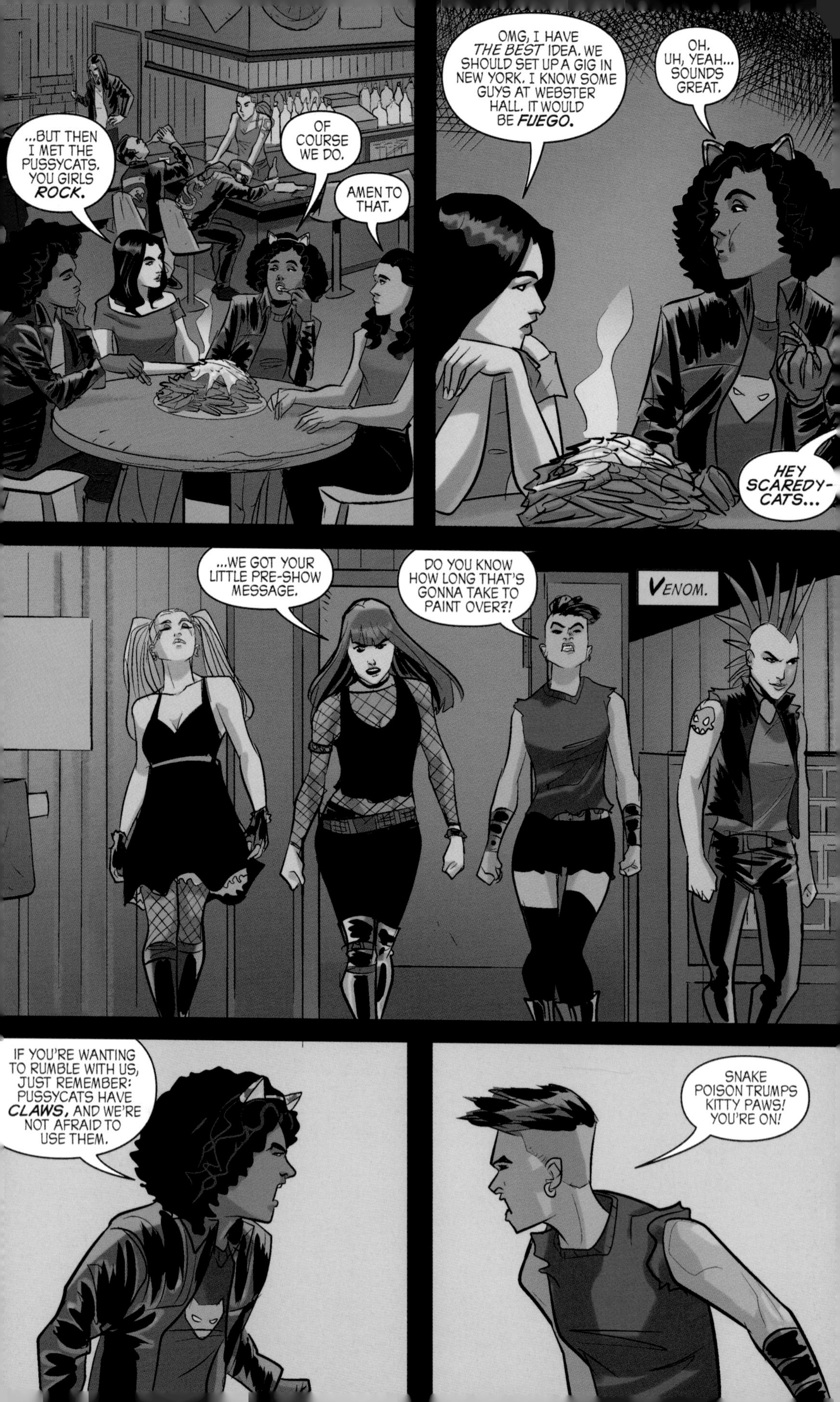
...BUT THEN I MET THE PUSSYCATS. YOU GIRLS ROCK.
OF COURSE WE DO.
AMEN TO THAT.
OMG, I HAVE THE BEST IDEA. WE SHOULD SET UP A GIG IN NEW YORK. I KNOW SOME GUYS AT WEBSTER HALL. IT WOULD BE FUEGO.
OH. UH, YEAH... SOUNDS GREAT.
HEY SCAREDY-CATS...
...WE GOT YOUR LITTLE PRE-SHOW MESSAGE.
DO YOU KNOW HOW LONG THAT'S GONNA TAKE TO PAINT OVER?!
VENOM.
IF YOU'RE WANTING TO RUMBLE WITH US, JUST REMEMBER: PUSSYCATS HAVE CLAWS, AND WE'RE NOT AFRAID TO USE THEM.
SNAKE POISON TRUMPS KITTY PAWS! YOU'RE ON!

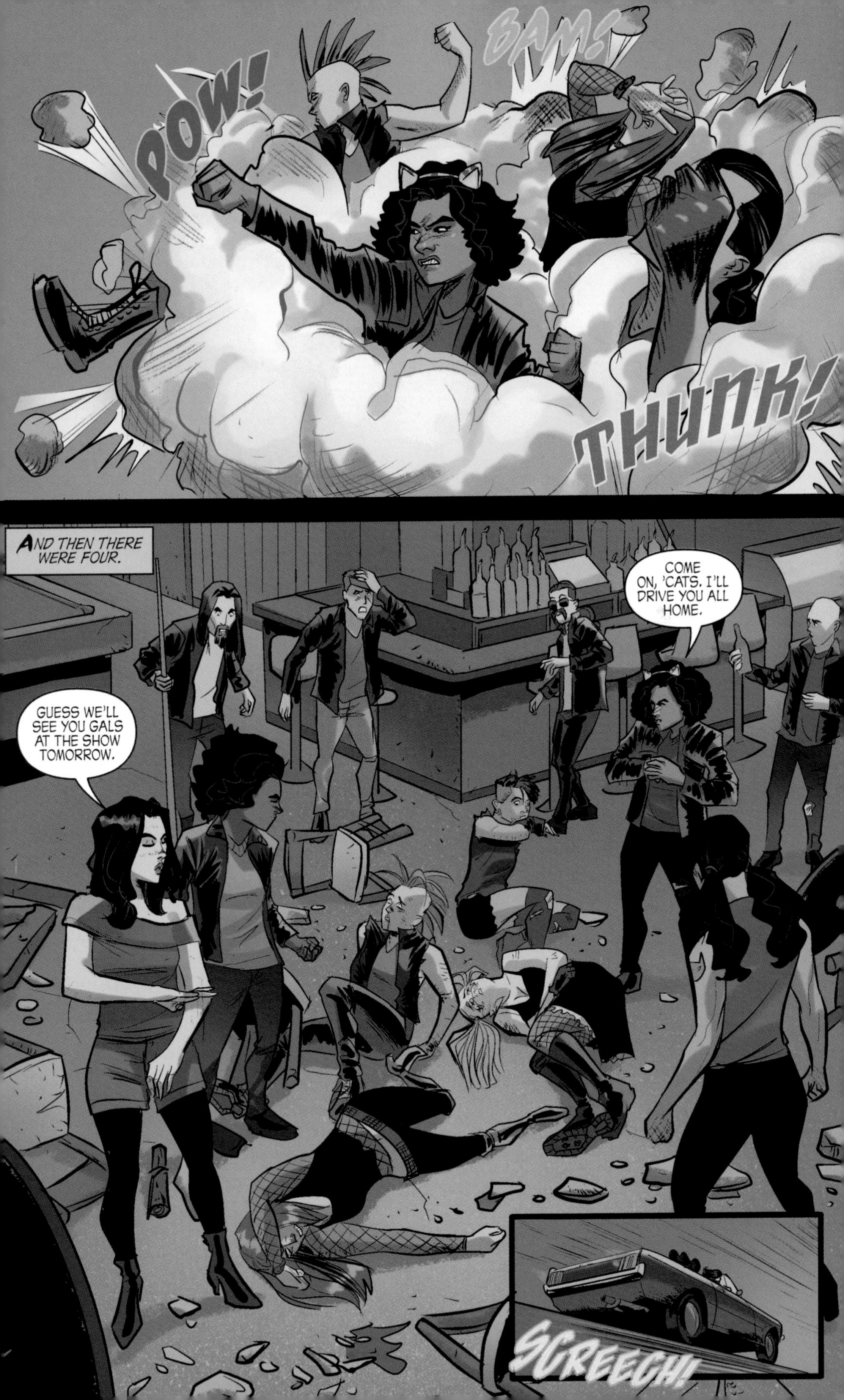
POW!
BAM!
THUNK!
AND THEN THERE WERE FOUR.
COME ON, 'CATS. I'LL DRIVE YOU ALL HOME.
GUESS WE'LL SEE YOU GALS AT THE SHOW TOMORROW.
SCREECH!

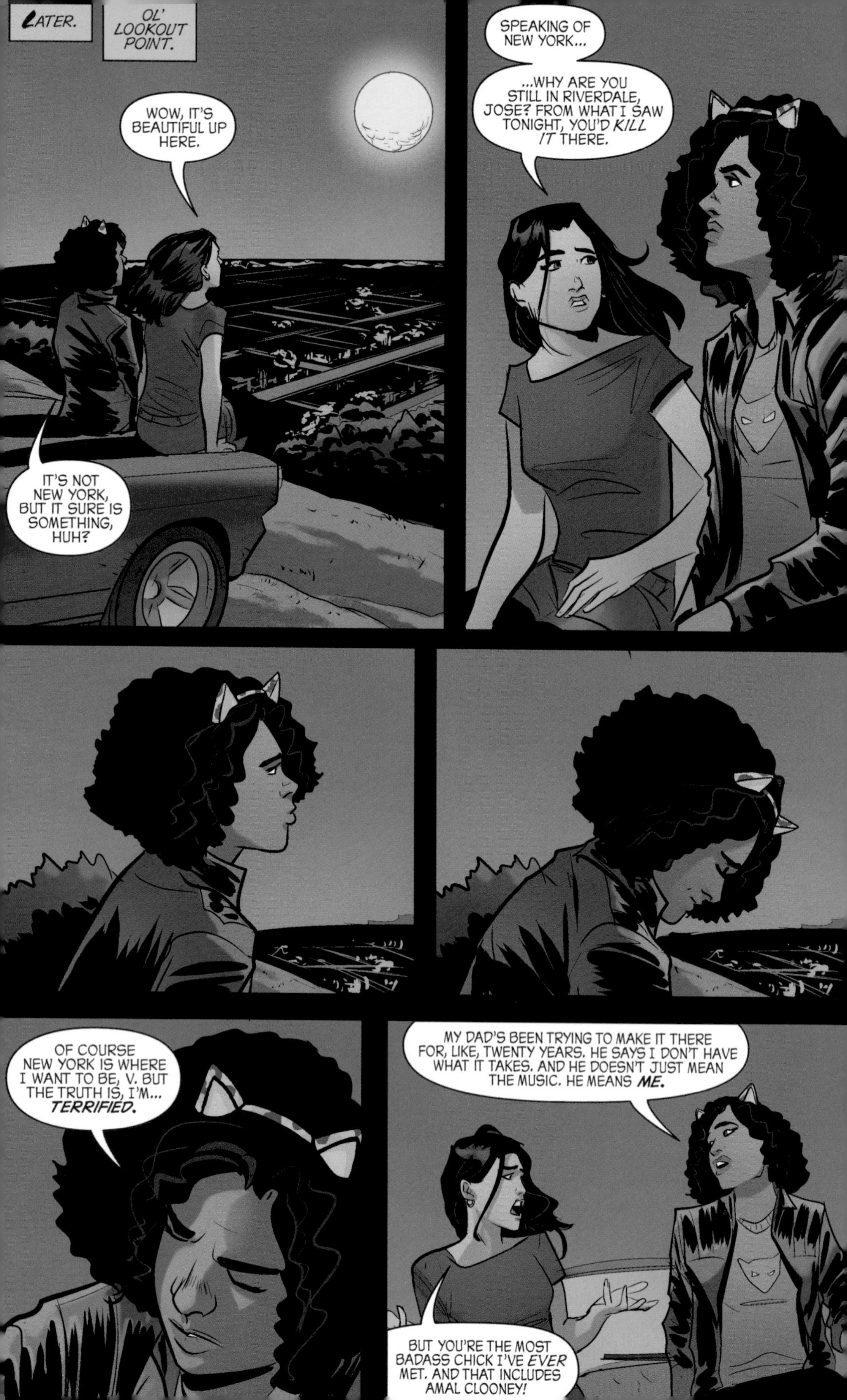
LATER.
OL' LOOKOUT POINT.
WOW, IT'S BEAUTIFUL UP HERE.
IT'S NOT NEW YORK, BUT IT SURE IS SOMETHING, HUH?
SPEAKING OF NEW YORK...
...WHY ARE YOU STILL IN RIVERDALE, JOSE? FROM WHAT I SAW TONIGHT, YOU'D *KILL IT* THERE.
OF COURSE NEW YORK IS WHERE I WANT TO BE, V. BUT THE TRUTH IS, I'M... ***TERRIFIED.***
MY DAD'S BEEN TRYING TO MAKE IT THERE FOR, LIKE, TWENTY YEARS. HE SAYS I DON'T HAVE WHAT IT TAKES. AND HE DOESN'T JUST MEAN THE MUSIC. HE MEANS ***ME.***
BUT YOU'RE THE MOST BADASS CHICK I'VE *EVER* MET. AND THAT INCLUDES AMAL CLOONEY!

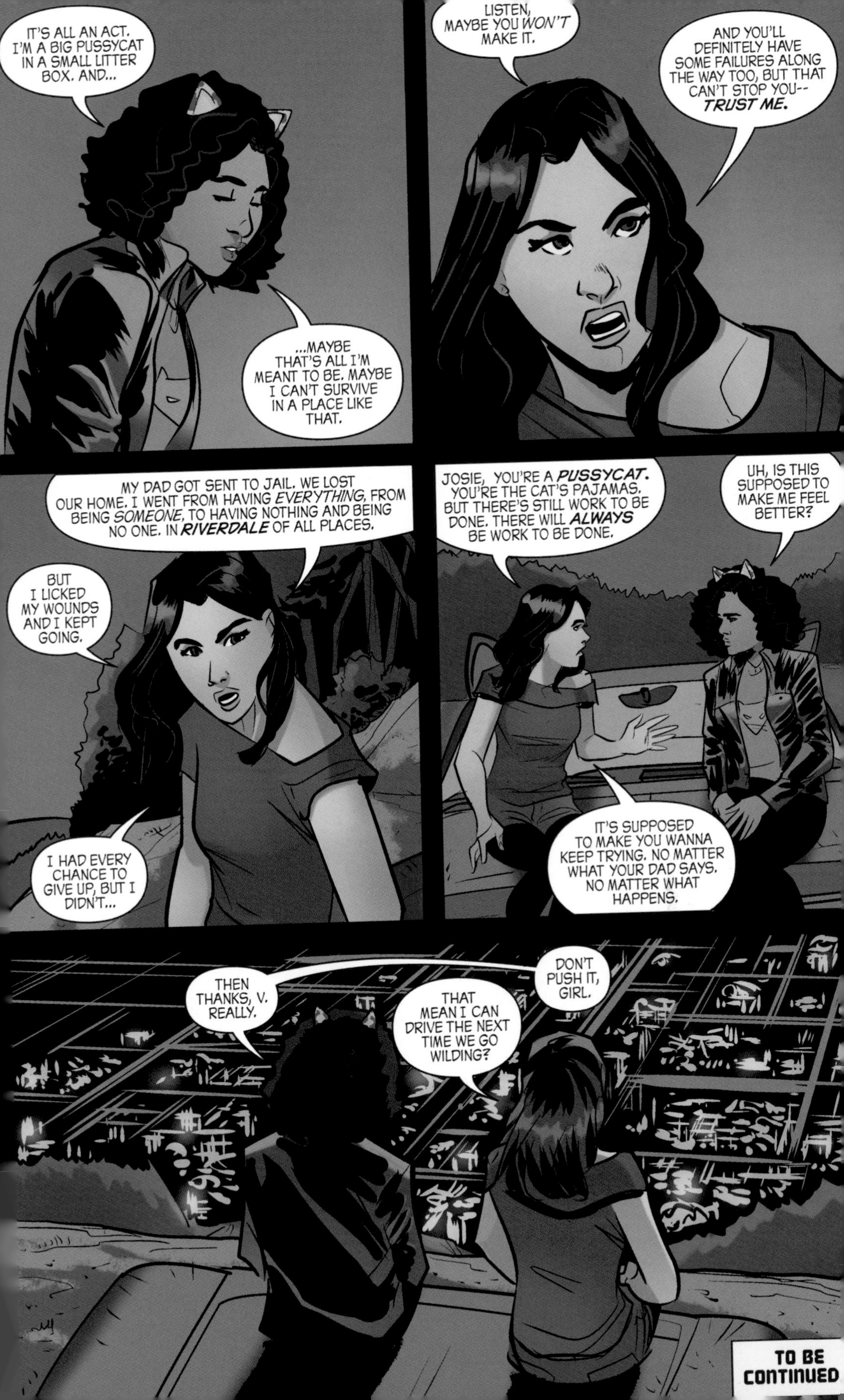

IT'S ALL AN ACT. I'M A BIG PUSSYCAT IN A SMALL LITTER BOX. AND...
...MAYBE THAT'S ALL I'M MEANT TO BE. MAYBE I CAN'T SURVIVE IN A PLACE LIKE THAT.
LISTEN, MAYBE YOU WON'T MAKE IT.
AND YOU'LL DEFINITELY HAVE SOME FAILURES ALONG THE WAY TOO, BUT THAT CAN'T STOP YOU-- TRUST ME.
MY DAD GOT SENT TO JAIL. WE LOST OUR HOME. I WENT FROM HAVING EVERYTHING, FROM BEING SOMEONE, TO HAVING NOTHING AND BEING NO ONE. IN RIVERDALE OF ALL PLACES.
BUT I LICKED MY WOUNDS AND I KEPT GOING.
I HAD EVERY CHANCE TO GIVE UP, BUT I DIDN'T...
JOSIE, YOU'RE A PUSSYCAT. YOU'RE THE CAT'S PAJAMAS. BUT THERE'S STILL WORK TO BE DONE. THERE WILL ALWAYS BE WORK TO BE DONE.
UH, IS THIS SUPPOSED TO MAKE ME FEEL BETTER?
IT'S SUPPOSED TO MAKE YOU WANNA KEEP TRYING. NO MATTER WHAT YOUR DAD SAYS. NO MATTER WHAT HAPPENS.
THEN THANKS, V. REALLY.
THAT MEAN I CAN DRIVE THE NEXT TIME WE GO WILDING?
DON'T PUSH IT, GIRL.
TO BE CONTINUED

CHAPTER NINE

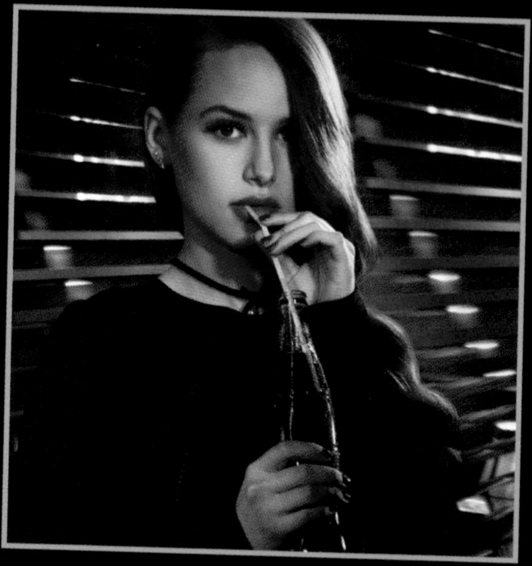

THE CASE OF THE SORREL ROAN

WRITER:
WILL EWING

ART:
THOMAS PITILLI

COLORS:
ANDRE SZYMANOWICZ

LETTERS:
JOHN WORKMAN

STARRING
CHERYL BLOSSOM

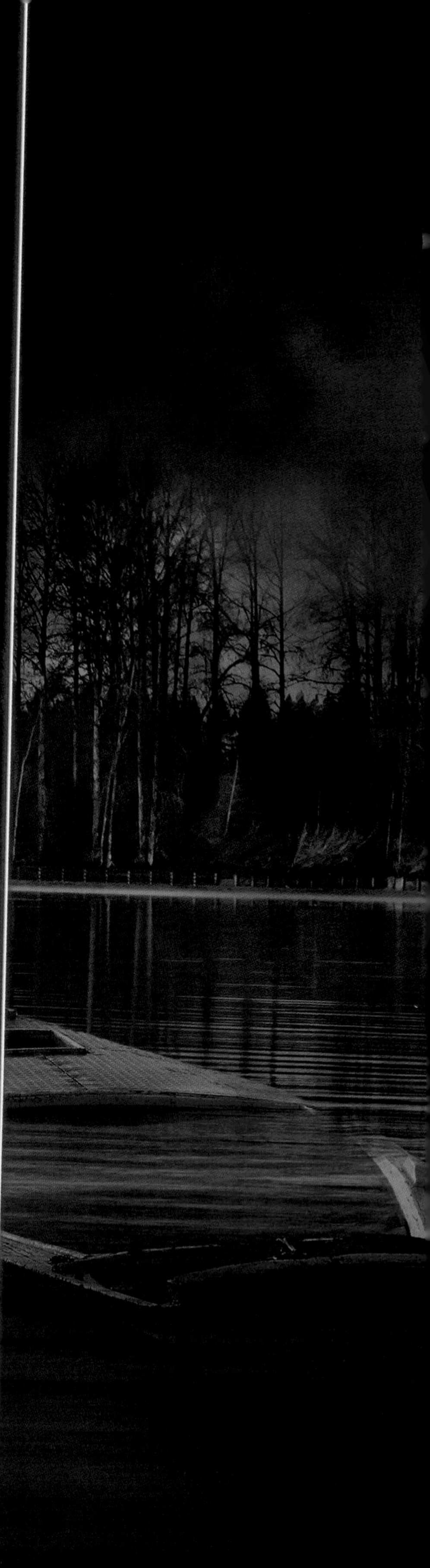

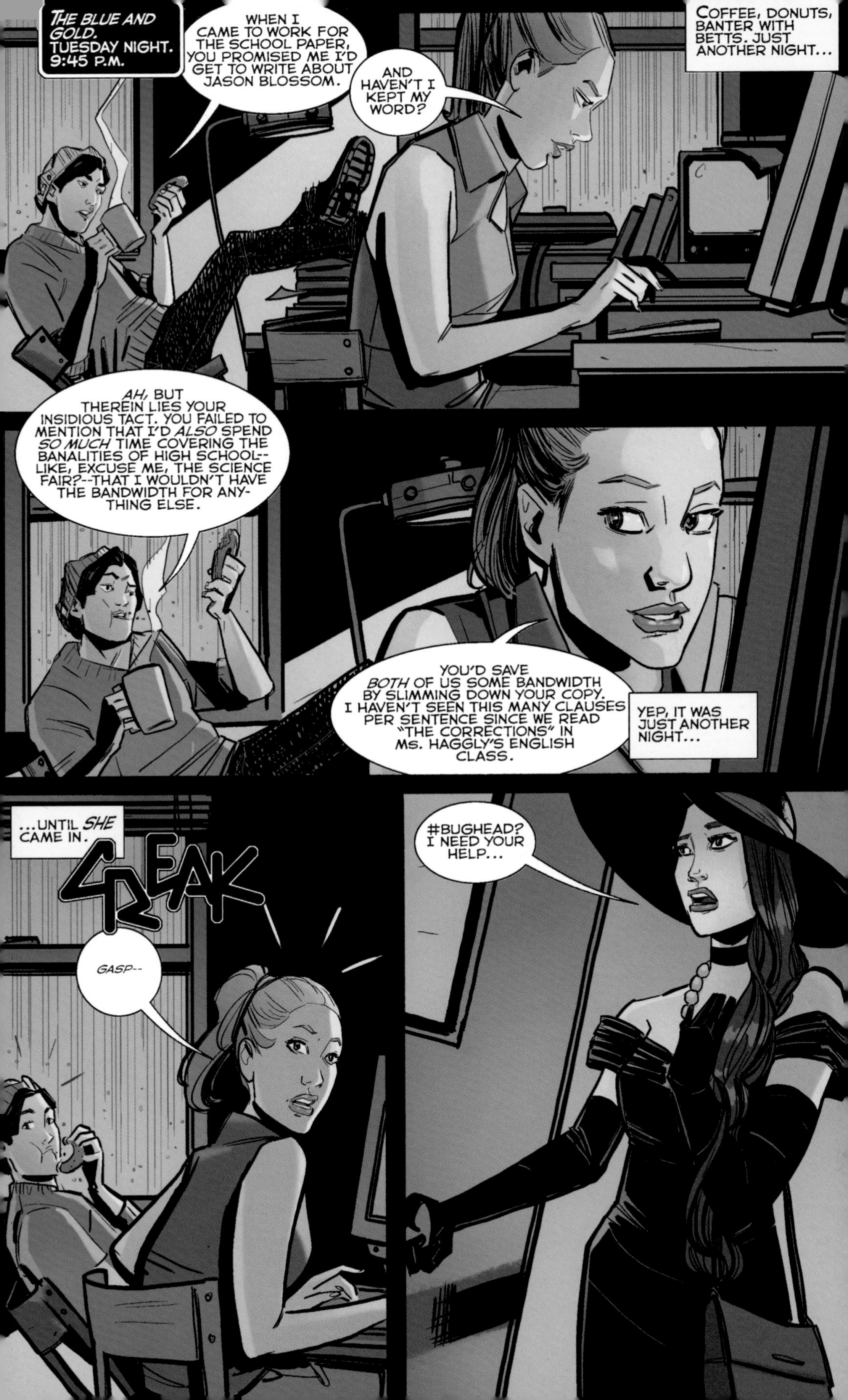
THE BLUE AND GOLD. TUESDAY NIGHT. 9:45 P.M.
WHEN I CAME TO WORK FOR THE SCHOOL PAPER, YOU PROMISED ME I'D GET TO WRITE ABOUT JASON BLOSSOM.
AND HAVEN'T I KEPT MY WORD?
COFFEE, DONUTS, BANTER WITH BETTS. JUST ANOTHER NIGHT...
AH, BUT THEREIN LIES YOUR INSIDIOUS TACT. YOU FAILED TO MENTION THAT I'D ALSO SPEND SO MUCH TIME COVERING THE BANALITIES OF HIGH SCHOOL--LIKE, EXCUSE ME, THE SCIENCE FAIR?--THAT I WOULDN'T HAVE THE BANDWIDTH FOR ANYTHING ELSE.
YOU'D SAVE BOTH OF US SOME BANDWIDTH BY SLIMMING DOWN YOUR COPY. I HAVEN'T SEEN THIS MANY CLAUSES PER SENTENCE SINCE WE READ "THE CORRECTIONS" IN MS. HAGGLY'S ENGLISH CLASS.
YEP, IT WAS JUST ANOTHER NIGHT...
...UNTIL SHE CAME IN.
CREAK
GASP--
#BUGHEAD? I NEED YOUR HELP...

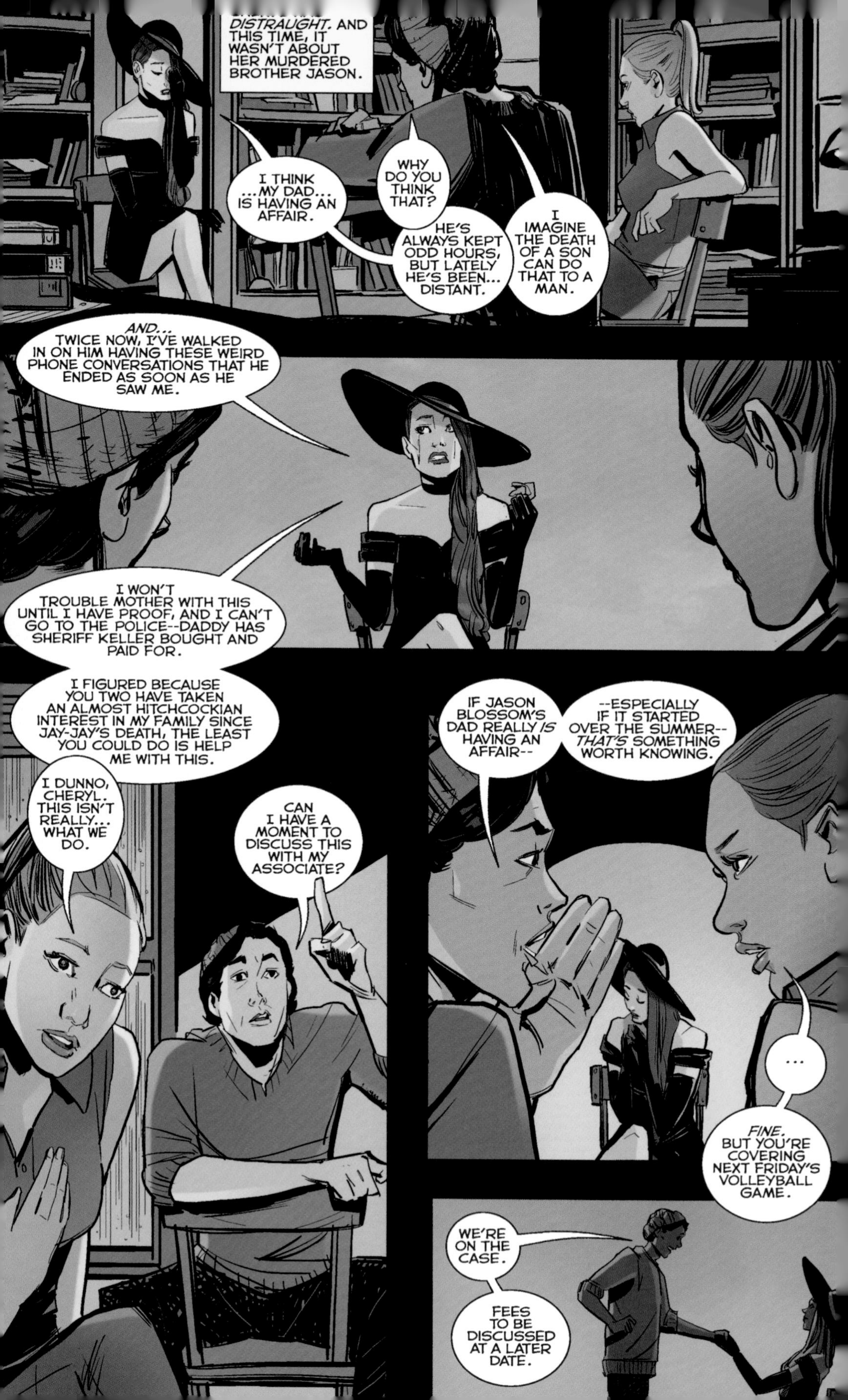
DISTRAUGHT. AND THIS TIME, IT WASN'T ABOUT HER MURDERED BROTHER JASON.
I THINK ...MY DAD... IS HAVING AN AFFAIR.
WHY DO YOU THINK THAT?
HE'S ALWAYS KEPT ODD HOURS, BUT LATELY HE'S BEEN... DISTANT.
I IMAGINE THE DEATH OF A SON CAN DO THAT TO A MAN.
AND... TWICE NOW, I'VE WALKED IN ON HIM HAVING THESE WEIRD PHONE CONVERSATIONS THAT HE ENDED AS SOON AS HE SAW ME.
I WON'T TROUBLE MOTHER WITH THIS UNTIL I HAVE PROOF, AND I CAN'T GO TO THE POLICE--DADDY HAS SHERIFF KELLER BOUGHT AND PAID FOR.
I FIGURED BECAUSE YOU TWO HAVE TAKEN AN ALMOST HITCHCOCKIAN INTEREST IN MY FAMILY SINCE JAY-JAY'S DEATH, THE LEAST YOU COULD DO IS HELP ME WITH THIS.
I DUNNO, CHERYL. THIS ISN'T REALLY... WHAT WE DO.
CAN I HAVE A MOMENT TO DISCUSS THIS WITH MY ASSOCIATE?
IF JASON BLOSSOM'S DAD REALLY IS HAVING AN AFFAIR--
--ESPECIALLY IF IT STARTED OVER THE SUMMER-- THAT'S SOMETHING WORTH KNOWING.
...
FINE. BUT YOU'RE COVERING NEXT FRIDAY'S VOLLEYBALL GAME.
WE'RE ON THE CASE.
FEES TO BE DISCUSSED AT A LATER DATE.

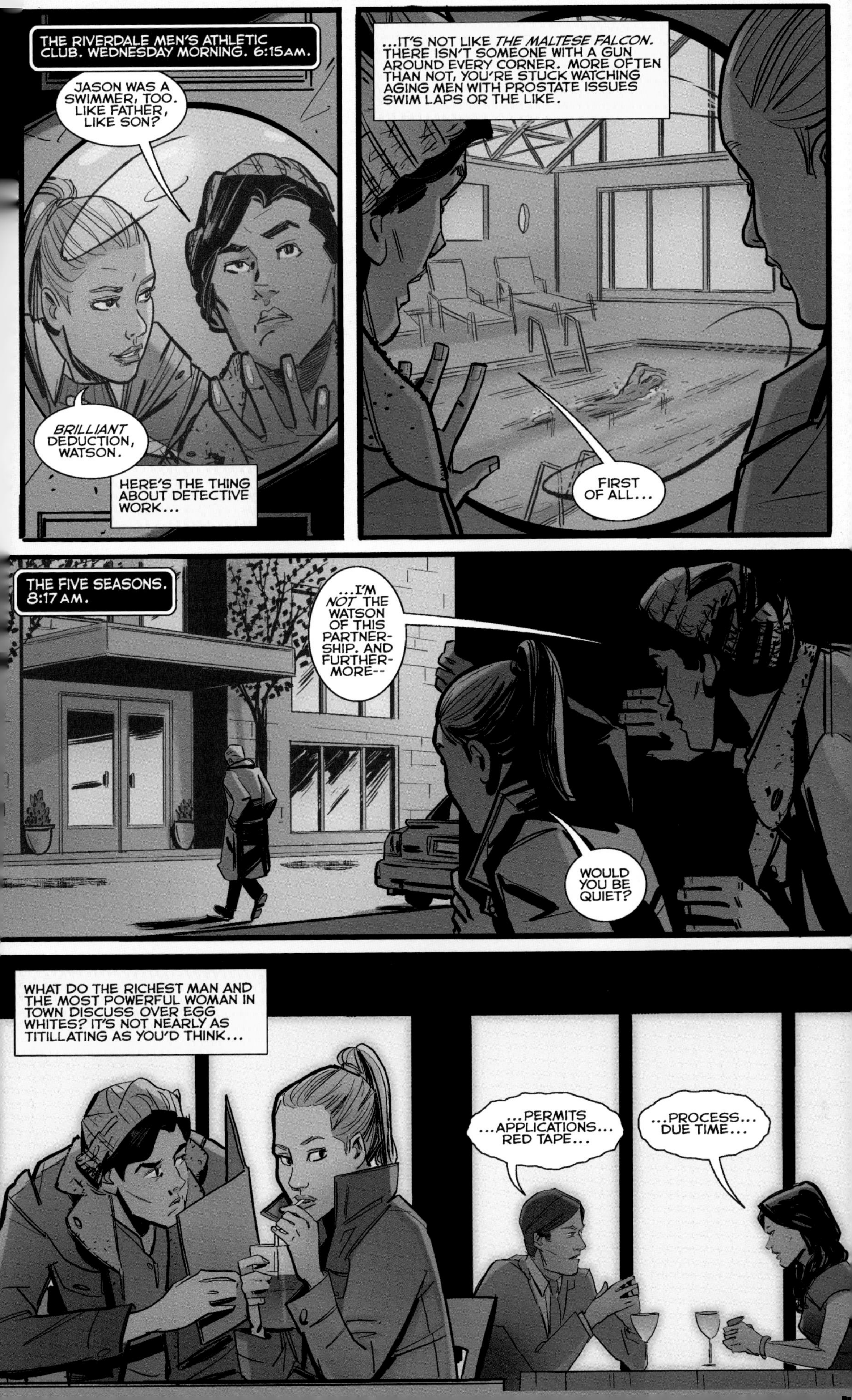
THE RIVERDALE MEN'S ATHLETIC CLUB. WEDNESDAY MORNING. 6:15AM.
JASON WAS A SWIMMER, TOO. LIKE FATHER, LIKE SON?
BRILLIANT DEDUCTION, WATSON.
HERE'S THE THING ABOUT DETECTIVE WORK...
...IT'S NOT LIKE *THE MALTESE FALCON.* THERE ISN'T SOMEONE WITH A GUN AROUND EVERY CORNER. MORE OFTEN THAN NOT, YOU'RE STUCK WATCHING AGING MEN WITH PROSTATE ISSUES SWIM LAPS OR THE LIKE.
FIRST OF ALL...
THE FIVE SEASONS. 8:17 AM.
...I'M *NOT* THE WATSON OF THIS PARTNERSHIP. AND FURTHERMORE--
WOULD YOU BE QUIET?
WHAT DO THE RICHEST MAN AND THE MOST POWERFUL WOMAN IN TOWN DISCUSS OVER EGG WHITES? IT'S NOT NEARLY AS TITILLATING AS YOU'D THINK...
...PERMITS ...APPLICATIONS... RED TAPE...
...PROCESS... DUE TIME...

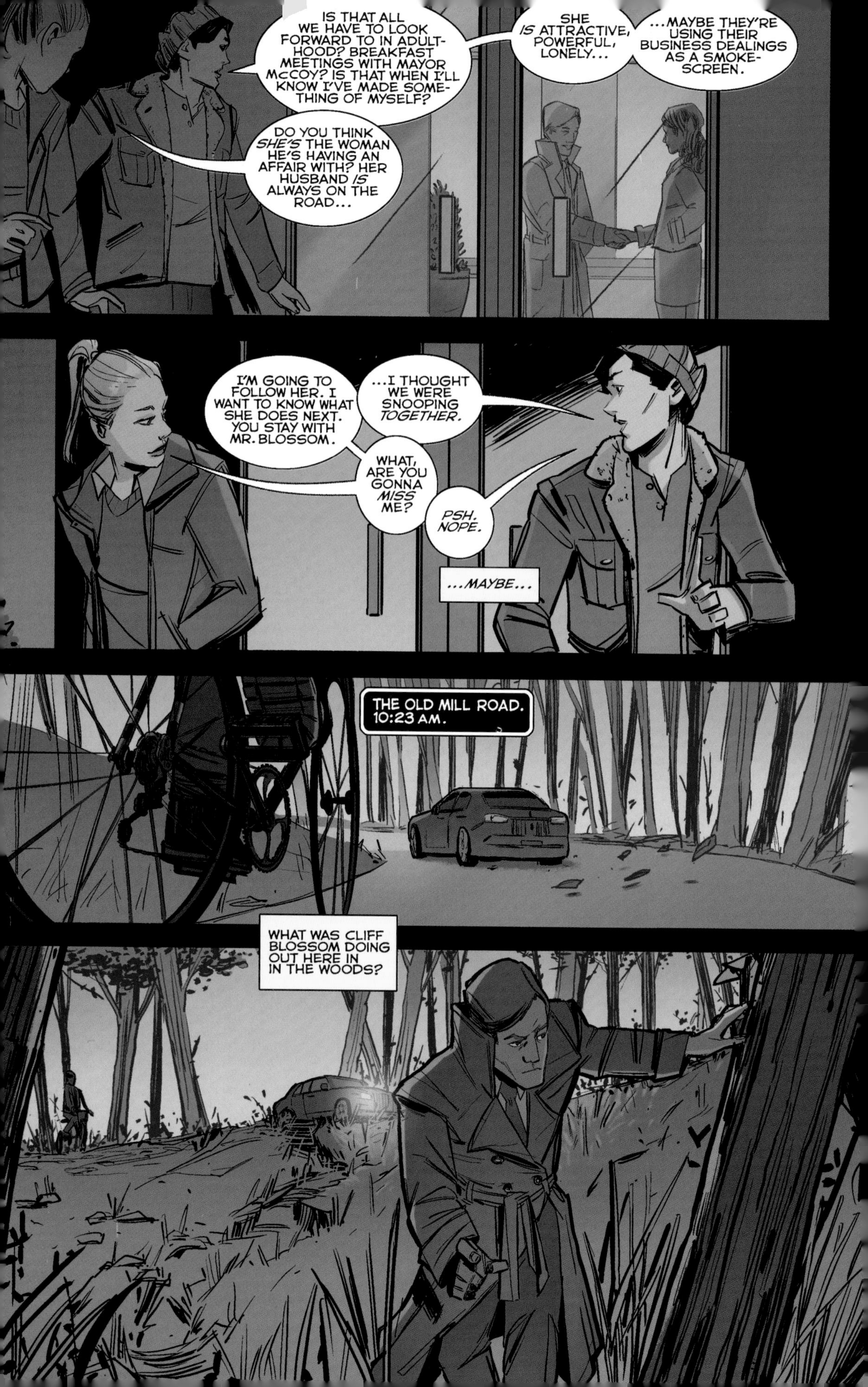
IS THAT ALL WE HAVE TO LOOK FORWARD TO IN ADULTHOOD? BREAKFAST MEETINGS WITH MAYOR McCOY? IS THAT WHEN I'LL KNOW I'VE MADE SOMETHING OF MYSELF?
DO YOU THINK *SHE'S* THE WOMAN HE'S HAVING AN AFFAIR WITH? HER HUSBAND *IS* ALWAYS ON THE ROAD...
SHE *IS* ATTRACTIVE, POWERFUL, LONELY...
...MAYBE THEY'RE USING THEIR BUSINESS DEALINGS AS A SMOKE-SCREEN.
I'M GOING TO FOLLOW HER. I WANT TO KNOW WHAT SHE DOES NEXT. YOU STAY WITH MR. BLOSSOM.
...I THOUGHT WE WERE SNOOPING *TOGETHER.*
WHAT, ARE YOU GONNA *MISS* ME?
PSH. NOPE.
...MAYBE...
THE OLD MILL ROAD. 10:23 AM.
WHAT WAS CLIFF BLOSSOM DOING OUT HERE IN IN THE WOODS?

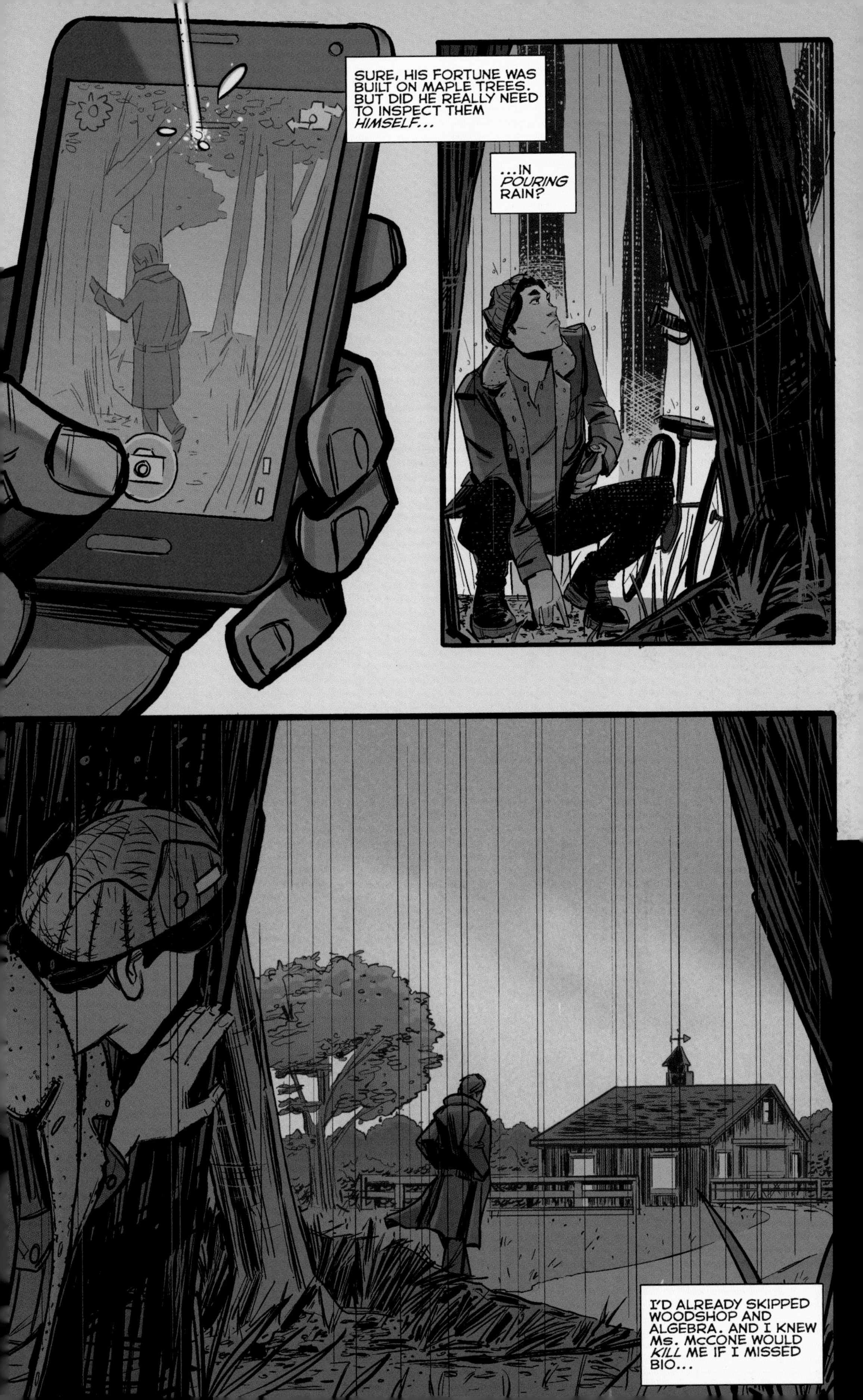
SURE, HIS FORTUNE WAS BUILT ON MAPLE TREES. BUT DID HE REALLY NEED TO INSPECT THEM *HIMSELF*...
...IN *POURING* RAIN?
I'D ALREADY SKIPPED WOODSHOP AND ALGEBRA. AND I KNEW Ms. McCONE WOULD *KILL* ME IF I MISSED BIO...

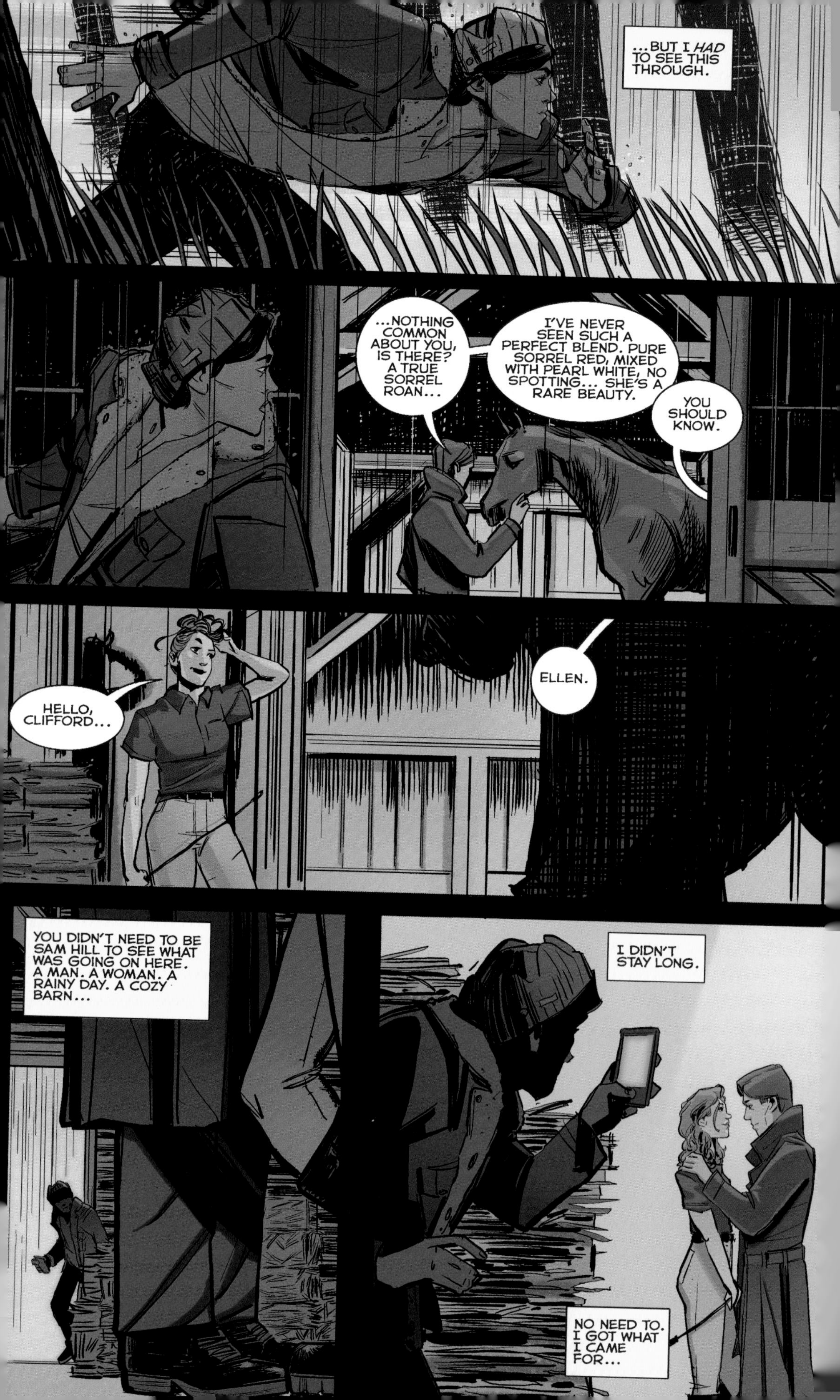
...BUT I *HAD* TO SEE THIS THROUGH.
...NOTHING COMMON ABOUT YOU, IS THERE? A TRUE SORREL ROAN...
I'VE NEVER SEEN SUCH A PERFECT BLEND. PURE SORREL RED, MIXED WITH PEARL WHITE, NO SPOTTING... SHE'S A RARE BEAUTY.
YOU SHOULD KNOW.
HELLO, CLIFFORD...
ELLEN.
YOU DIDN'T NEED TO BE SAM HILL TO SEE WHAT WAS GOING ON HERE. A MAN. A WOMAN. A RAINY DAY. A COZY BARN...
I DIDN'T STAY LONG.
NO NEED TO. I GOT WHAT I CAME FOR...

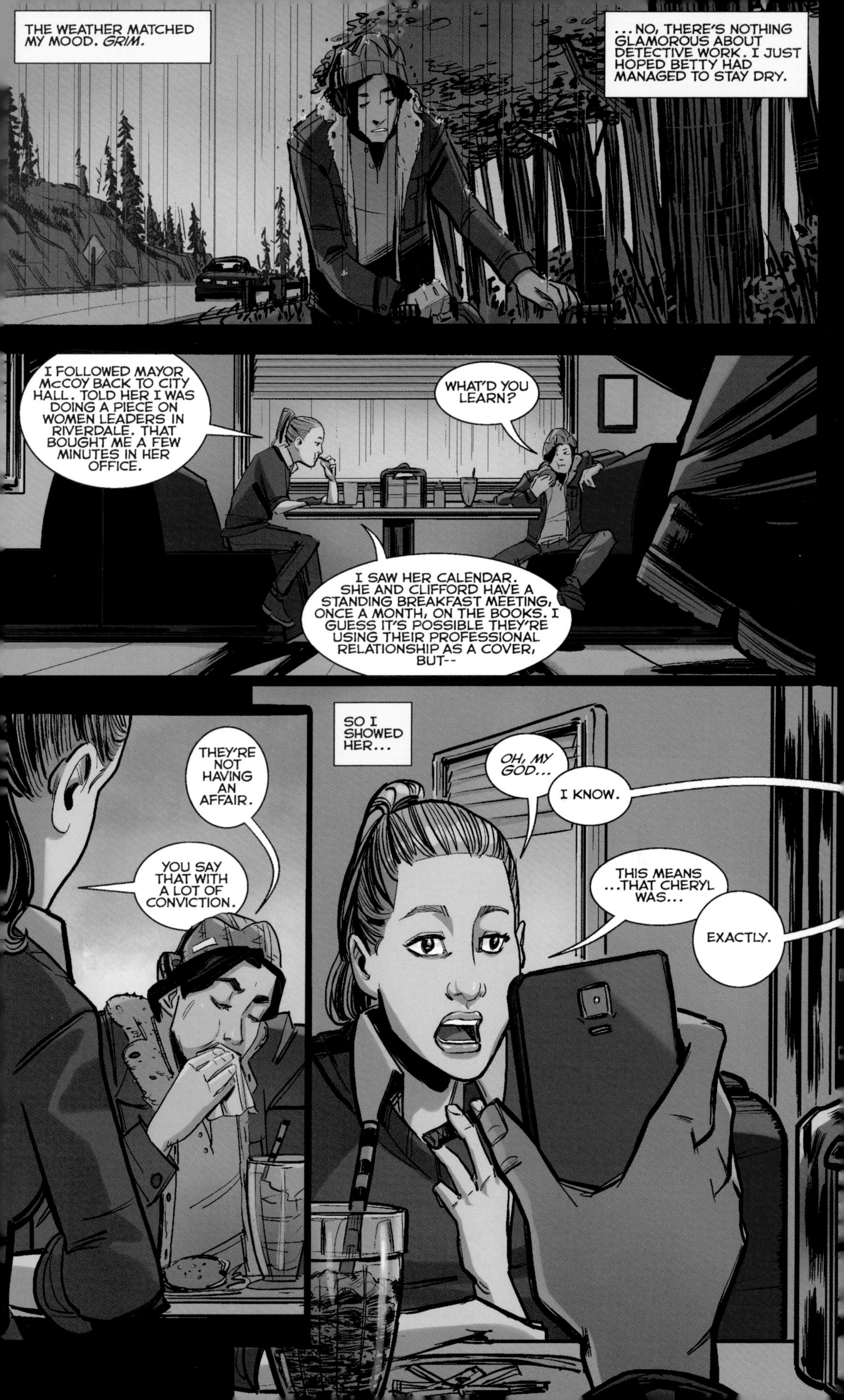
THE WEATHER MATCHED MY MOOD. GRIM.
...NO, THERE'S NOTHING GLAMOROUS ABOUT DETECTIVE WORK. I JUST HOPED BETTY HAD MANAGED TO STAY DRY.
I FOLLOWED MAYOR McCOY BACK TO CITY HALL. TOLD HER I WAS DOING A PIECE ON WOMEN LEADERS IN RIVERDALE. THAT BOUGHT ME A FEW MINUTES IN HER OFFICE.
WHAT'D YOU LEARN?
I SAW HER CALENDAR. SHE AND CLIFFORD HAVE A STANDING BREAKFAST MEETING, ONCE A MONTH, ON THE BOOKS. I GUESS IT'S POSSIBLE THEY'RE USING THEIR PROFESSIONAL RELATIONSHIP AS A COVER, BUT--
THEY'RE NOT HAVING AN AFFAIR.
YOU SAY THAT WITH A LOT OF CONVICTION.
SO I SHOWED HER...
OH, MY GOD...
I KNOW.
THIS MEANS ...THAT CHERYL WAS...
EXACTLY.

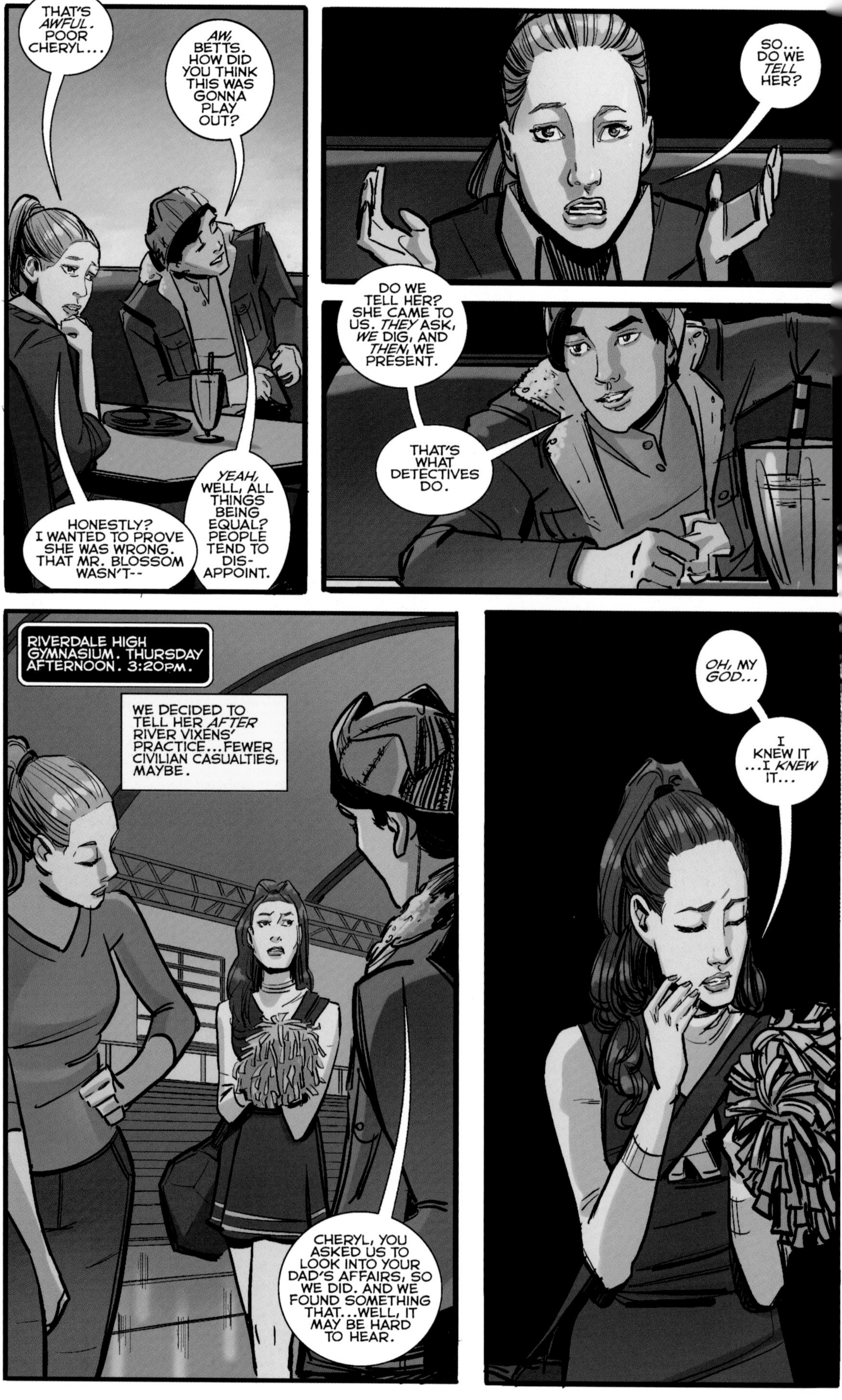
THAT'S AWFUL. POOR CHERYL...
AW, BETTS. HOW DID YOU THINK THIS WAS GONNA PLAY OUT?
HONESTLY? I WANTED TO PROVE SHE WAS WRONG. THAT MR. BLOSSOM WASN'T--
YEAH, WELL, ALL THINGS BEING EQUAL? PEOPLE TEND TO DIS-APPOINT.
SO... DO WE TELL HER?
DO WE TELL HER? SHE CAME TO US. THEY ASK, WE DIG, AND THEN, WE PRESENT.
THAT'S WHAT DETECTIVES DO.
RIVERDALE HIGH GYMNASIUM. THURSDAY AFTERNOON. 3:20PM.
WE DECIDED TO TELL HER AFTER RIVER VIXENS' PRACTICE...FEWER CIVILIAN CASUALTIES, MAYBE.
CHERYL, YOU ASKED US TO LOOK INTO YOUR DAD'S AFFAIRS, SO WE DID. AND WE FOUND SOMETHING THAT...WELL, IT MAY BE HARD TO HEAR.
OH, MY GOD...
I KNEW IT ...I KNEW IT...

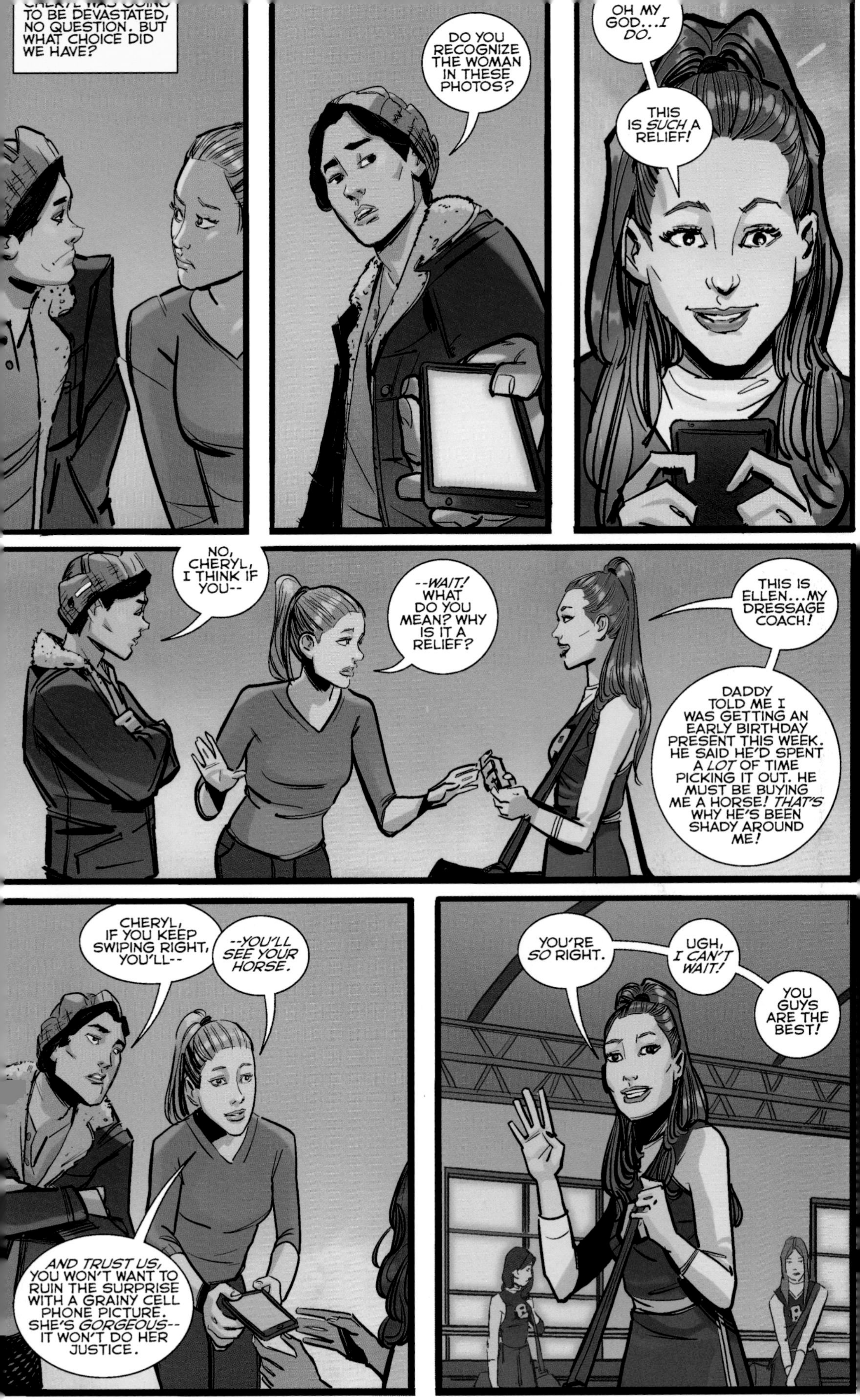

TO BE DEVASTATED, NO QUESTION. BUT WHAT CHOICE DID WE HAVE?
DO YOU RECOGNIZE THE WOMAN IN THESE PHOTOS?
OH MY GOD...*I DO.*
THIS IS *SUCH* A RELIEF!
NO, CHERYL, I THINK IF YOU--
--WAIT! WHAT DO YOU MEAN? WHY IS IT A RELIEF?
THIS IS ELLEN...MY DRESSAGE COACH!
DADDY TOLD ME I WAS GETTING AN EARLY BIRTHDAY PRESENT THIS WEEK. HE SAID HE'D SPENT A *LOT* OF TIME PICKING IT OUT. HE MUST BE BUYING ME A HORSE! *THAT'S* WHY HE'S BEEN SHADY AROUND ME!
CHERYL, IF YOU KEEP SWIPING RIGHT, YOU'LL--
--YOU'LL SEE YOUR HORSE.
AND TRUST US, YOU WON'T WANT TO RUIN THE SURPRISE WITH A GRAINY CELL PHONE PICTURE. SHE'S *GORGEOUS*-- IT WON'T DO HER JUSTICE.
YOU'RE *SO* RIGHT.
UGH, *I CAN'T WAIT!*
YOU GUYS ARE THE BEST!

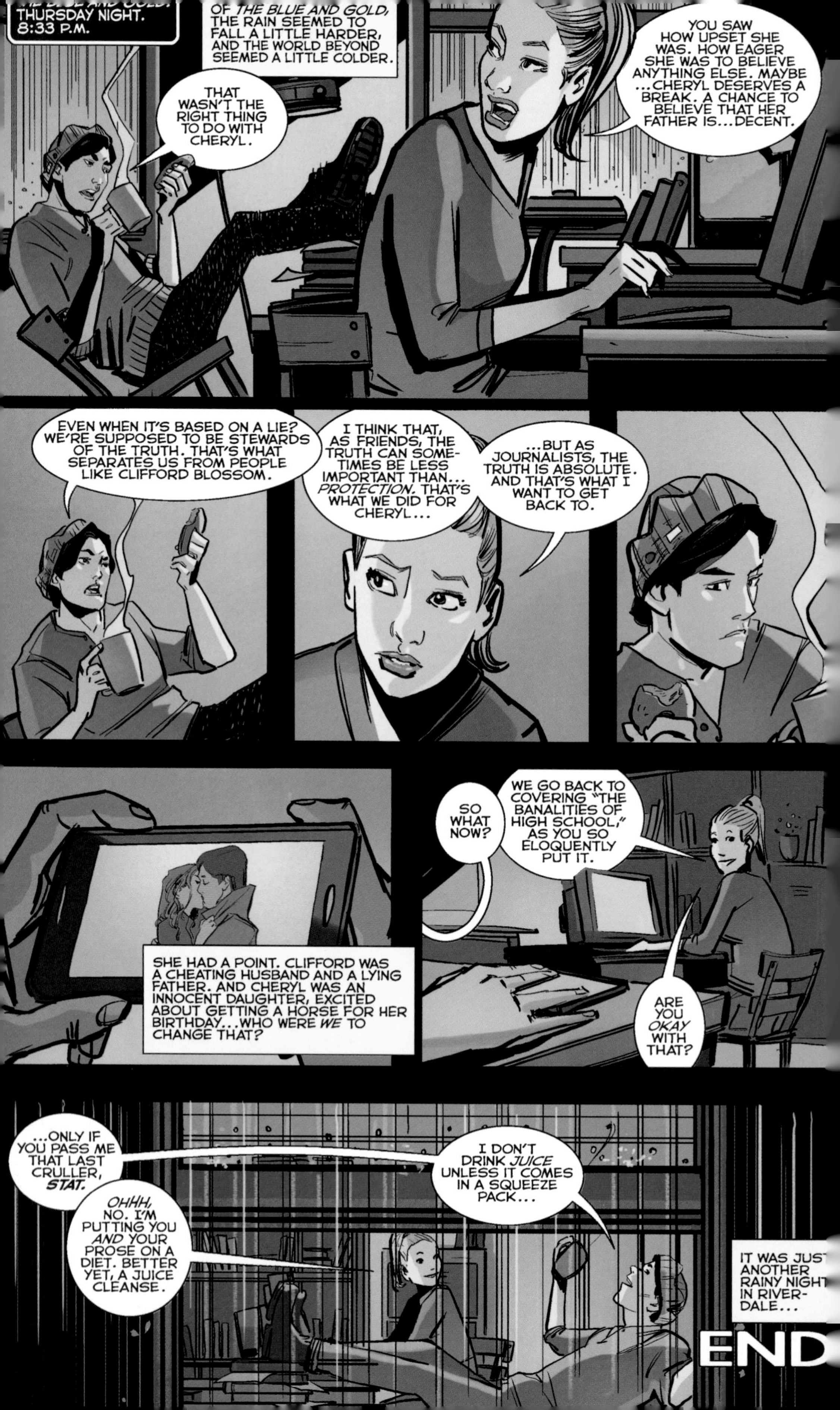
THURSDAY NIGHT.
8:33 P.M.
OF THE BLUE AND GOLD, THE RAIN SEEMED TO FALL A LITTLE HARDER, AND THE WORLD BEYOND SEEMED A LITTLE COLDER.
THAT WASN'T THE RIGHT THING TO DO WITH CHERYL.
YOU SAW HOW UPSET SHE WAS. HOW EAGER SHE WAS TO BELIEVE ANYTHING ELSE. MAYBE ...CHERYL DESERVES A BREAK. A CHANCE TO BELIEVE THAT HER FATHER IS...DECENT.
EVEN WHEN IT'S BASED ON A LIE? WE'RE SUPPOSED TO BE STEWARDS OF THE TRUTH. THAT'S WHAT SEPARATES US FROM PEOPLE LIKE CLIFFORD BLOSSOM.
I THINK THAT, AS FRIENDS, THE TRUTH CAN SOMETIMES BE LESS IMPORTANT THAN... PROTECTION. THAT'S WHAT WE DID FOR CHERYL...
...BUT AS JOURNALISTS, THE TRUTH IS ABSOLUTE. AND THAT'S WHAT I WANT TO GET BACK TO.
SHE HAD A POINT. CLIFFORD WAS A CHEATING HUSBAND AND A LYING FATHER. AND CHERYL WAS AN INNOCENT DAUGHTER, EXCITED ABOUT GETTING A HORSE FOR HER BIRTHDAY...WHO WERE WE TO CHANGE THAT?
SO WHAT NOW?
WE GO BACK TO COVERING "THE BANALITIES OF HIGH SCHOOL," AS YOU SO ELOQUENTLY PUT IT.
ARE YOU OKAY WITH THAT?
...ONLY IF YOU PASS ME THAT LAST CRULLER, STAT.
OHHH, NO. I'M PUTTING YOU AND YOUR PROSE ON A DIET. BETTER YET, A JUICE CLEANSE.
I DON'T DRINK JUICE UNLESS IT COMES IN A SQUEEZE PACK...
IT WAS JUST ANOTHER RAINY NIGHT IN RIVERDALE...
END

RIVERDALE®

SPECIAL FEATURES

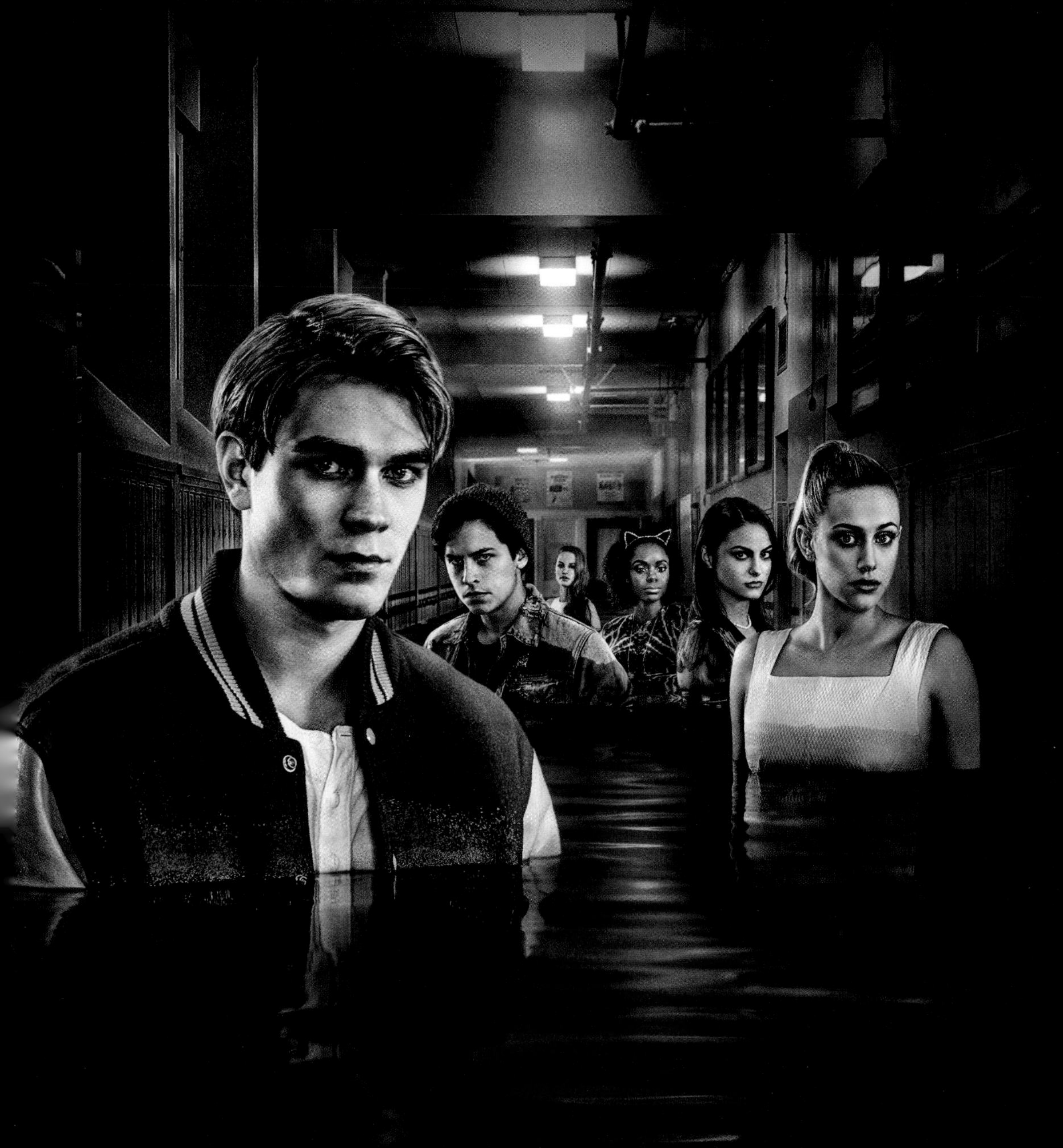

COVER GALLERY

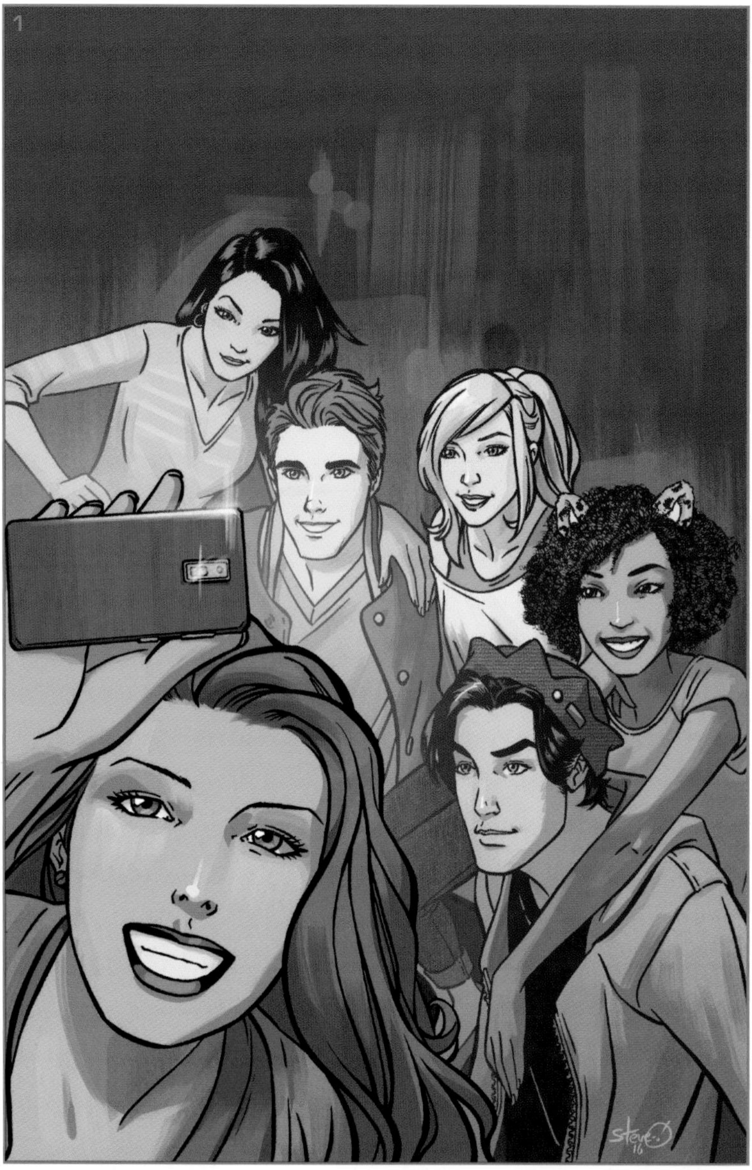

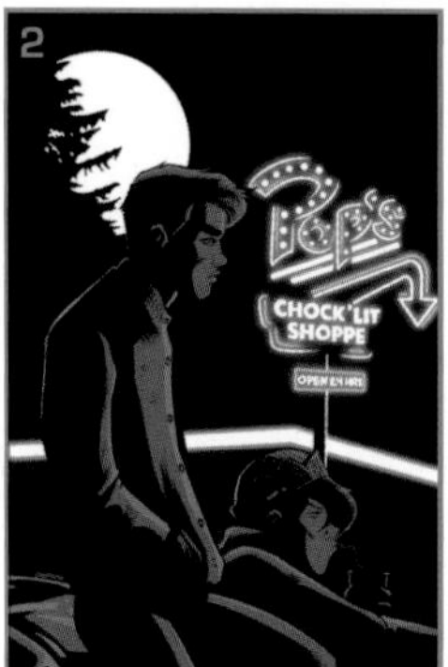
CHOCK'LIT SHOPPE
OPEN 24 HRS

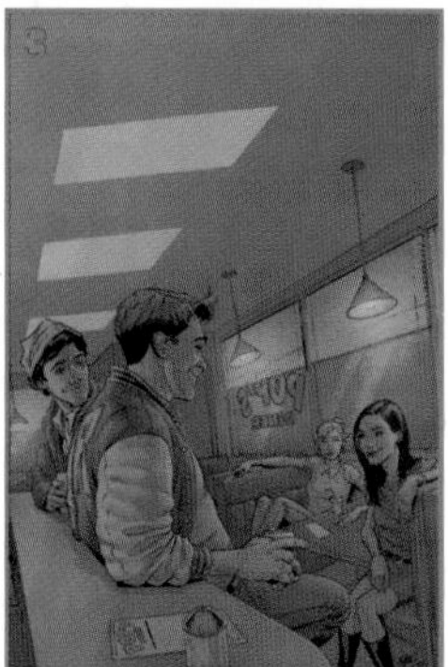

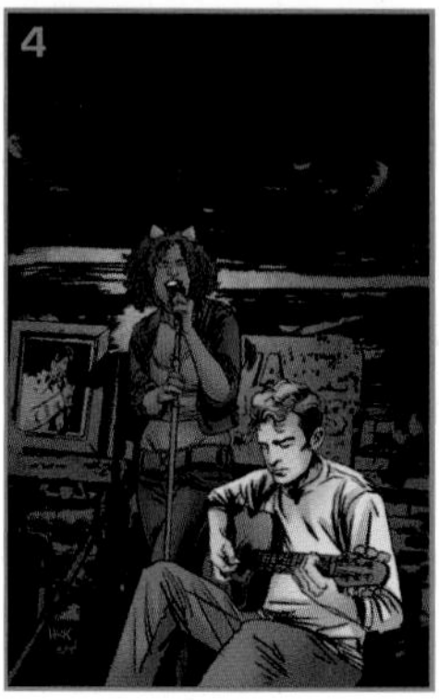

ONE SHOT

1 ALITHA MARTINEZ

2 DEREK CHARM

3 ADAM GORHAM

4 ROBERT HACK

5
SANDRA LANZ

6
MORITAT

7
DAN PARENT

8
THOMAS PITILLI

9
MATTHEW DOW SMITH

10
CORY SMITH

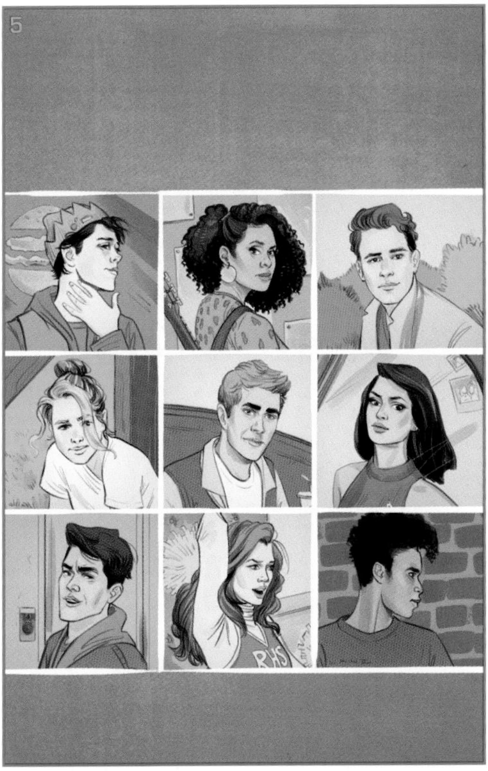
5

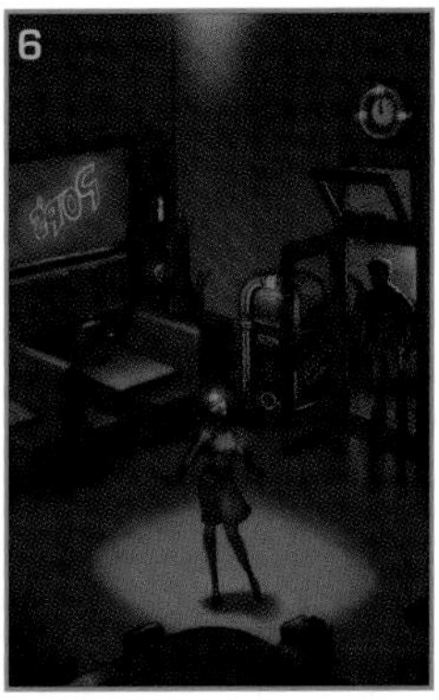
6

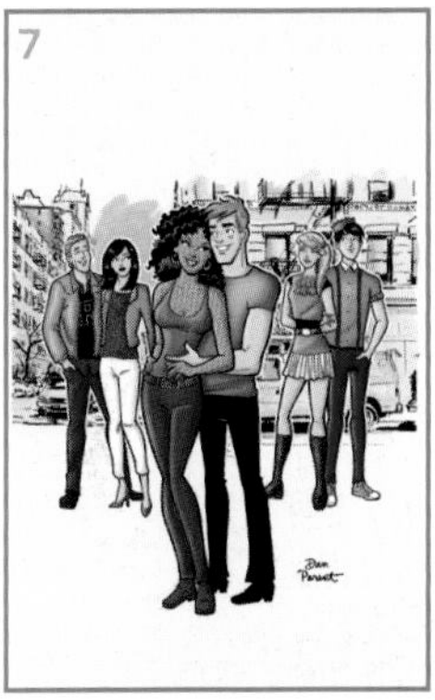
7
Dan Parent

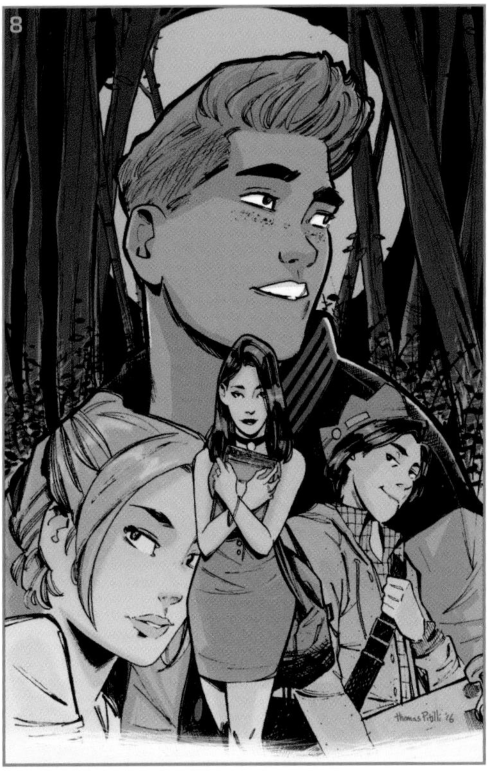
8
thomas Pitilli '16

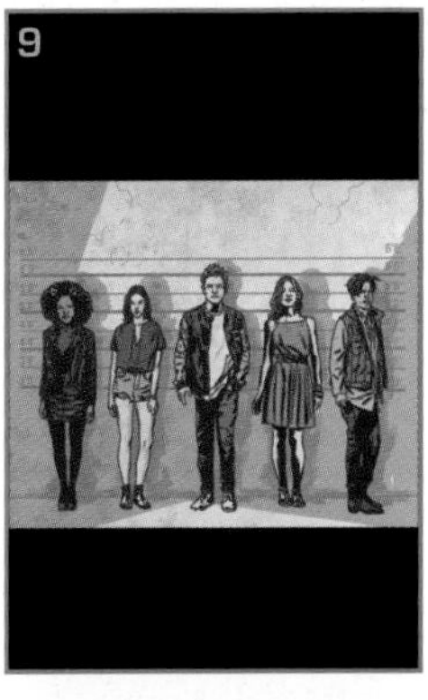
9

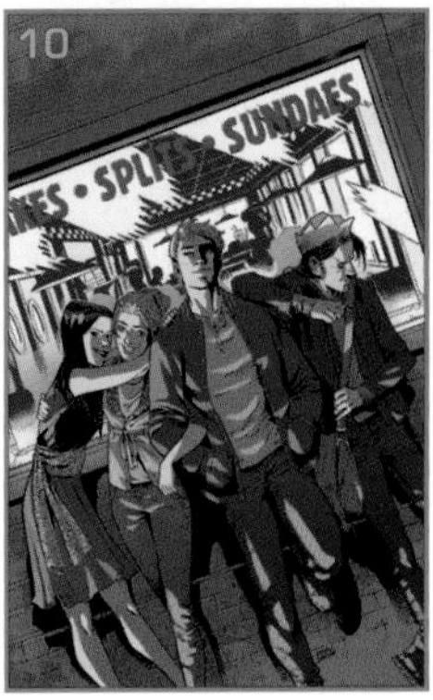
10
SUNDAES

ISSUE ONE

1
FRANCESCO FRANCAVILLA

2
ELLIOT FERNANDEZ

3
PETER KRAUSE

4
ALITHA MARTINEZ

5
DJIBRIL MORISSETTE-PHAN

6
RON SALAS

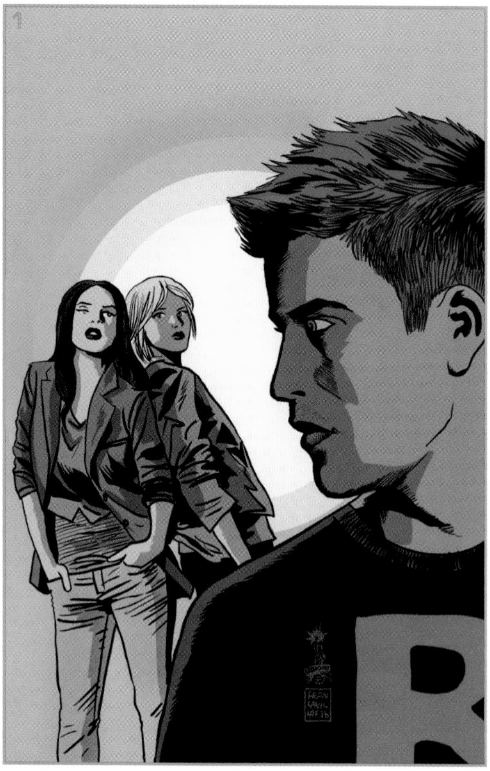

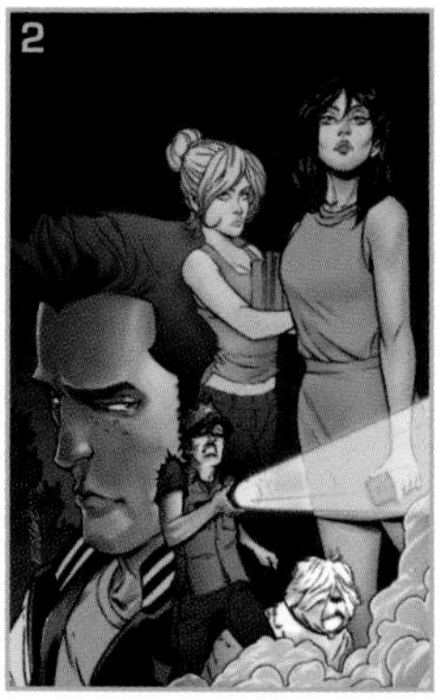

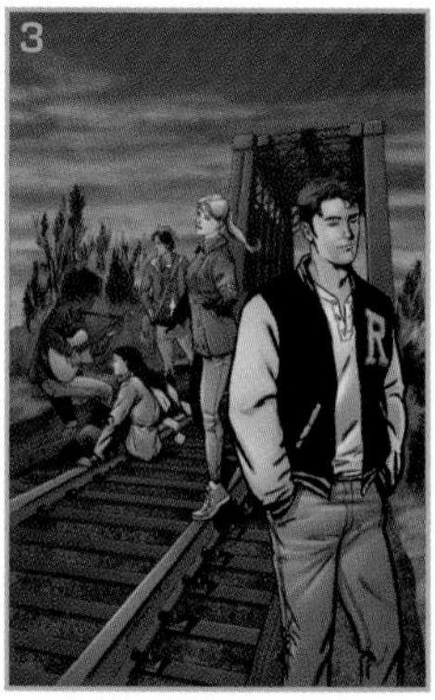

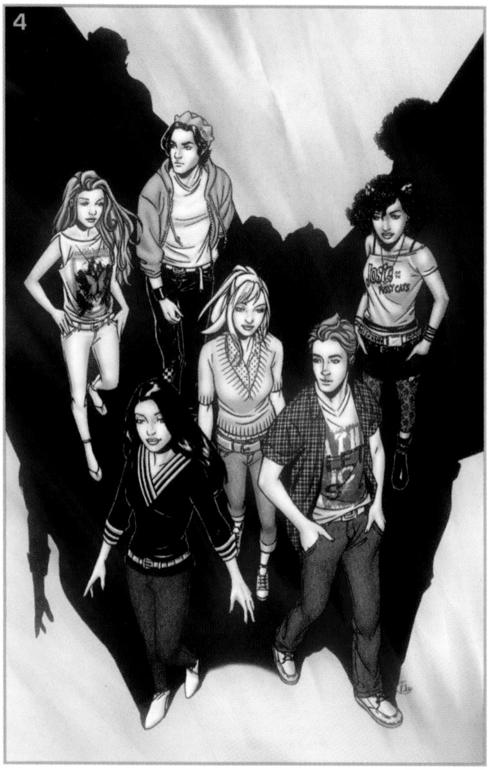

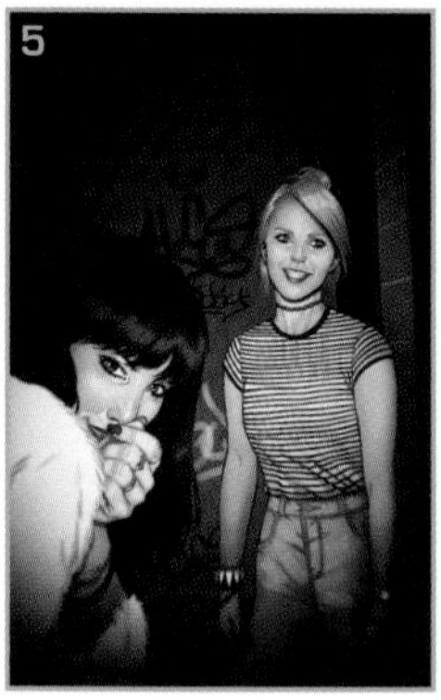

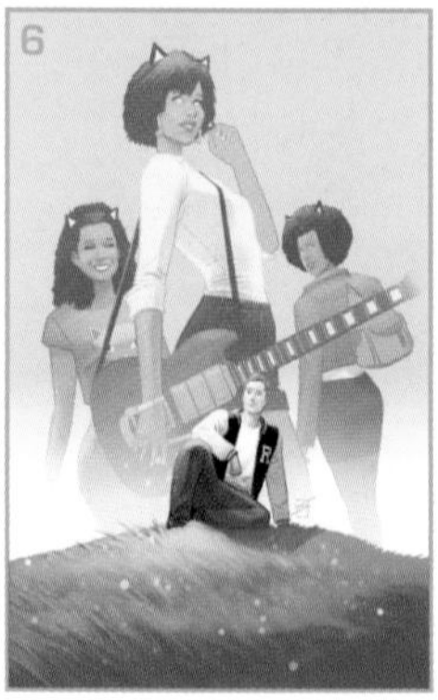

ISSUE TWO

1
FRANCESCO FRANCAVILLA

2
MICHAEL DOONEY

3
MATTHEW SOUTHWORTH

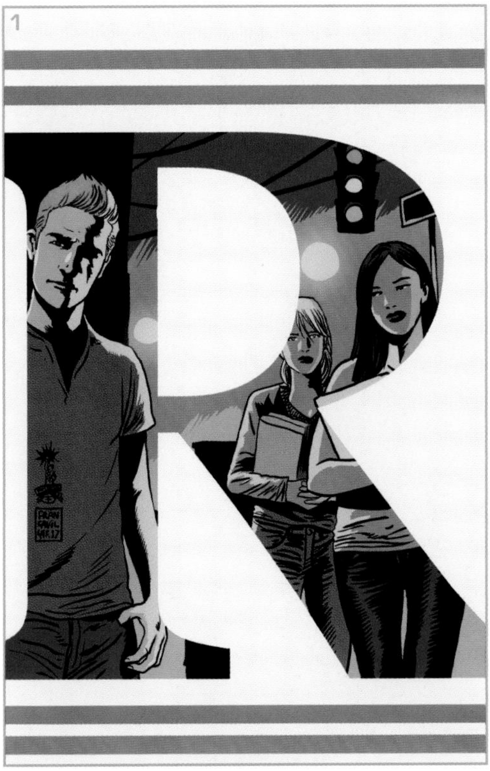

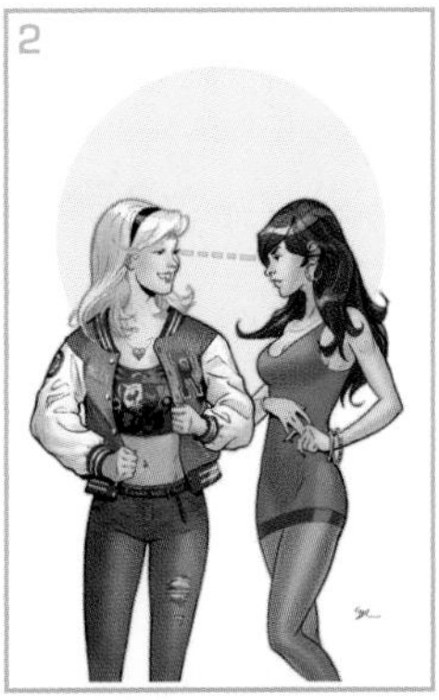

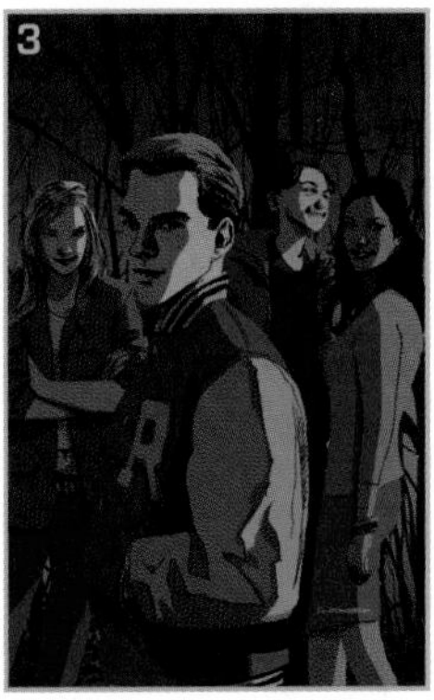

ISSUE THREE

1
FRANCESCO FRANCAVILLA

2
MARGUERITE SAUVAGE

3
WILFREDO TORRES

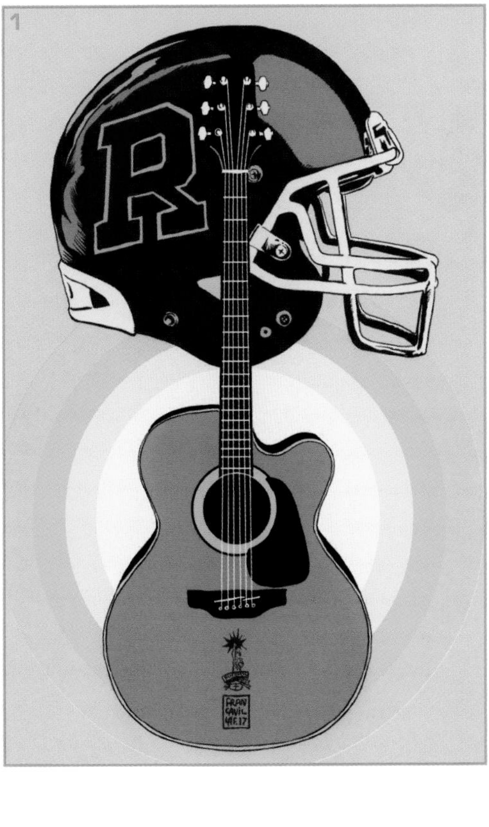

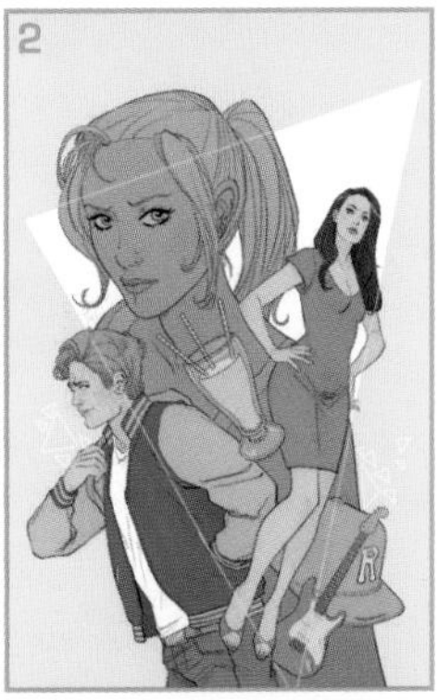

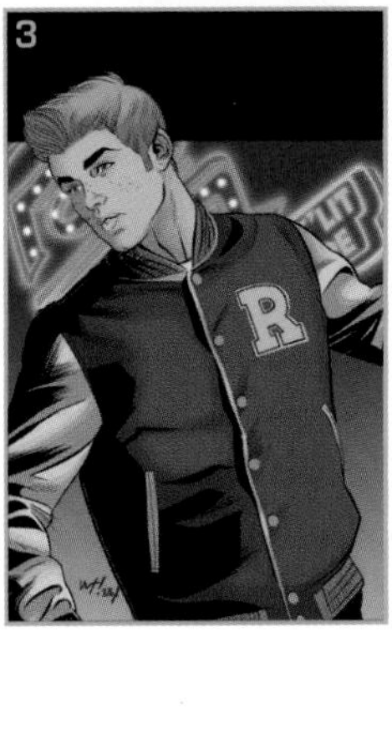

RIVERDALE®

THE EVOLUTION OF ARCHIE COMICS

Archie and his best friends have been around for over 75 years—and as you'd probably expect, they've changed a lot in that time! While each character's style has evolved, and certain aspects of their personalities have developed, the core Archie crew has held true to much of what's made them so notable over the years. From comics to TV, Archie, Betty, Veronica and Jughead have always been recognizable figures with distinct personalities, interests and styles.

Here's a look at the many faces of Archie and the gang.

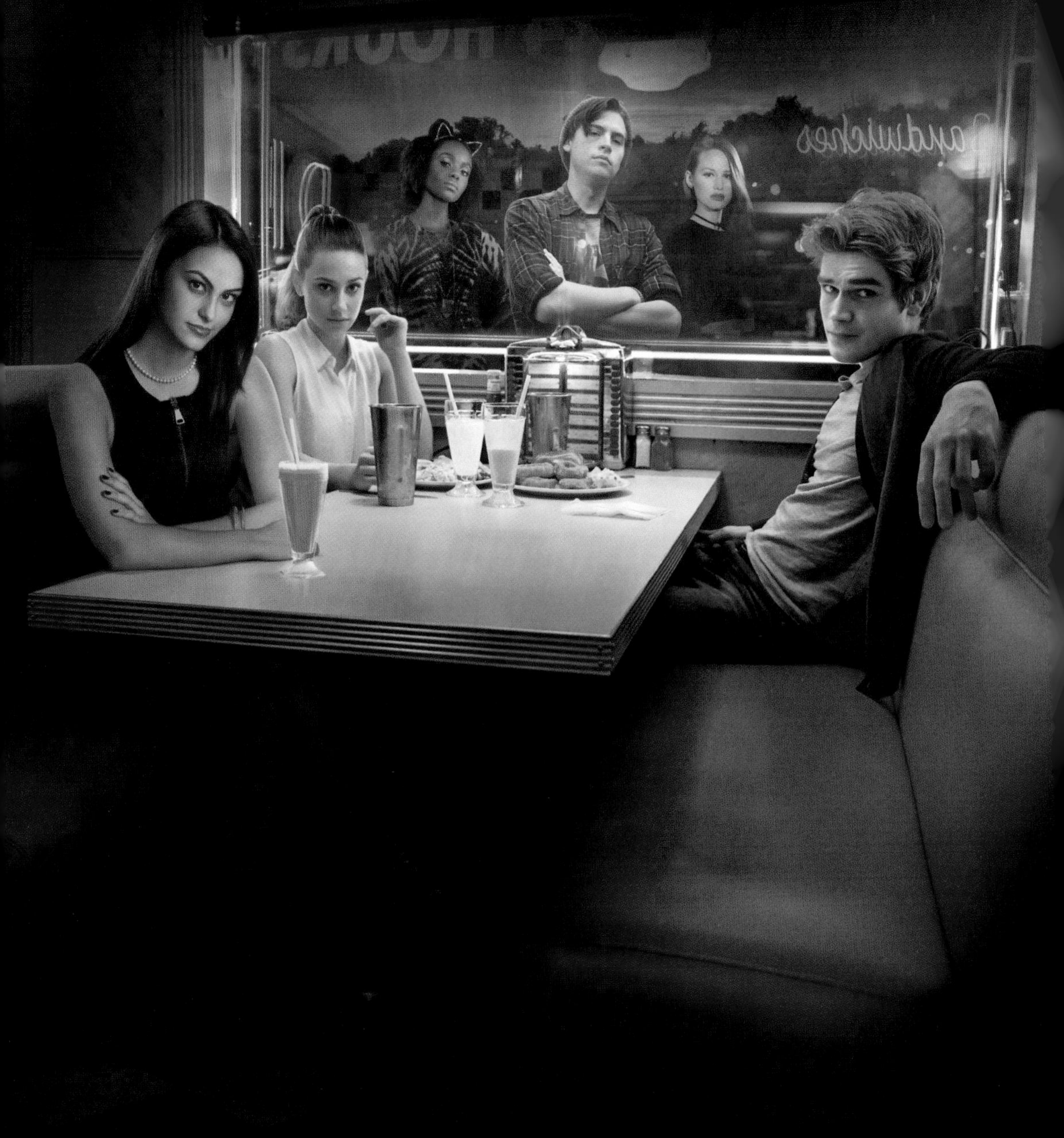

1940s 2017

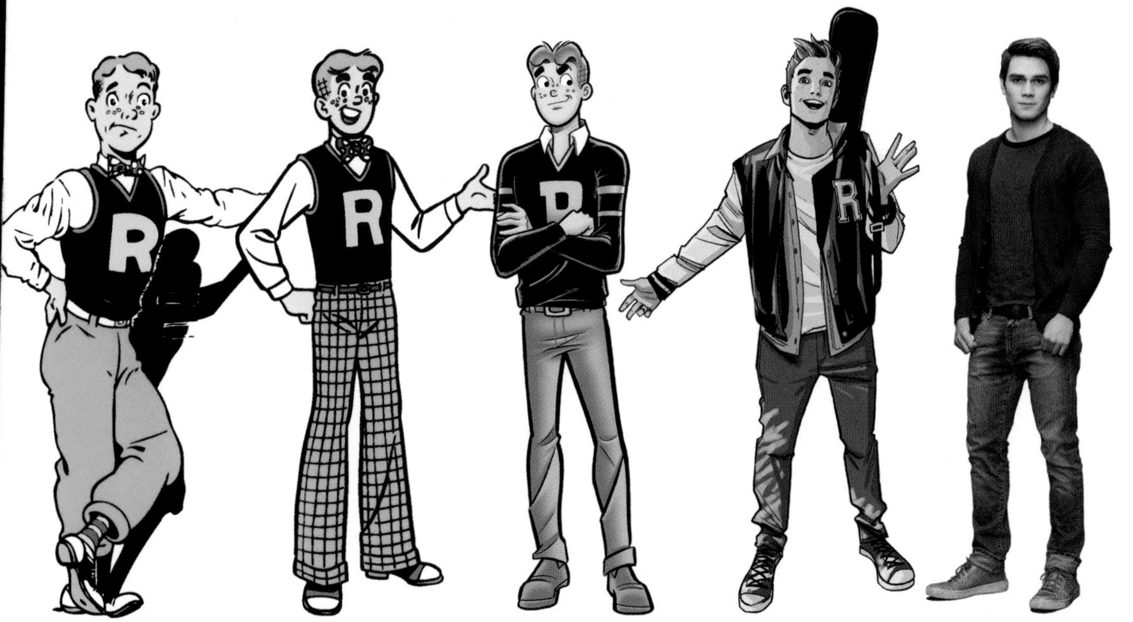

ARCHIE: From goofy-yet-lovable troublemaker to a handsome, thoughtful teen hero, Archie Andrews has always been the star of the show with one of the most recognizable faces and hairstyles in pop culture! Pictured here are the different looks Archie's had since his inception in 1941, leading up to his revamped image courtesy of Fiona Staples and then as a small-screen star portrayed by KJ Apa. As you'll notice, his style has definitely improved!

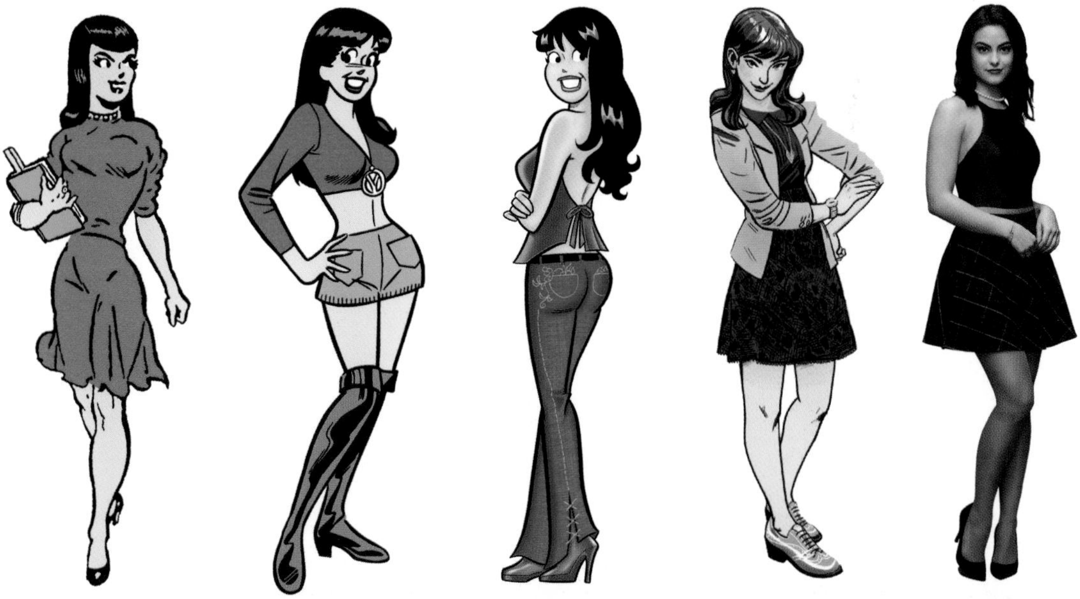

VERONICA: Even from her first appearance in the 1940s, Veronica's always had a stunning, eye-catching look. Despite a few hairstyle changes, there's no mistaking Veronica Lodge. Camila Mendes knocks it out of the park while playing the affluent yet down-to-earth teen!

1940s 2017

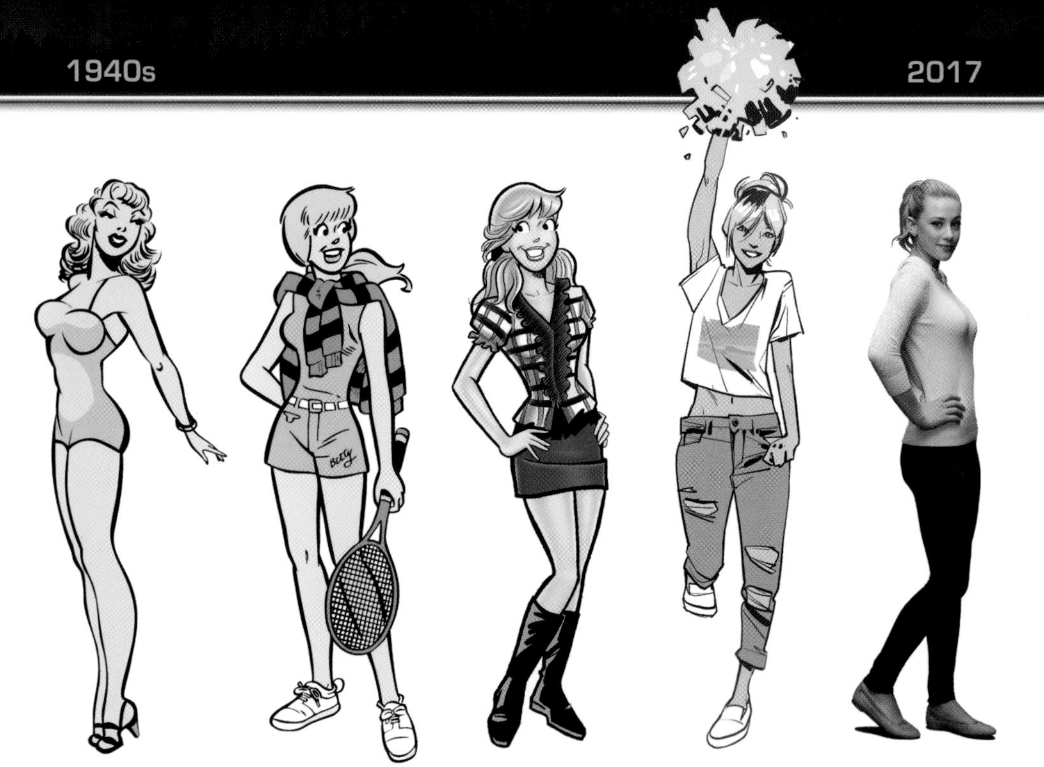
Betty

BETTY: Betty Cooper's look was very sultry when she first appeared in 1941 and throughout the '50s/'60s, but we can still see elements of her shy, sweet nature. Betty's morphed into America's Sweetheart, but with a darker side that only a few people know about—this is expertly portrayed by Lili Reinhart on *Riverdale*!

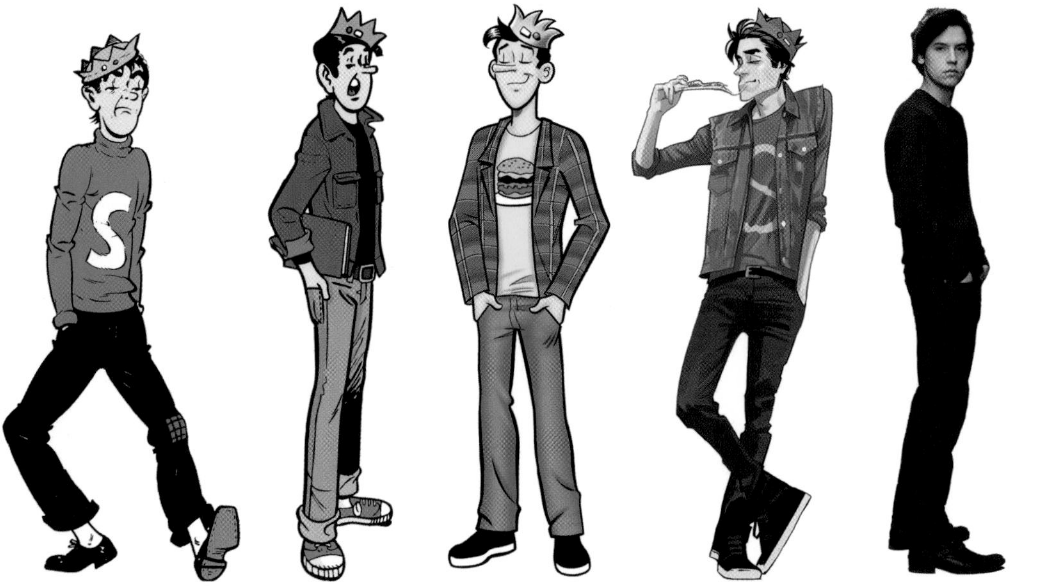

JUGHEAD: No one can deny that if there's any character who's maintained his recognizable look and style since the very beginning, it's Jughead Jones! Never without his bejeweled beanie, Jughead's casual, laid-back look has held strong for 75+ years. Now, Cole Sprouse does an amazing job of not only playing Jughead as aloof but also adding elements of intrigue to his persona!

BONUS ISSUE

ARCHIE®

If you like Riverdale, then you'll love the rest of the new Archie Comics series! From *Archie* to *Jughead* to *Betty and Veronica*, *Josie and the Pussycats* and *Reggie and Me*, the new line of comics keeps on growing. It started with an all-new #1 issue of *Archie* after a 666-issue run spanning over 70 years. The series launched with a bang thanks to this clever and charming story courtesy of legendary comics writer Mark Waid featuring the beautiful and striking art of Fiona Staples. Here's your chance to get a special look at the first issue!

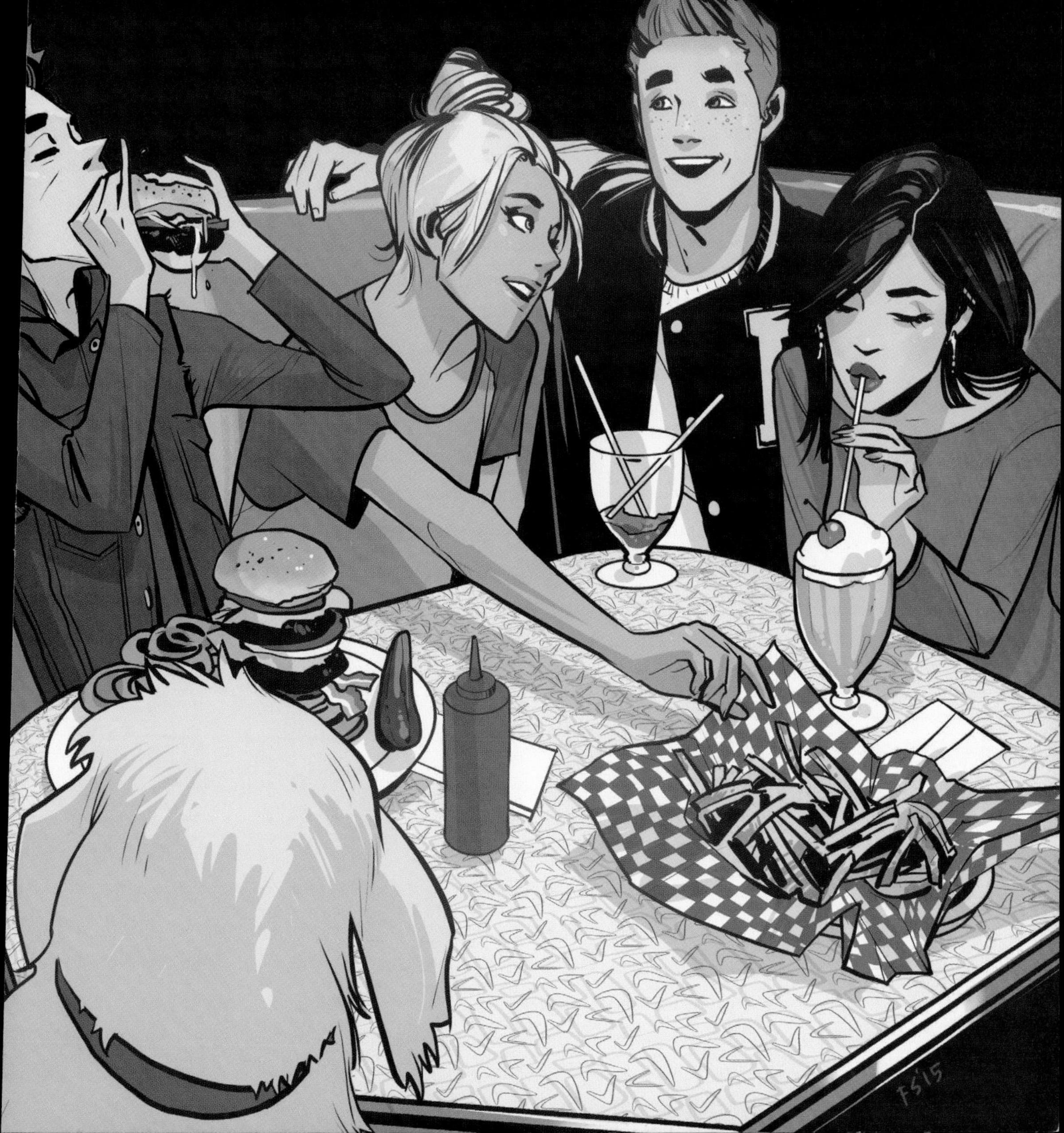

ISSUE ONE

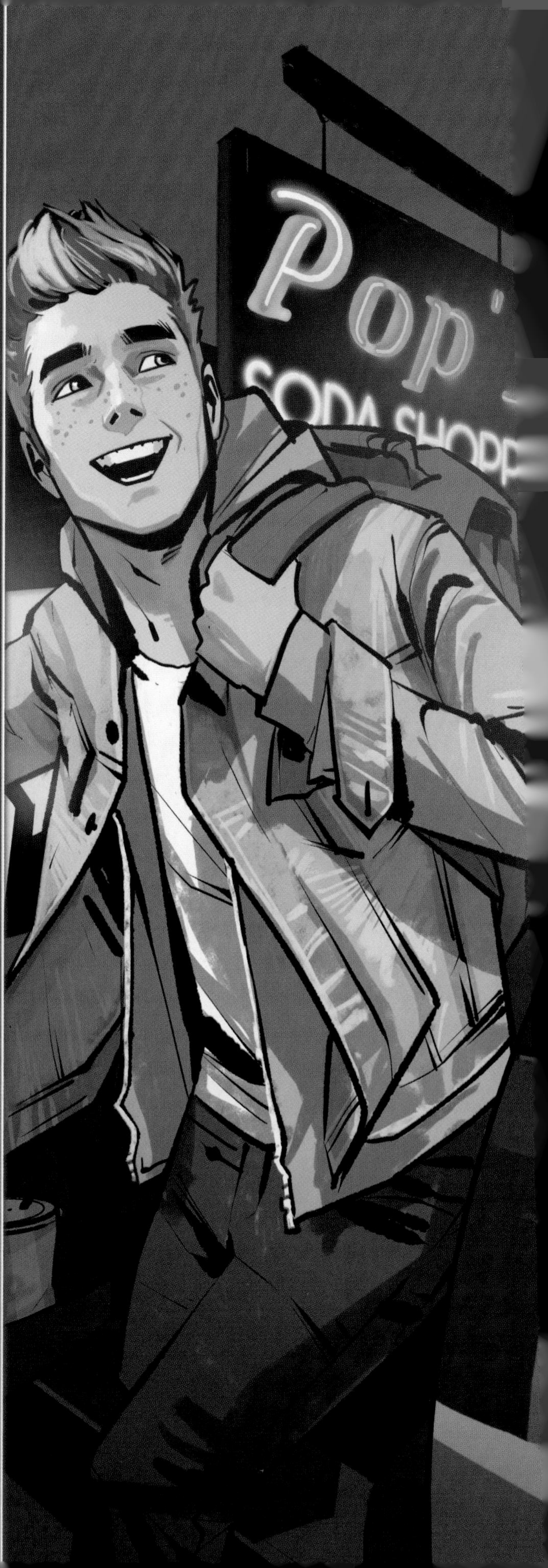
Pop'
SODA SHOPP

WRITER:
MARK WAID

ART:
FIONA STAPLES

COLORS:
ANDRE SZYMANOWICZ WITH **JEN VAUGHN**

LETTERS:
JACK MORELLI

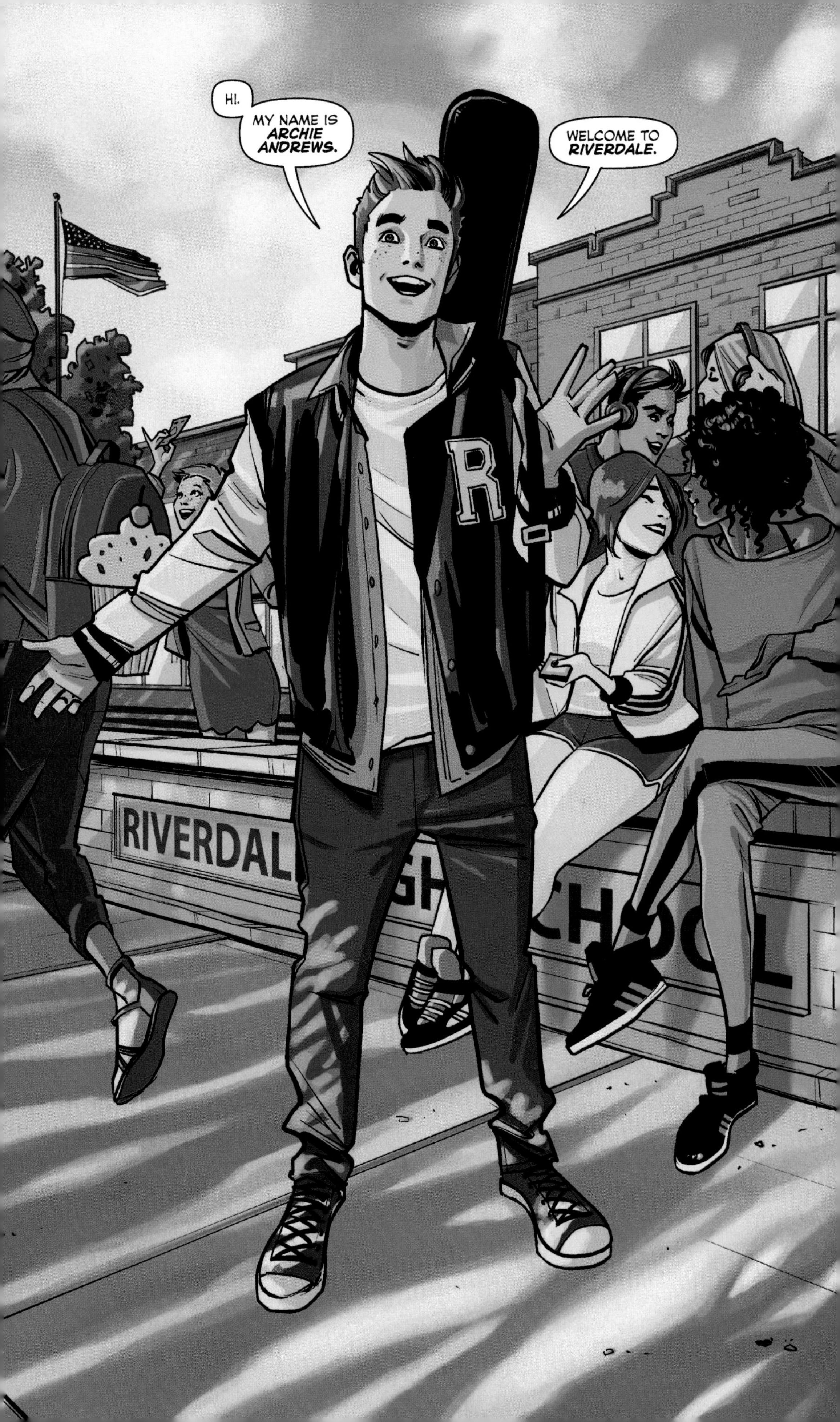
HI.
MY NAME IS ARCHIE ANDREWS.
WELCOME TO RIVERDALE.
RIVERDAL
CHOOL

CHAPTER ONE: There is this Girl

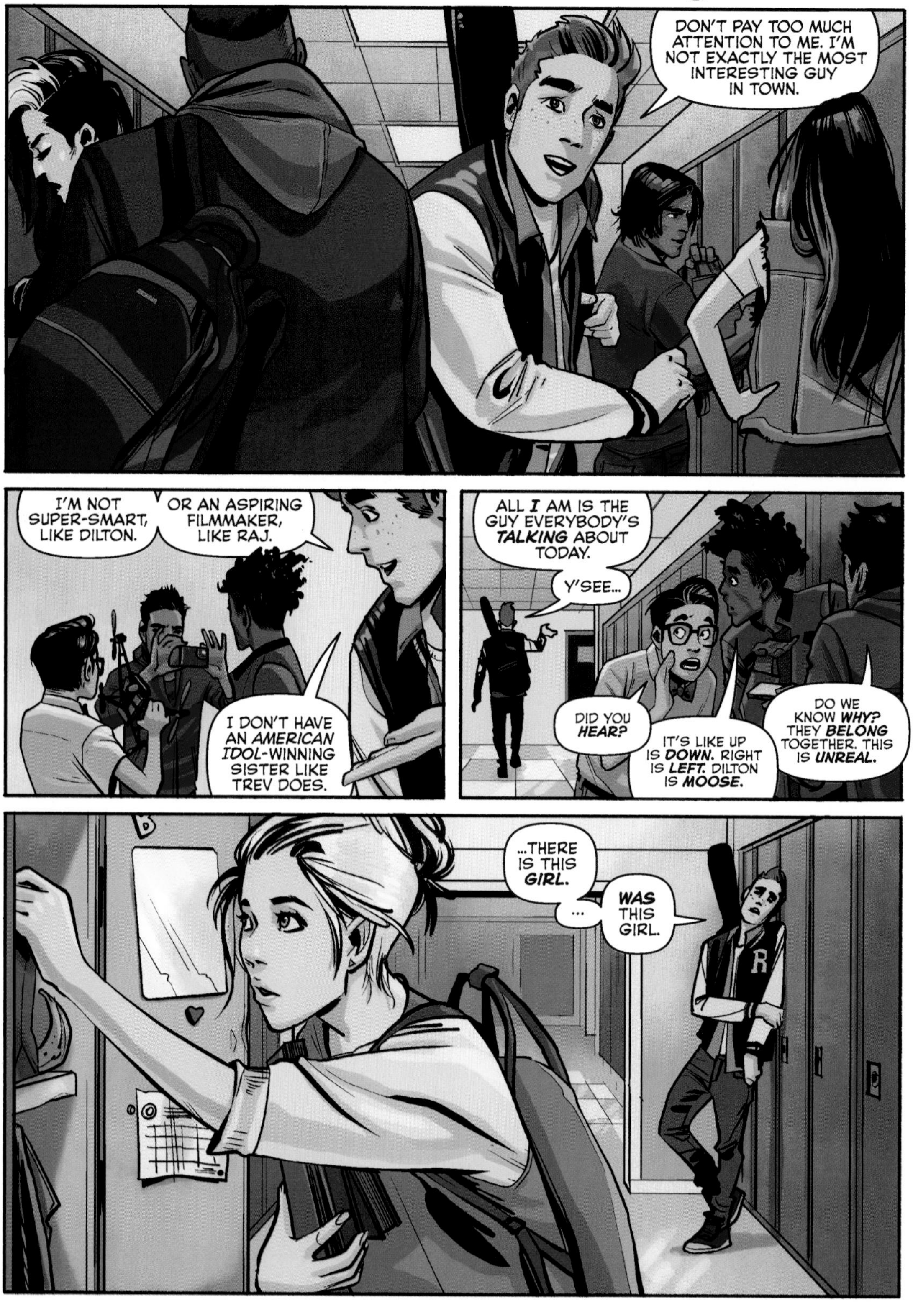

DON'T PAY TOO MUCH ATTENTION TO ME. I'M NOT EXACTLY THE MOST INTERESTING GUY IN TOWN.
I'M NOT SUPER-SMART, LIKE DILTON.
OR AN ASPIRING FILMMAKER, LIKE RAJ.
I DON'T HAVE AN *AMERICAN IDOL*-WINNING SISTER LIKE TREV DOES.
ALL ***I*** AM IS THE GUY EVERYBODY'S ***TALKING*** ABOUT TODAY.
Y'SEE...
DID YOU ***HEAR?***
IT'S LIKE UP IS ***DOWN.*** RIGHT IS ***LEFT.*** DILTON IS ***MOOSE.***
DO WE KNOW ***WHY?*** THEY ***BELONG*** TOGETHER. THIS IS ***UNREAL.***
...THERE IS THIS ***GIRL.***
...
WAS THIS GIRL.

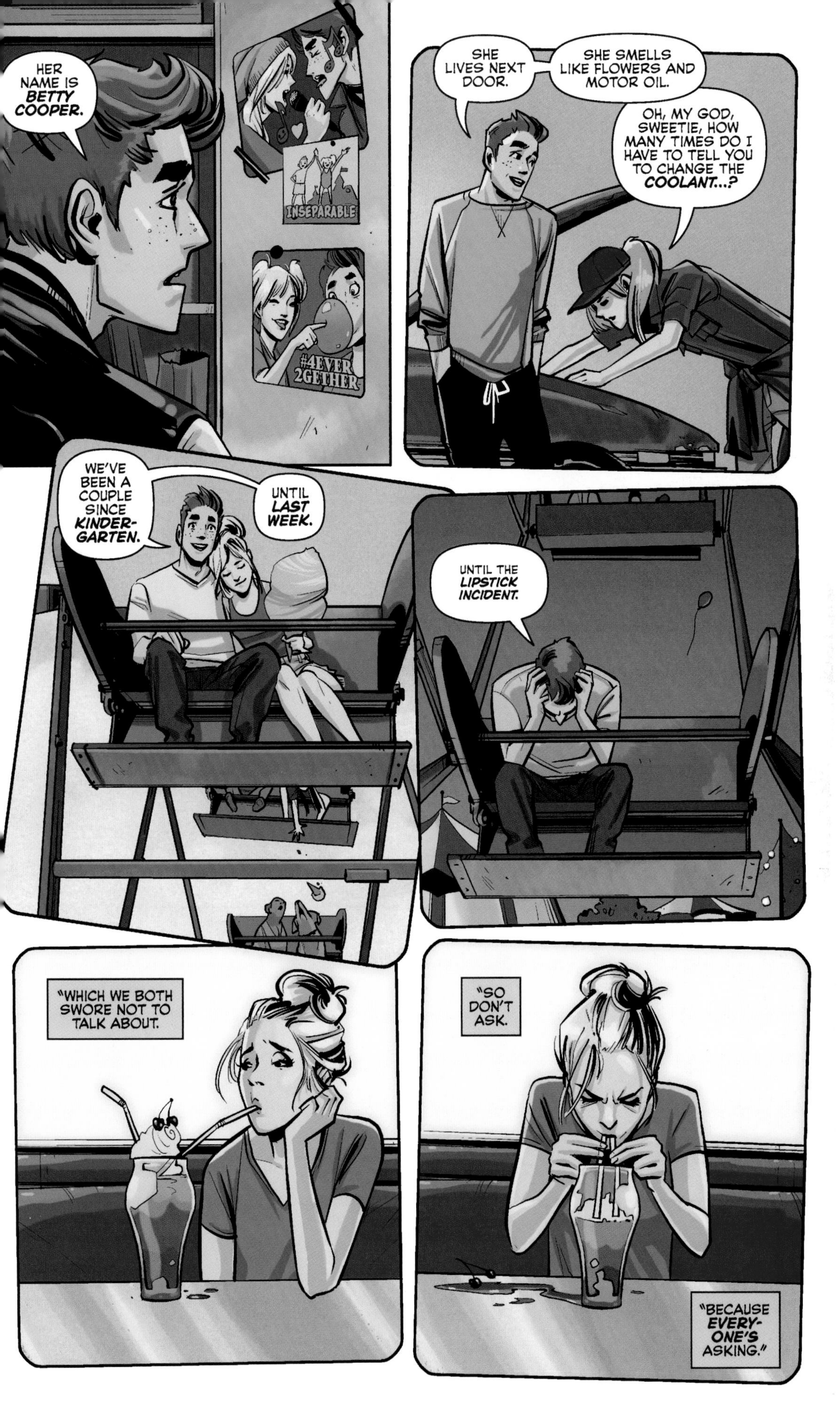
HER NAME IS BETTY COOPER.
INSEPARABLE
#4EVER 2GETHER
SHE LIVES NEXT DOOR.
SHE SMELLS LIKE FLOWERS AND MOTOR OIL.
OH, MY GOD, SWEETIE, HOW MANY TIMES DO I HAVE TO TELL YOU TO CHANGE THE COOLANT...?
WE'VE BEEN A COUPLE SINCE KINDER-GARTEN.
UNTIL LAST WEEK.
UNTIL THE LIPSTICK INCIDENT.
"WHICH WE BOTH SWORE NOT TO TALK ABOUT.
"SO DON'T ASK.
"BECAUSE EVERY-ONE'S ASKING."

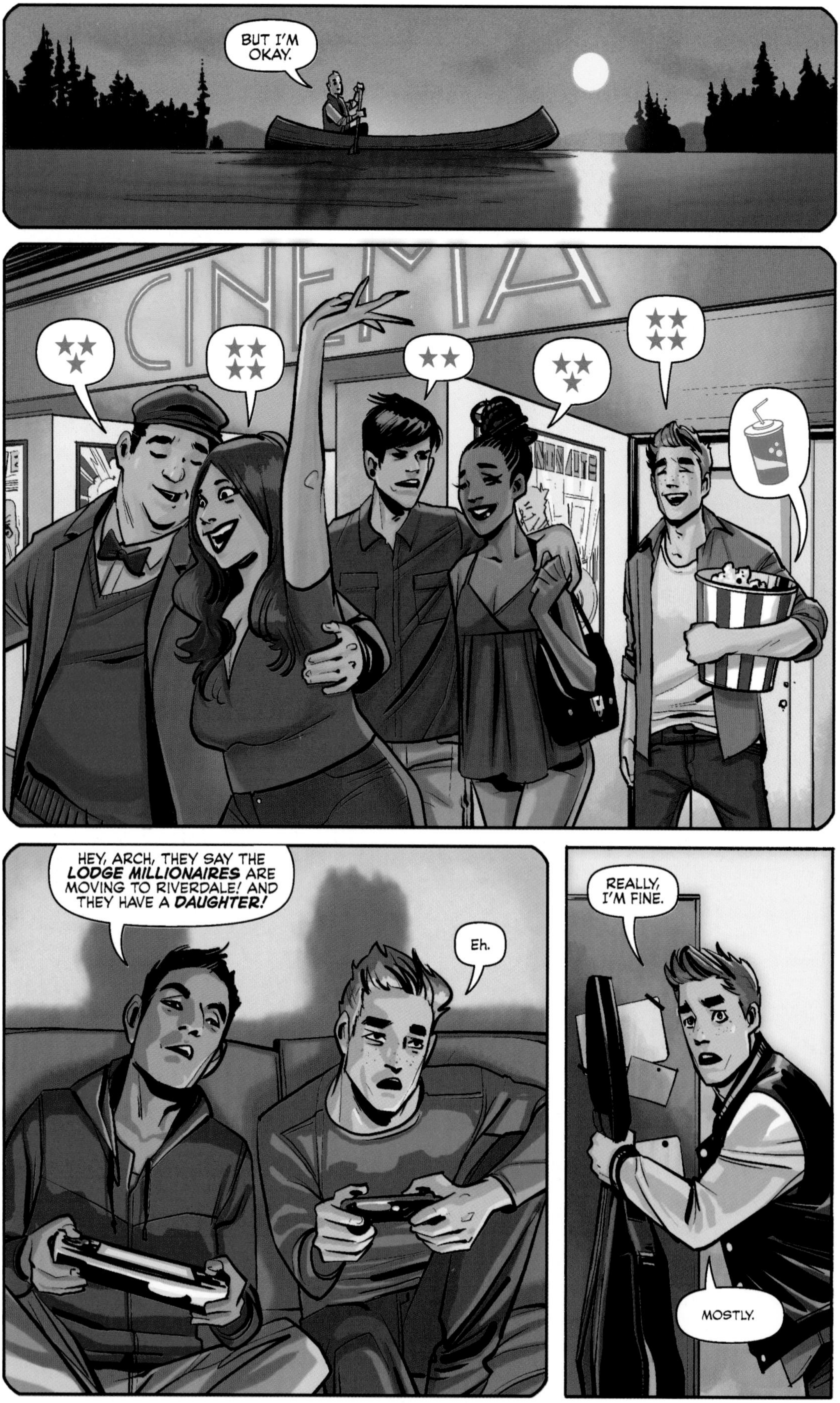
BUT I'M OKAY.
HEY, ARCH, THEY SAY THE **LODGE MILLIONAIRES** ARE MOVING TO RIVERDALE! AND THEY HAVE A **DAUGHTER!**
Eh.
REALLY, I'M FINE.
MOSTLY.

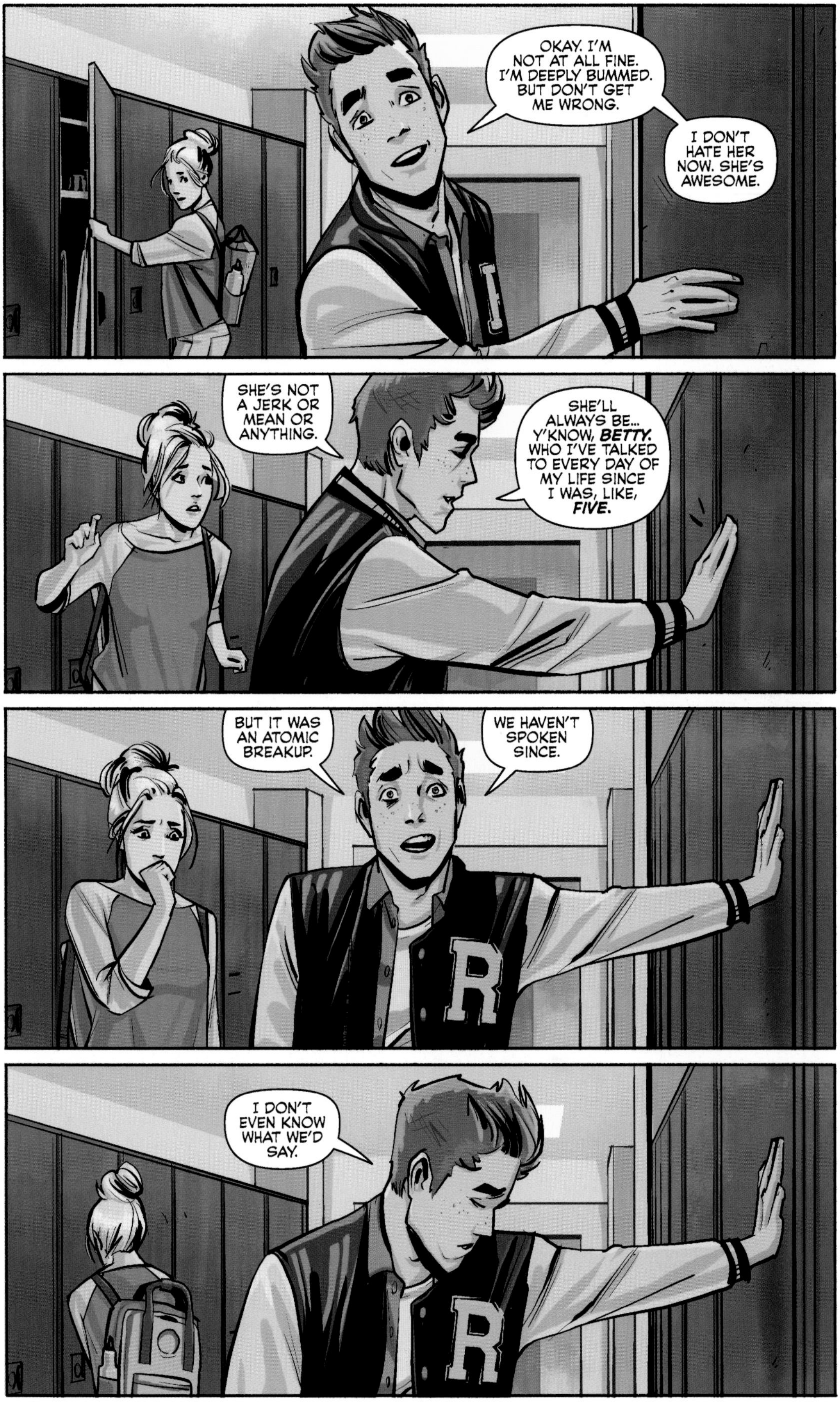
OKAY. I'M NOT AT ALL FINE. I'M DEEPLY BUMMED. BUT DON'T GET ME WRONG.
I DON'T HATE HER NOW. SHE'S AWESOME.
SHE'S NOT A JERK OR MEAN OR ANYTHING.
SHE'LL ALWAYS BE... Y'KNOW, BETTY. WHO I'VE TALKED TO EVERY DAY OF MY LIFE SINCE I WAS, LIKE, FIVE.
BUT IT WAS AN ATOMIC BREAKUP.
WE HAVEN'T SPOKEN SINCE.
I DON'T EVEN KNOW WHAT WE'D SAY.

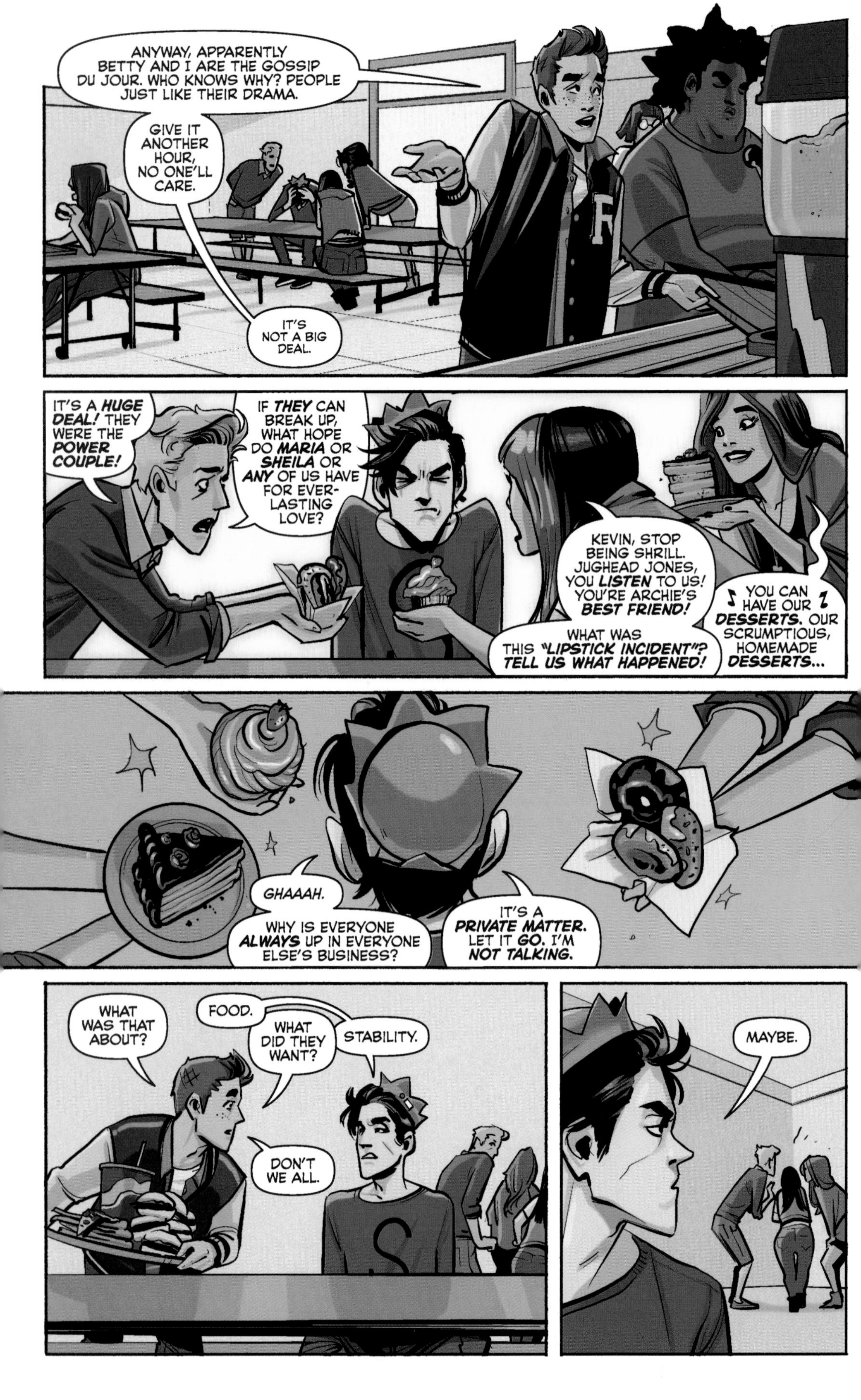
ANYWAY, APPARENTLY BETTY AND I ARE THE GOSSIP DU JOUR. WHO KNOWS WHY? PEOPLE JUST LIKE THEIR DRAMA.
GIVE IT ANOTHER HOUR, NO ONE'LL CARE.
IT'S NOT A BIG DEAL.
IT'S A HUGE DEAL! THEY WERE THE POWER COUPLE!
IF THEY CAN BREAK UP, WHAT HOPE DO MARIA OR SHEILA OR ANY OF US HAVE FOR EVER-LASTING LOVE?
KEVIN, STOP BEING SHRILL. JUGHEAD JONES, YOU LISTEN TO US! YOU'RE ARCHIE'S BEST FRIEND!
WHAT WAS THIS "LIPSTICK INCIDENT"? TELL US WHAT HAPPENED!
YOU CAN HAVE OUR DESSERTS. OUR SCRUMPTIOUS, HOMEMADE DESSERTS...
GHAAAH.
WHY IS EVERYONE ALWAYS UP IN EVERYONE ELSE'S BUSINESS?
IT'S A PRIVATE MATTER. LET IT GO. I'M NOT TALKING.
WHAT WAS THAT ABOUT?
FOOD.
WHAT DID THEY WANT?
STABILITY.
DON'T WE ALL.
MAYBE.

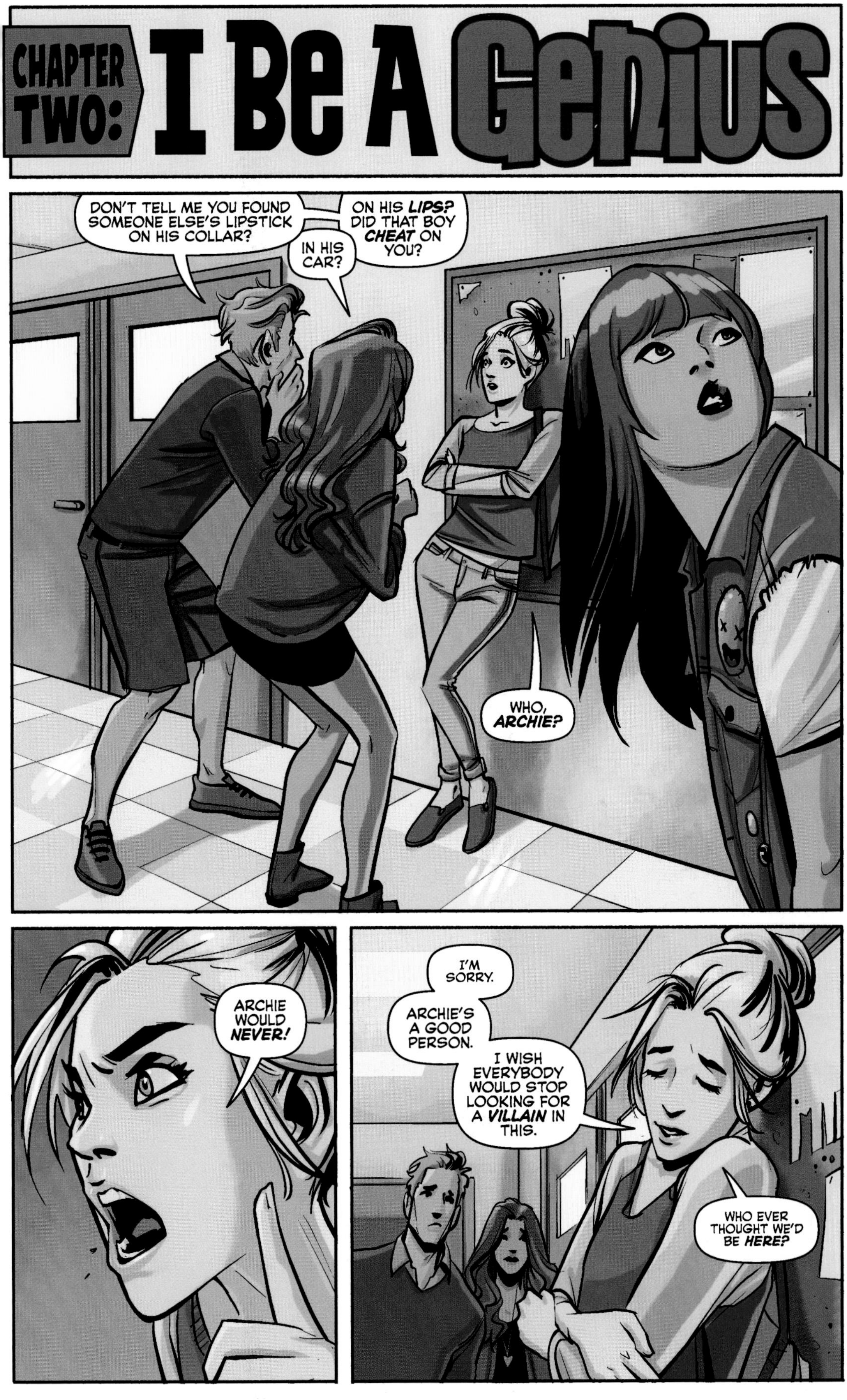
CHAPTER TWO: I Be A Genius
DON'T TELL ME YOU FOUND SOMEONE ELSE'S LIPSTICK ON HIS COLLAR?
IN HIS CAR?
ON HIS *LIPS?* DID THAT BOY *CHEAT* ON YOU?
WHO, *ARCHIE?*
ARCHIE WOULD *NEVER!*
I'M SORRY.
ARCHIE'S A GOOD PERSON.
I WISH EVERYBODY WOULD STOP LOOKING FOR A *VILLAIN* IN THIS.
WHO EVER THOUGHT WE'D BE *HERE?*

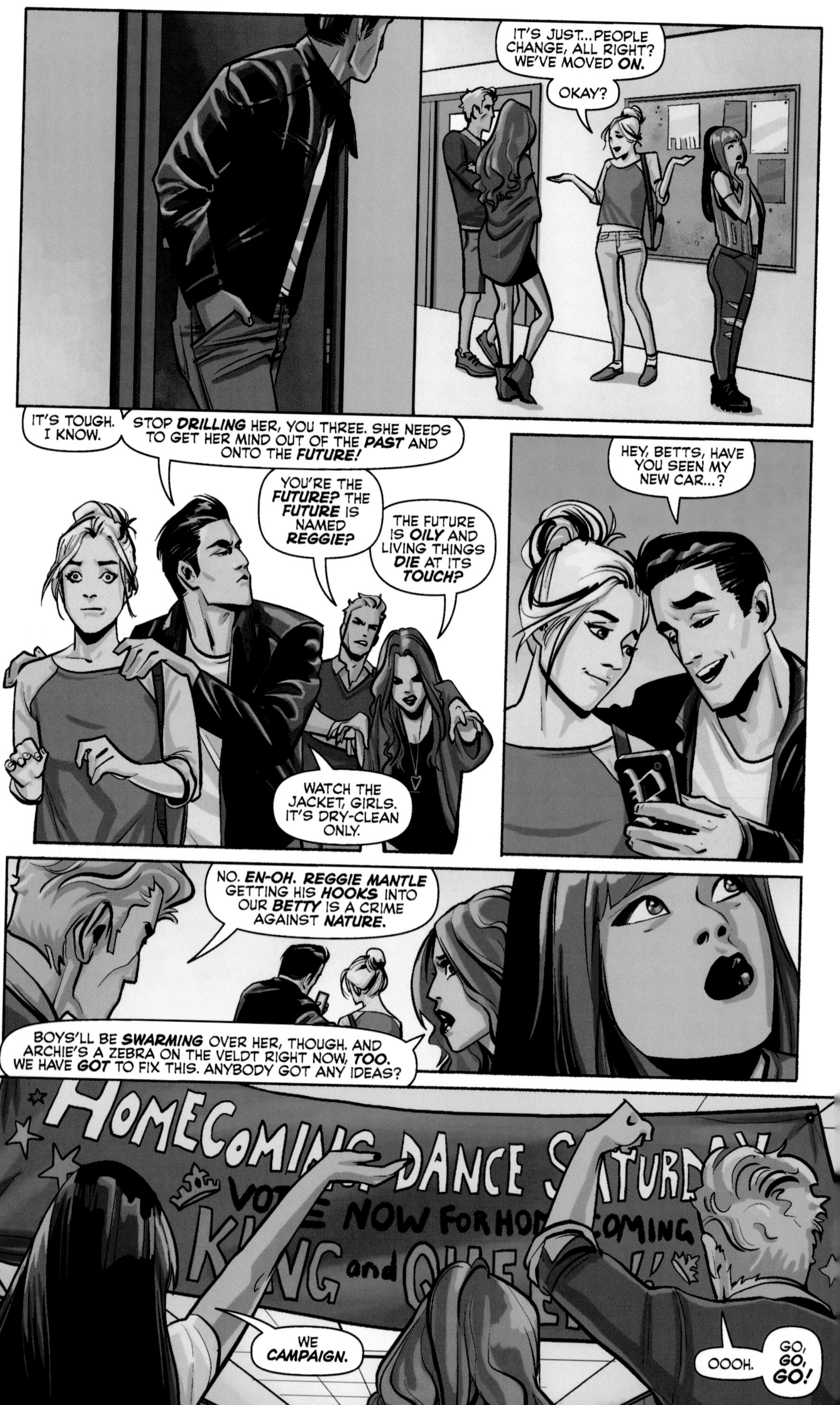
IT'S JUST...PEOPLE CHANGE, ALL RIGHT? WE'VE MOVED ON.
OKAY?
IT'S TOUGH. I KNOW.
STOP DRILLING HER, YOU THREE. SHE NEEDS TO GET HER MIND OUT OF THE PAST AND ONTO THE FUTURE!
YOU'RE THE FUTURE? THE FUTURE IS NAMED REGGIE?
THE FUTURE IS OILY AND LIVING THINGS DIE AT ITS TOUCH?
WATCH THE JACKET, GIRLS. IT'S DRY-CLEAN ONLY.
HEY, BETTS, HAVE YOU SEEN MY NEW CAR...?
NO. EN-OH. REGGIE MANTLE GETTING HIS HOOKS INTO OUR BETTY IS A CRIME AGAINST NATURE.
BOYS'LL BE SWARMING OVER HER, THOUGH. AND ARCHIE'S A ZEBRA ON THE VELDT RIGHT NOW, TOO. WE HAVE GOT TO FIX THIS. ANYBODY GOT ANY IDEAS?
HOMECOMING DANCE SATURDAY
NOW FOR HOMECOMING
WE CAMPAIGN.
OOOH.
GO, GO, GO!

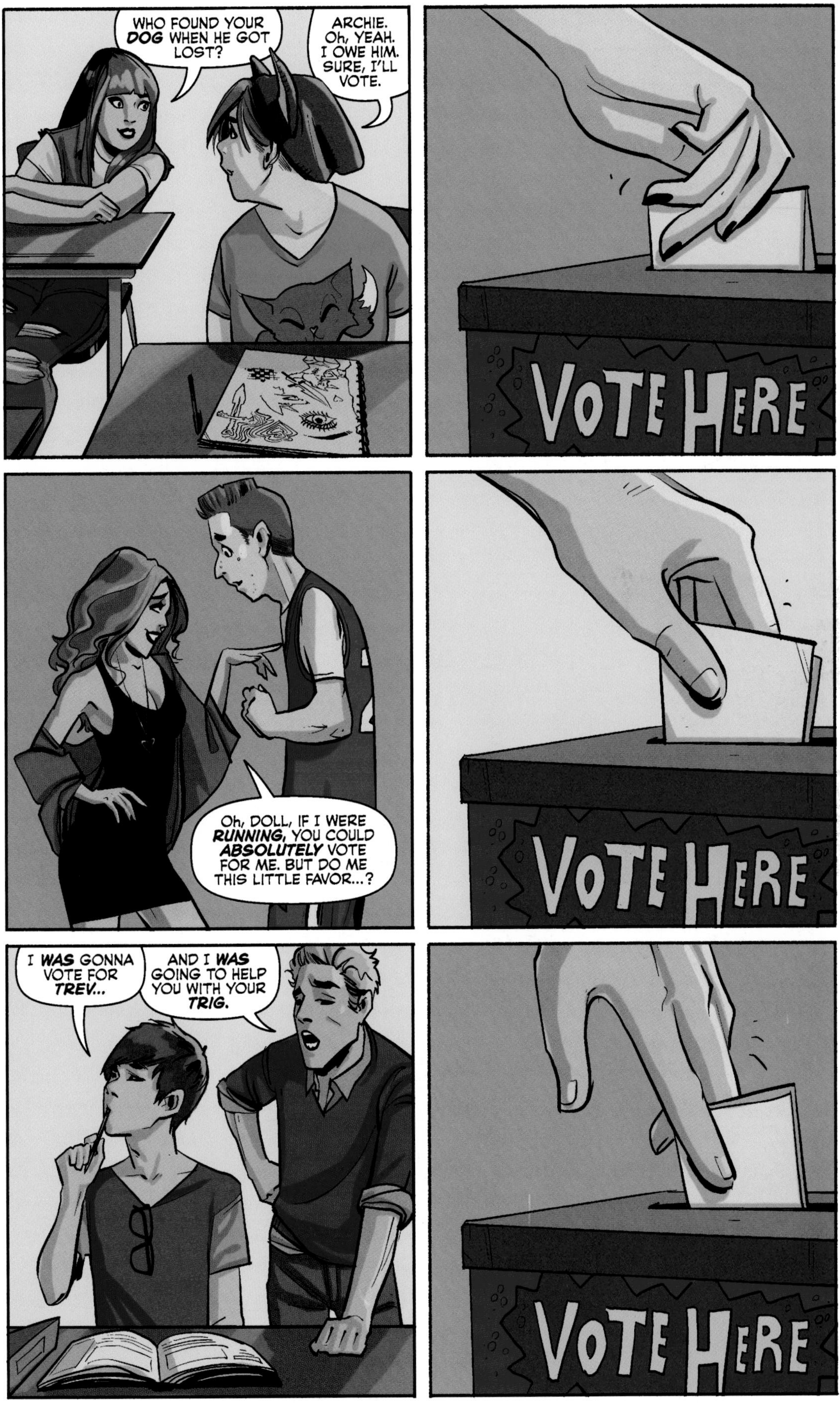

WHO FOUND YOUR DOG WHEN HE GOT LOST?
ARCHIE. Oh, YEAH. I OWE HIM. SURE, I'LL VOTE.
VOTE HERE
Oh, DOLL, IF I WERE RUNNING, YOU COULD ABSOLUTELY VOTE FOR ME. BUT DO ME THIS LITTLE FAVOR...?
VOTE HERE
I WAS GONNA VOTE FOR TREV...
AND I WAS GOING TO HELP YOU WITH YOUR TRIG.
VOTE HERE

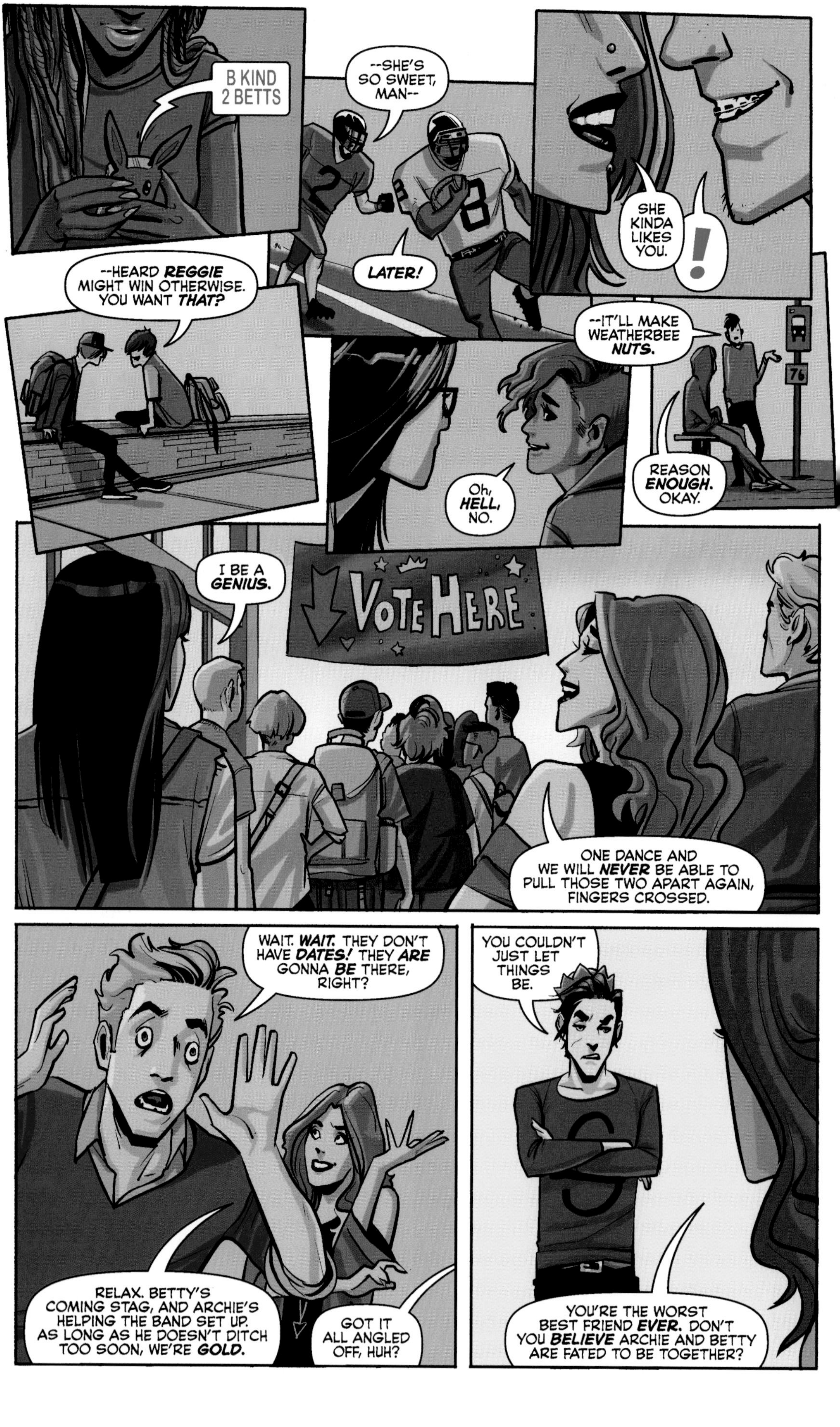
B KIND 2 BETTS
--SHE'S SO SWEET, MAN--
LATER!
SHE KINDA LIKES YOU.
!
--HEARD **REGGIE** MIGHT WIN OTHERWISE. YOU WANT **THAT?**
Oh, **HELL,** NO.
--IT'LL MAKE WEATHERBEE **NUTS.**
REASON **ENOUGH.** OKAY.
76
I BE A **GENIUS.**
VOTE HERE
ONE DANCE AND WE WILL **NEVER** BE ABLE TO PULL THOSE TWO APART AGAIN, FINGERS CROSSED.
WAIT. **WAIT.** THEY DON'T HAVE **DATES!** THEY **ARE** GONNA **BE** THERE, RIGHT?
RELAX. BETTY'S COMING STAG, AND ARCHIE'S HELPING THE BAND SET UP. AS LONG AS HE DOESN'T DITCH TOO SOON, WE'RE **GOLD.**
GOT IT ALL ANGLED OFF, HUH?
YOU COULDN'T JUST LET THINGS BE.
YOU'RE THE WORST BEST FRIEND **EVER.** DON'T YOU **BELIEVE** ARCHIE AND BETTY ARE FATED TO BE TOGETHER?

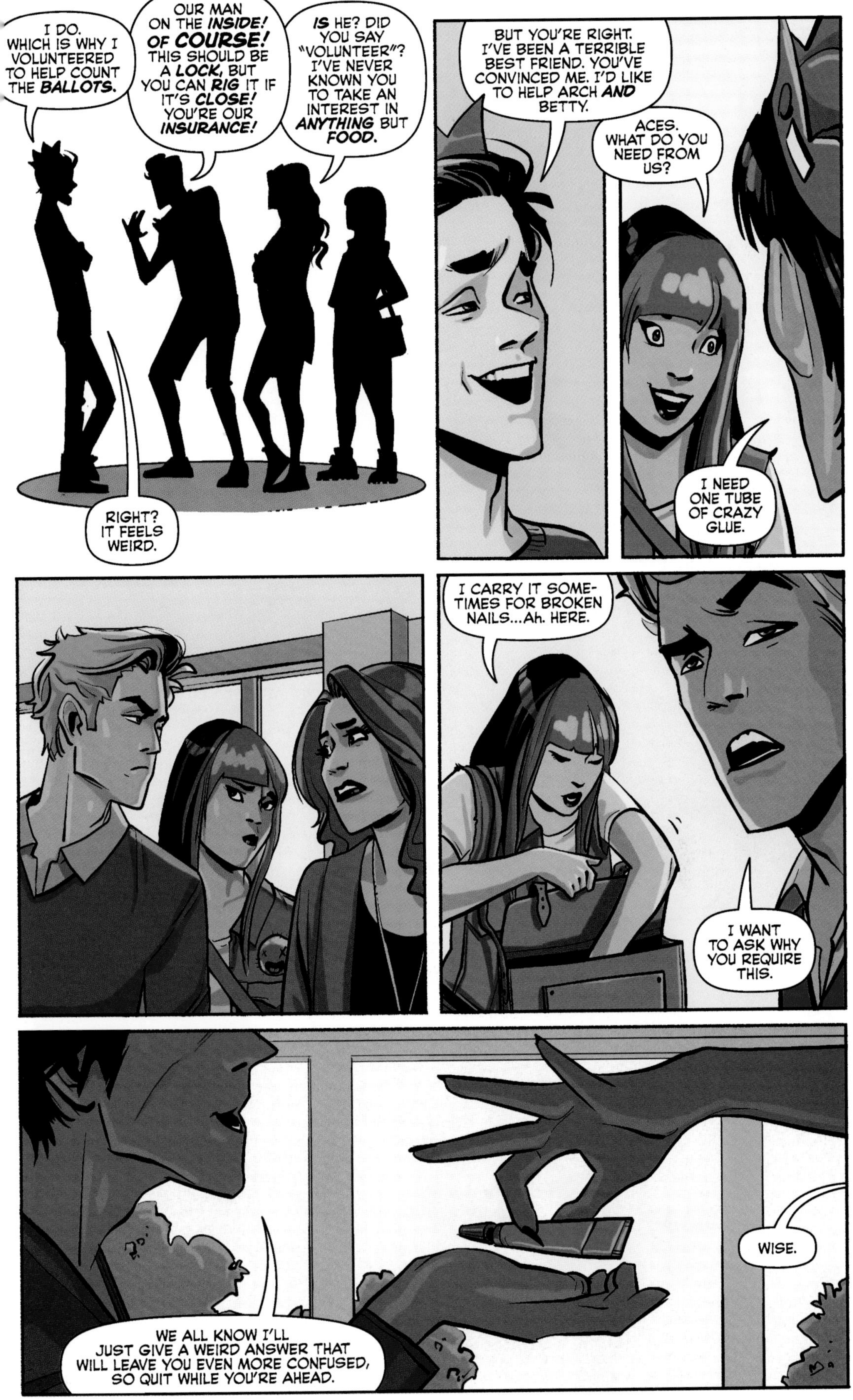
I DO. WHICH IS WHY I VOLUNTEERED TO HELP COUNT THE BALLOTS.
OUR MAN ON THE INSIDE! OF COURSE! THIS SHOULD BE A LOCK, BUT YOU CAN RIG IT IF IT'S CLOSE! YOU'RE OUR INSURANCE!
IS HE? DID YOU SAY "VOLUNTEER"? I'VE NEVER KNOWN YOU TO TAKE AN INTEREST IN ANYTHING BUT FOOD.
RIGHT? IT FEELS WEIRD.
BUT YOU'RE RIGHT. I'VE BEEN A TERRIBLE BEST FRIEND. YOU'VE CONVINCED ME. I'D LIKE TO HELP ARCH AND BETTY.
ACES. WHAT DO YOU NEED FROM US?
I NEED ONE TUBE OF CRAZY GLUE.
I CARRY IT SOMETIMES FOR BROKEN NAILS...Ah. HERE.
I WANT TO ASK WHY YOU REQUIRE THIS.
WE ALL KNOW I'LL JUST GIVE A WEIRD ANSWER THAT WILL LEAVE YOU EVEN MORE CONFUSED, SO QUIT WHILE YOU'RE AHEAD.
WISE.

CHAPTER THREE:

THAT'S MY DAD.

HE TAUGHT ME EVERYTHING I KNOW ABOUT HIS THREE PASSIONS: HOME REPAIR, BOWLING, AND THE GUITAR.

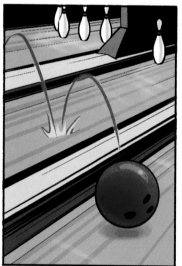

THANK GOD THAT ONE STUCK, OR WE'D HAVE *NOTHING* IN COMMON.

HEY, *ANGUS YOUNG*, HAND OVER THE AXE.

ARE YOU PLAYING TONIGHT? IN *PUBLIC*, FINALLY? CAN I COME?

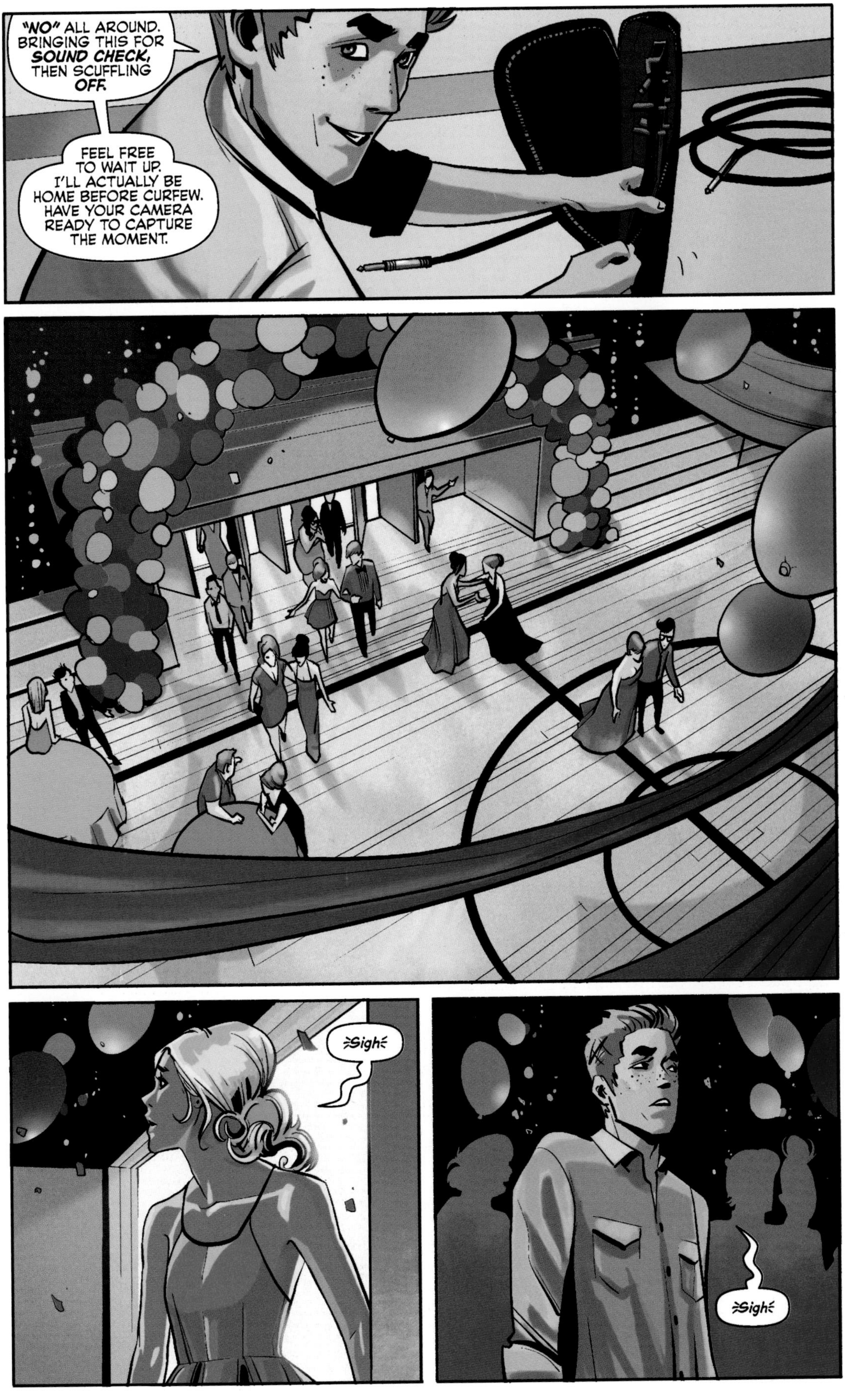
"NO" ALL AROUND. BRINGING THIS FOR SOUND CHECK, THEN SCUFFLING OFF.
FEEL FREE TO WAIT UP. I'LL ACTUALLY BE HOME BEFORE CURFEW. HAVE YOUR CAMERA READY TO CAPTURE THE MOMENT.
Sigh
Sigh

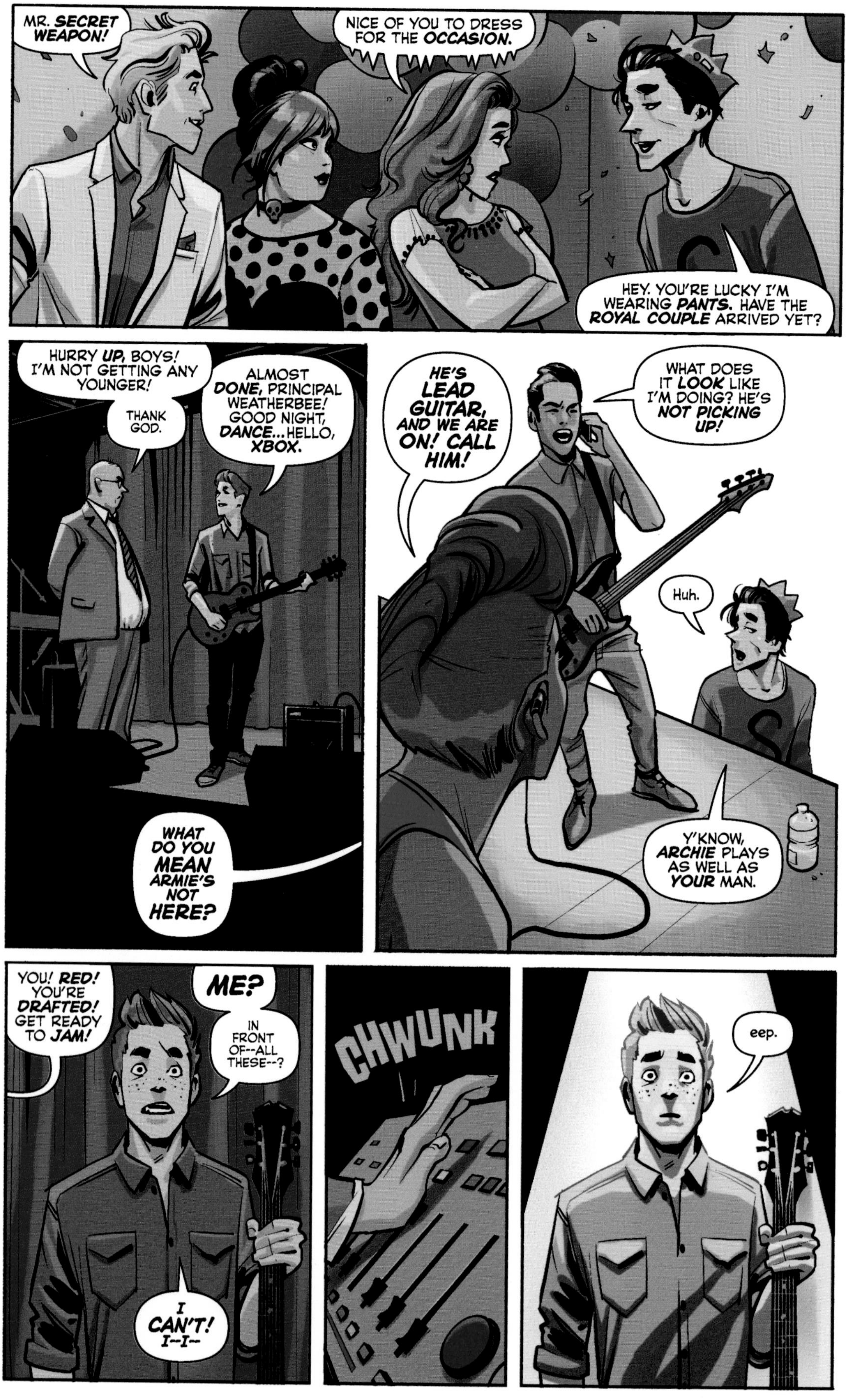
MR. SECRET WEAPON!
NICE OF YOU TO DRESS FOR THE OCCASION.
HEY. YOU'RE LUCKY I'M WEARING PANTS. HAVE THE ROYAL COUPLE ARRIVED YET?
HURRY UP, BOYS! I'M NOT GETTING ANY YOUNGER!
THANK GOD.
ALMOST DONE, PRINCIPAL WEATHERBEE! GOOD NIGHT, DANCE...HELLO, XBOX.
WHAT DO YOU MEAN ARMIE'S NOT HERE?
HE'S LEAD GUITAR, AND WE ARE ON! CALL HIM!
WHAT DOES IT LOOK LIKE I'M DOING? HE'S NOT PICKING UP!
Huh.
Y'KNOW, ARCHIE PLAYS AS WELL AS YOUR MAN.
YOU! RED! YOU'RE DRAFTED! GET READY TO JAM!
ME?
IN FRONT OF--ALL THESE--?
I CAN'T! I--I--
CHWUNK
eep.

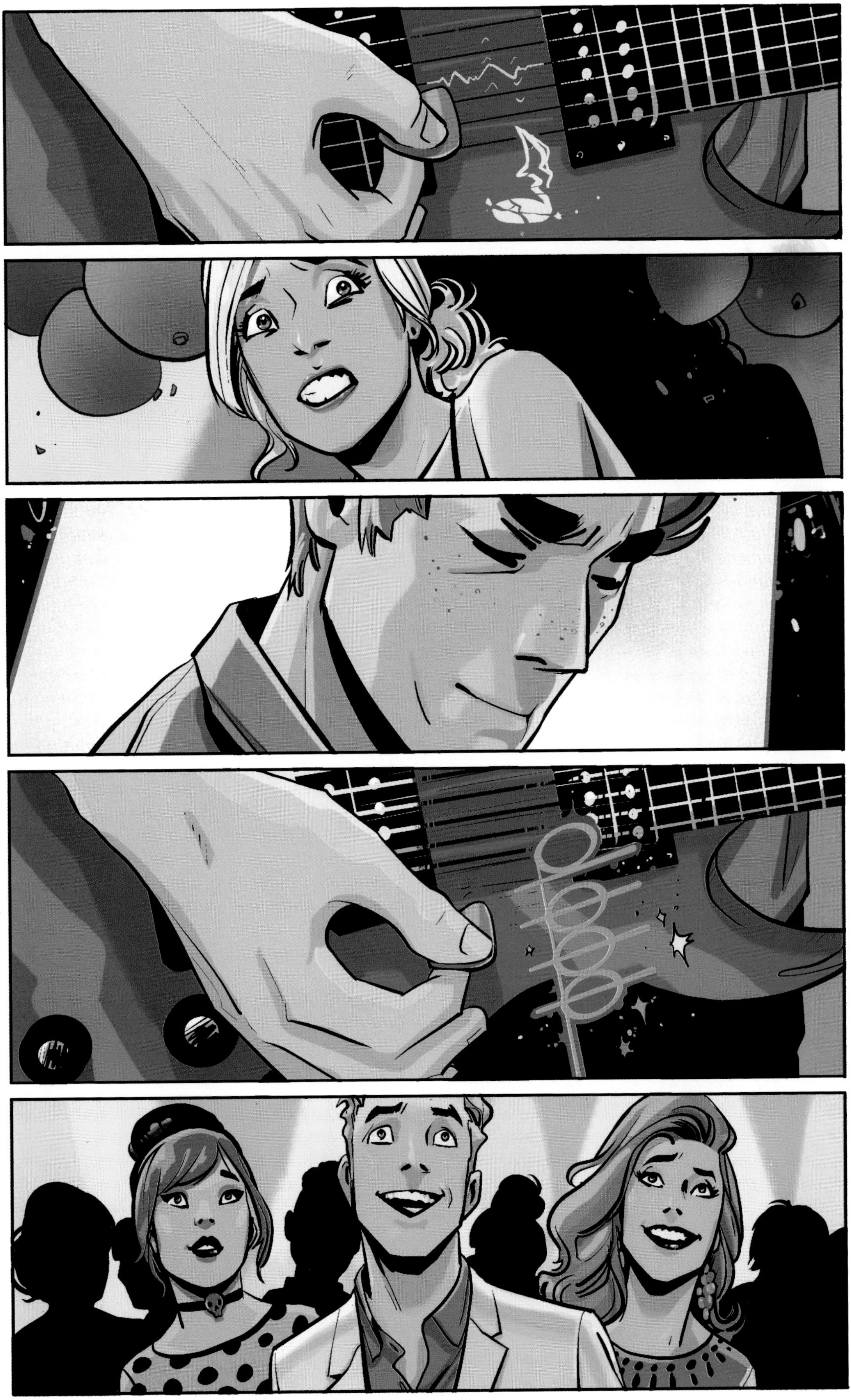

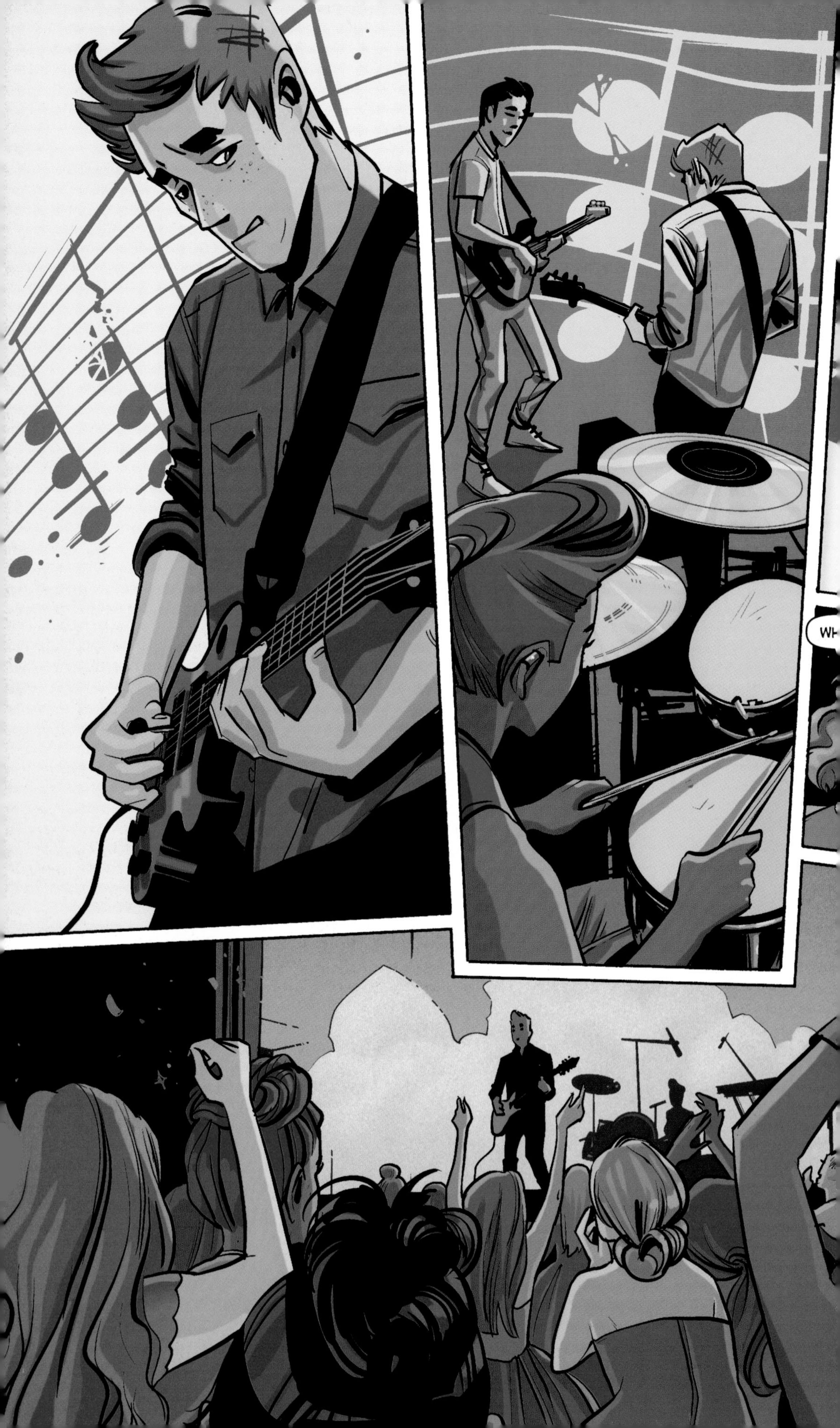

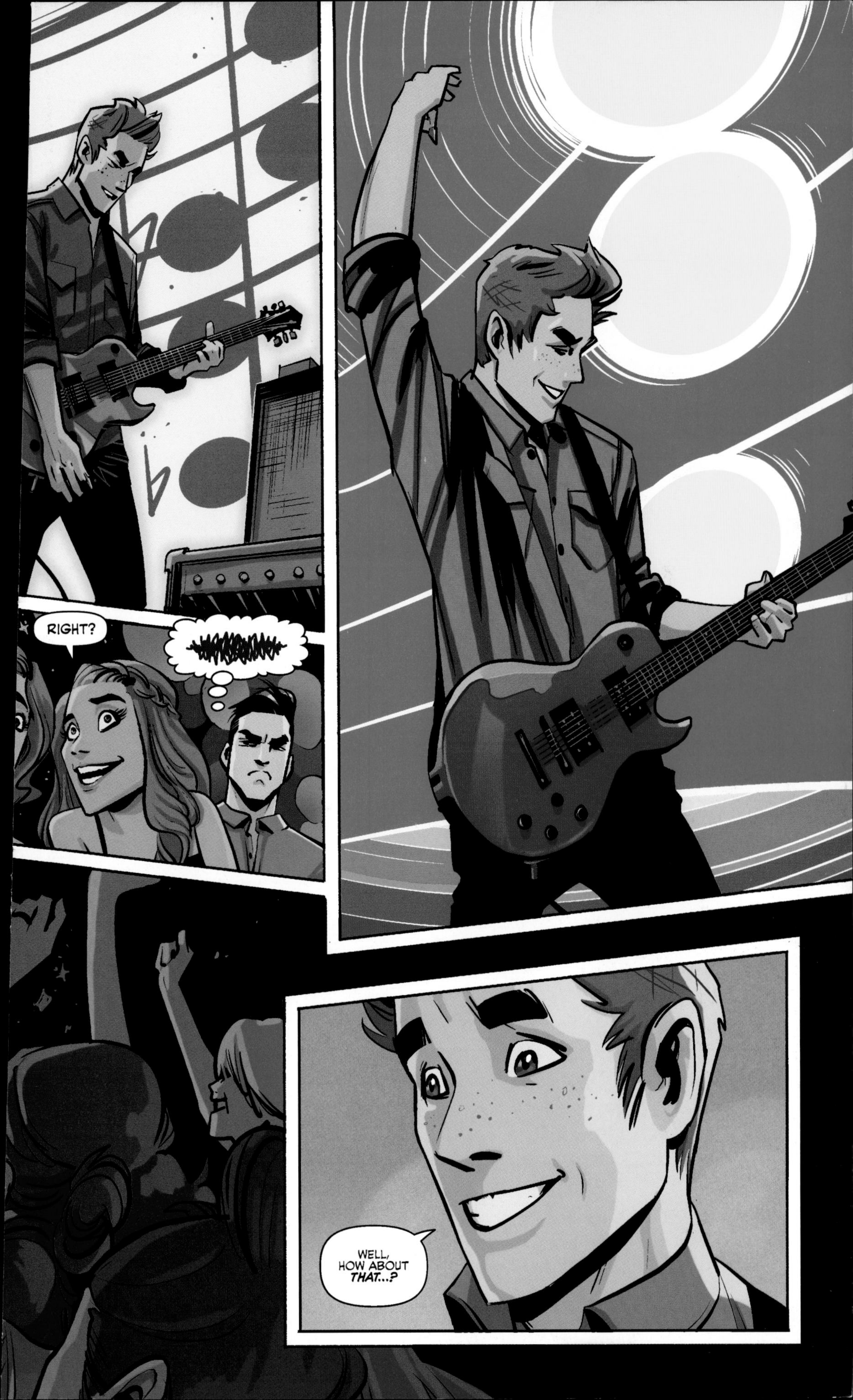
RIGHT?
WELL, HOW ABOUT THAT...?

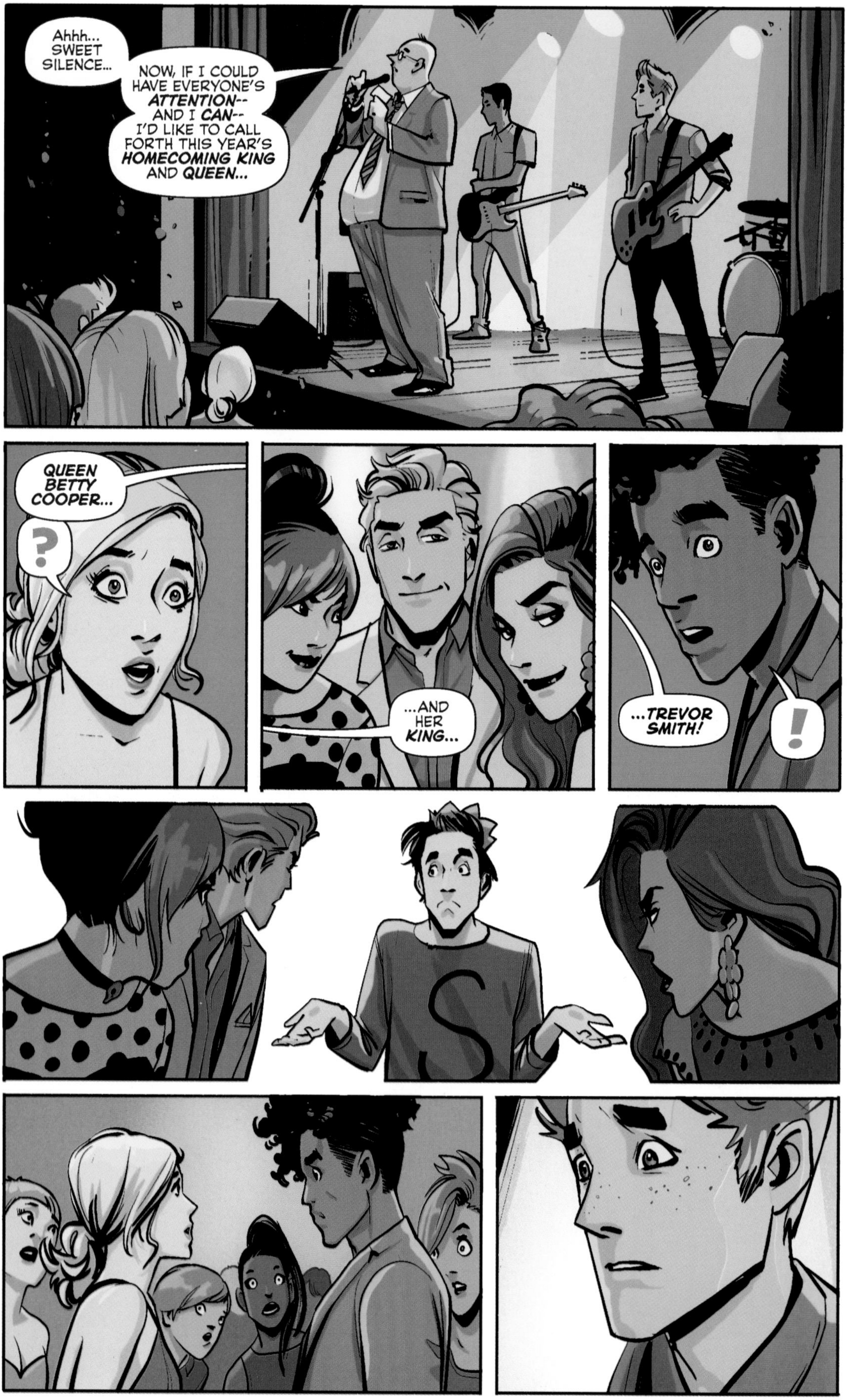
Ahhh... SWEET SILENCE...
NOW, IF I COULD HAVE EVERYONE'S ATTENTION-- AND I CAN-- I'D LIKE TO CALL FORTH THIS YEAR'S HOMECOMING KING AND QUEEN...
QUEEN BETTY COOPER...
?
...AND HER KING...
...TREVOR SMITH!
!
S

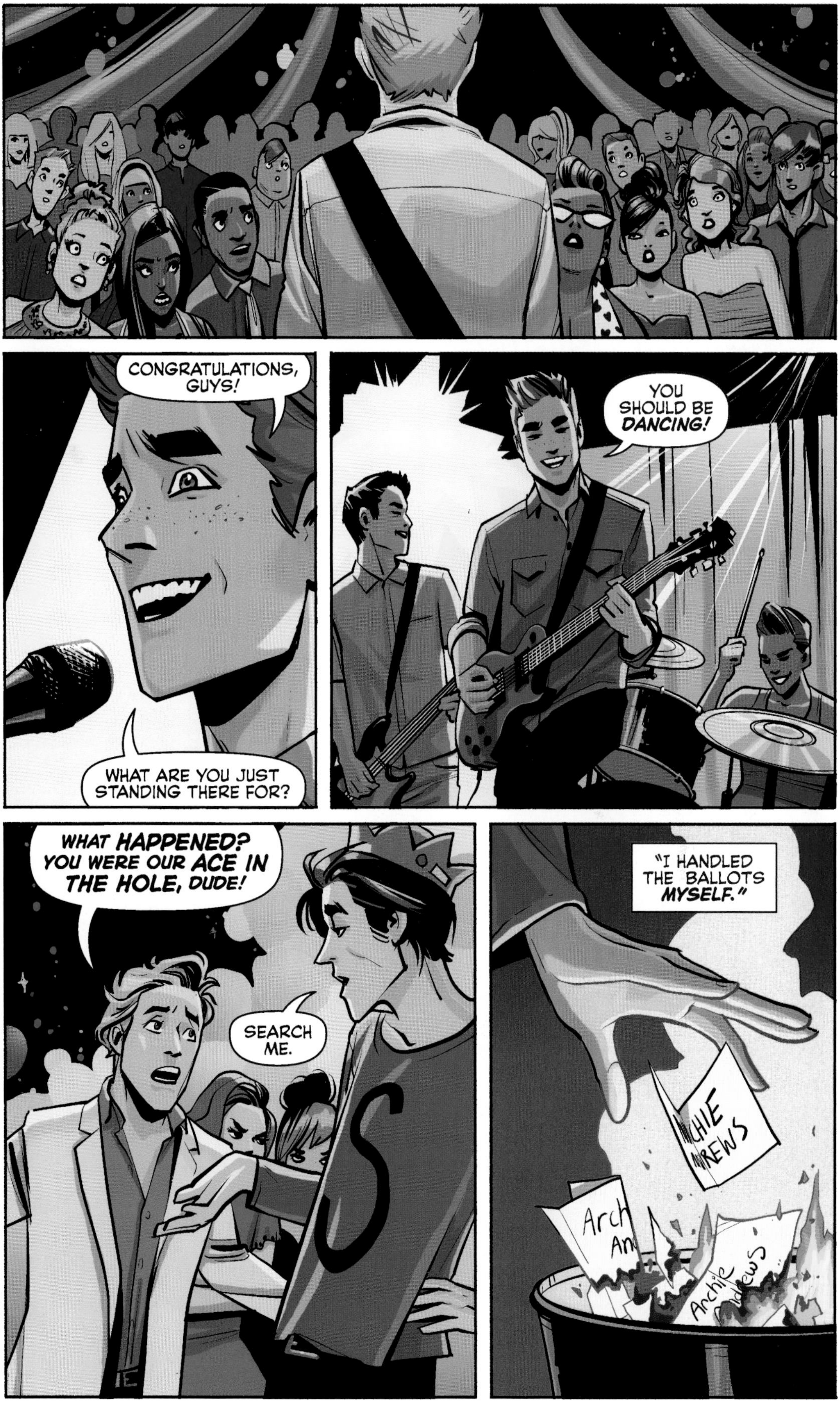
CONGRATULATIONS, GUYS!
WHAT ARE YOU JUST STANDING THERE FOR?
YOU SHOULD BE DANCING!
WHAT HAPPENED? YOU WERE OUR ACE IN THE HOLE, DUDE!
SEARCH ME.
"I HANDLED THE BALLOTS MYSELF."

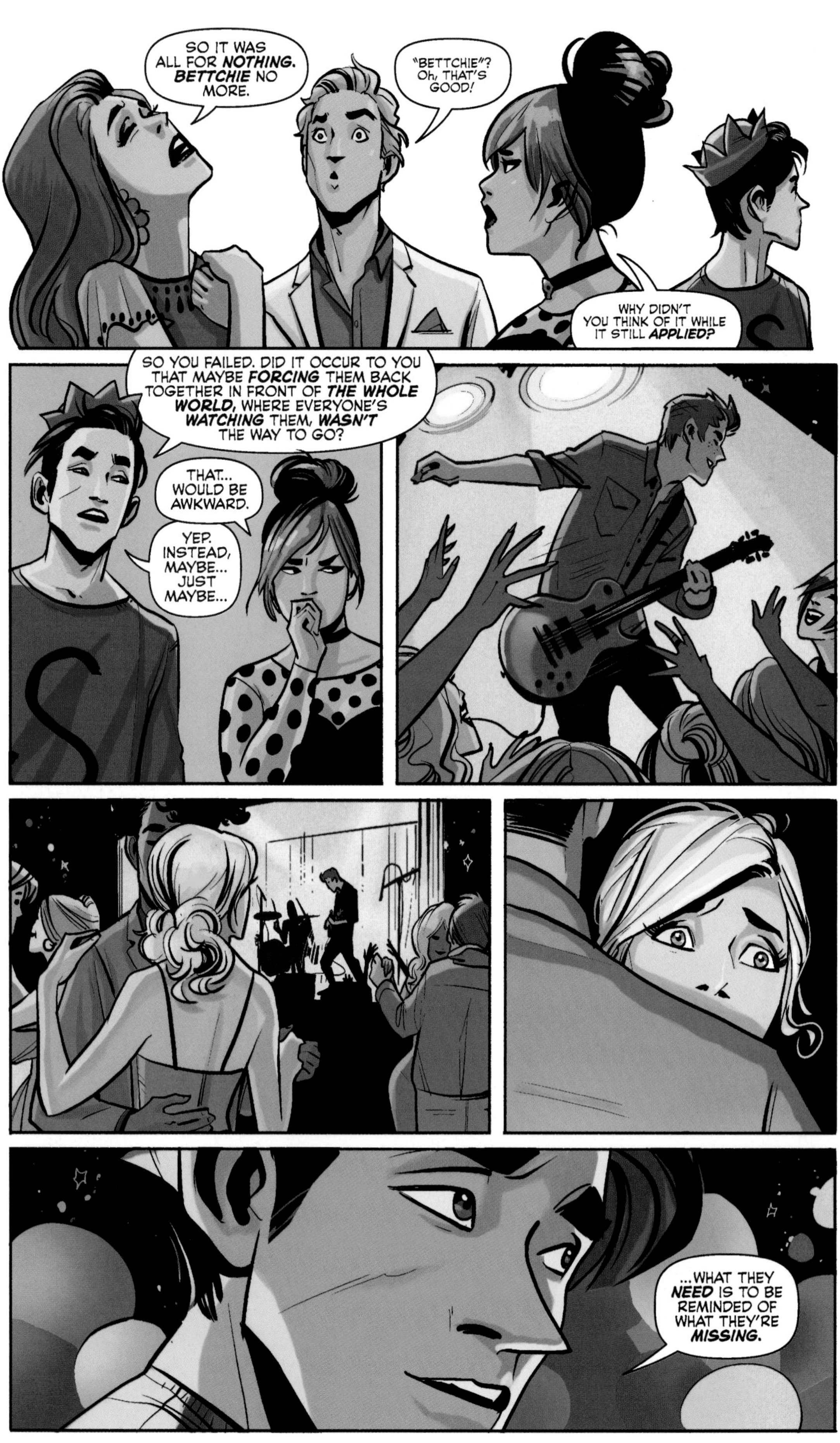
SO IT WAS ALL FOR NOTHING. BETTCHIE NO MORE.
"BETTCHIE"? Oh, THAT'S GOOD!
WHY DIDN'T YOU THINK OF IT WHILE IT STILL APPLIED?
SO YOU FAILED. DID IT OCCUR TO YOU THAT MAYBE FORCING THEM BACK TOGETHER IN FRONT OF THE WHOLE WORLD, WHERE EVERYONE'S WATCHING THEM, WASN'T THE WAY TO GO?
THAT... WOULD BE AWKWARD.
YEP. INSTEAD, MAYBE... JUST MAYBE...
...WHAT THEY NEED IS TO BE REMINDED OF WHAT THEY'RE MISSING.

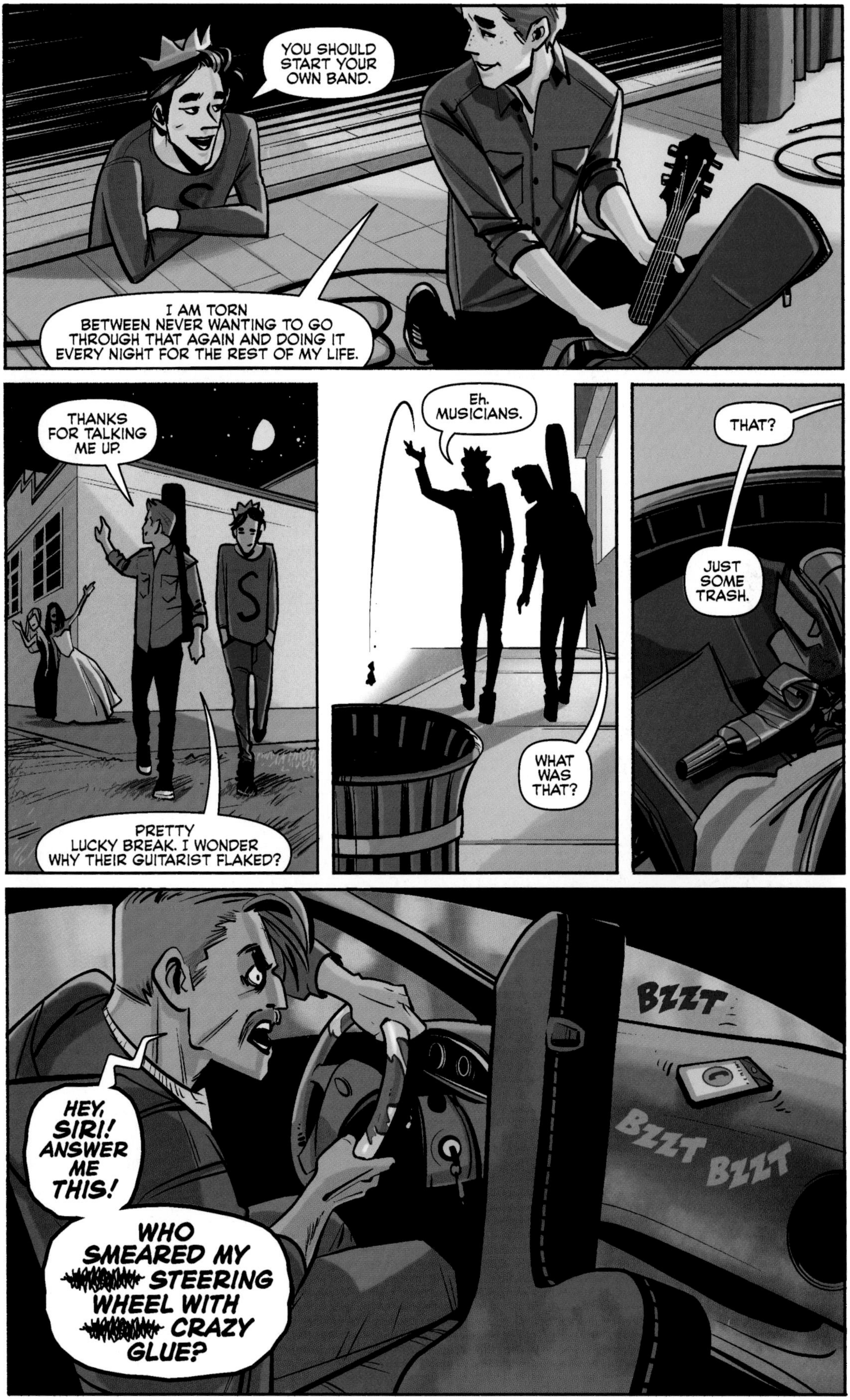

YOU SHOULD START YOUR OWN BAND.
I AM TORN BETWEEN NEVER WANTING TO GO THROUGH THAT AGAIN AND DOING IT EVERY NIGHT FOR THE REST OF MY LIFE.
THANKS FOR TALKING ME UP.
PRETTY LUCKY BREAK. I WONDER WHY THEIR GUITARIST FLAKED?
Eh. MUSICIANS.
WHAT WAS THAT?
THAT?
JUST SOME TRASH.
BZZT
BZZT BZZT
HEY, SIRI! ANSWER ME THIS!
WHO SMEARED MY STEERING WHEEL WITH CRAZY GLUE?

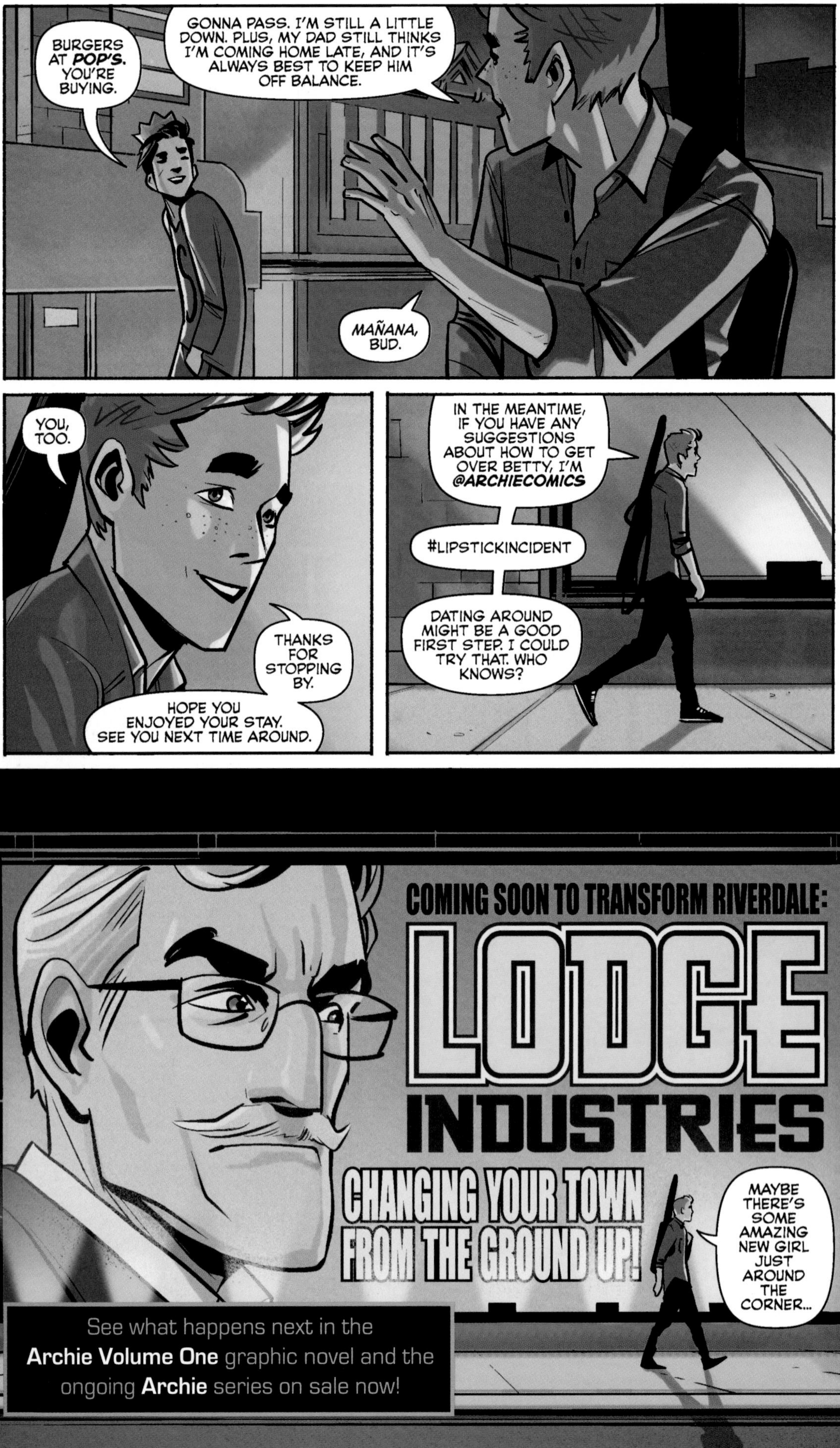
BURGERS AT **POP'S.** YOU'RE BUYING.
GONNA PASS. I'M STILL A LITTLE DOWN. PLUS, MY DAD STILL THINKS I'M COMING HOME LATE, AND IT'S ALWAYS BEST TO KEEP HIM OFF BALANCE.
MAÑANA, BUD.
YOU, TOO.
THANKS FOR STOPPING BY.
HOPE YOU ENJOYED YOUR STAY. SEE YOU NEXT TIME AROUND.
IN THE MEANTIME, IF YOU HAVE ANY SUGGESTIONS ABOUT HOW TO GET OVER BETTY, I'M **@ARCHIECOMICS**
#LIPSTICKINCIDENT
DATING AROUND MIGHT BE A GOOD FIRST STEP. I COULD TRY THAT. WHO KNOWS?
COMING SOON TO TRANSFORM RIVERDALE:
LODGE
INDUSTRIES
CHANGING YOUR TOWN FROM THE GROUND UP!
MAYBE THERE'S SOME AMAZING NEW GIRL JUST AROUND THE CORNER...
See what happens next in the **Archie Volume One** graphic novel and the ongoing **Archie** series on sale now!